Wittgenstein: From Mysticism to Ordinary Language

SUNY Series in Philosophy
Robert C. Neville, Editor

Wittgenstein: From Mysticism to Ordinary Language

A Study of Viennese Positivism and the Thought of Ludwig Wittgenstein

Russell Nieli

State University of New York Press

Published by
State University of New York Press, Albany

Printed in the United States of America

For information, address State University of New York Press, State University Plaza, Albany, N.Y., 12246

Library of Congress Cataloging in Publication Data

Nieli, Russell, 1948–
Wittgenstein: from mysticism to ordinary language.

(SUNY series in philosophy)
Includes index.
1. Wittgenstein, Ludwig, 1889–1951. 2. Logical positivism. I. Title. II. Series.
B3376.W564N53 1987 192 86-23144
ISBN 0-88706-397-7
ISBN 0-88706-398-5 (pbk.)

10 9 8 7 6 5 4 3 2 1

To My Mother

I have much to tell you that is of interest. I leave here today after a fortnight's stay, during a week of which Wittgenstein was here, and we discussed his book every day. I came to think even better of it than I had done; I feel sure it is really a great book, though I do not feel sure it is right . . .

I had felt in his book a flavour of mysticism, but was astonished when I found that he has become a complete mystic. He reads people like Kierkegaard and Angelus Silesius, and he seriously contemplates becoming a monk. It all started from William James's Varieties of Religious Experience, and grew (not unnaturally) during the winter he spent alone in Norway before the war, when he was nearly mad. Then during the war a curious thing happened. He went on duty to the town of Tarnov in Galicia, and happened to come upon a bookshop, which, however, seemed to contain nothing but picture postcards. However, he went inside and found that it contained just one book: Tolstoy on The Gospels. He bought it merely because there was no other. He read it and re-read it, and thenceforth had it always with him, under fire and at all times. But on the whole he likes Tolstoy less than Dostoevski (especially Karamazov). He has penetrated deep into mystical ways of thought and feeling, but I think (though he wouldn't agree) that what he likes best in mysticism is its power to make him stop thinking. I don't much think he will really become a monk—it is an idea, not an intention. His intention is to be a teacher. He gave all his money to his brothers and sisters, because he found earthly possessions a burden. I wish you had seen him . . .

Bertrand Russell

(Letter to Lady Ottoline Morrell, 20 December 1919, The Hague)

Contents

Preface ***ix***

I Positivism and Metaphysics: The Vienna Circle and the Dispute over the Nothing **1**

The Vienna Circle, 3/ Heidegger's Nothing and the Experience of Radical Derealization-Depersonalization, 15/ Freak-out in a French Town: Sartre and the Nothing, 29/ The Nothing and the Christian Purgatorial Night, 39/ Who's on First?, 54/

II Metaphysics as Profanation: Wittgenstein Reconsidered **59**

The Philistine and the Prophet, 61/ The Tractatus*: Preliminary Characterization, 69/ Mystic Flight: Theophanic Encounter, 70/ The Symbolization of the Mystic Peak: Unbefittingness, Inadequacy, Profanation, 75/ The Theophanic Encounter and the Rejection of Metaphysics, 82/ Silence, 88/ Being Absolutely Safe, 91/ The World-Symbol of the* Tractatus*, 97/* Ekstasis *and* Apatheia*, 99/ God and the World, 107/ Of What One Can and Cannot Speak: The Say/Show-Itself Distinction, 108/ The Solipsism of the* Tractatus*, 118/ Existential Yearning: The Urge to the Mystical, 123/ Profanation and Obscurantism: The Judgment on Metaphysics, 127/ Some Problems with the* Tractatus*: A Theocentric Ethic Without Fallen Man, 139/ Problems II: "Legislative Linguistics", 148/ Problems III: The Rejection of History, 152/ Problems IV: The Rejection of a Hierarchical Ontology, 156/ The* Tractatus*: Final Characterization, 159/*

III From Prophecy to Scripture: The Canonization of Ordinary Language 161

Showing the Truth of the Tractatus*: A Choice of Vocations, 163/ Breaking Silence—Wittgenstein's Encounter with Paul Engelmann, 168/ Creating a Monster, 170/ Remarks on Frazer, 174/ The Shift to Ordinary Language: A Celebration of the Common Man, 176/ From Prophetism to the Spirit of Jamnia: A New Conservatism and a New Epoch, 182/ Off to Russia, 187/ The Triumph of Ordinary Language Philosophy in Britain, 190/*

IV Linguistic Tribalism and the Revolt Against *Innerlichkeit* 195

Saving Society/ Saving Oneself, 197/ "Our *Language*"*, 198/ Coming in Out of the Storm: Metaphysics, Mysticism, and the Significance of the Mental Health Metaphors, 202/ Towards a Behaviorist View of Mind: The Revolt Against Inwardness, 211/ Towards a Behaviorist View of Mind: The Revolt Against Privacy, 220/ Work Therapy vs Language Therapy, 225/ The Attack on the Notion of Universal Essences, 229/ A Comparison with Augustine, 235/ Linguistic Tribalism and the Ultimate Failure of Ordinary Language Philosophy: An Evaluation 237/ An Exoteric Philosophy: Wittgenstein's Relationship to His Later Thought, 246/*

V Concluding Remarks on the Nature of Language as *Spiel* 249

Index ***259***

Preface

The Prophet Who Became a Rabbi

The following study began completely by accident. In the late summer of 1974 I returned to the United States from West Germany, having completed a year of study as a Fulbright Scholar at the University of Bochum. I was due to return to Princeton that fall, where I was enrolled as a doctoral candidate in the Department of Politics, and begin the writing of my dissertation on the thought of Eric Voegelin. While in Germany, I had given a good deal of thought to the question of how I would begin the dissertation, and one of the ideas I toyed with was the possibility of including some preliminary material on the philosophical and cultural situation in Vienna during the years when Eric Voegelin was connected with the University there (1920-1938). It so happened that at the time I returned to the United States there was going the rounds in the paperback bookstores Allan Janik's and Stephen Toulmin's *Wittgenstein's Vienna.* Though I had no interest at all at the time in the thought of Ludwig Wittgenstein, the late pre-World War I Vienna of Wittgenstein, I assumed, must have had a lot in common with Voegelin's early post-World War I Vienna, so I quickly bought a copy of the book and eagerly began to read it. I would, of course, have been no less eager to read the work had it borne such a title as *Popper's Vienna, Hayek's Vienna, Loos's Vienna,* or anything comparable, for it was Viennese culture, and not Wittgenstein, which interested me. It could almost be said that the name of Wittgenstein tended to discourage me from reading the book. As an undergraduate, I had taken a number of philosophy courses at a university with an analytically oriented department, and had developed an early dislike for this manner of philosophizing. (I can still remember reading a work of Professor Ryle in which he divides 20th Century philosophers into journeymen and pontiffs, the former category subsuming the positivists, logicians, and language analysts, the latter, the existentialists, Thomists, and Marxists. My own interest in philosophy was always more in line with those in the second category than in the first). And when I attended Princeton for the first time in 1971, what had originally been a dislike for analytic philosophy was soon to develop into an outright loathing following a disasterous experience in the Philosophy Department with a linguistically oriented course on Plato. So as the man whose later works I knew to be closely identified with the language/analytic mode of doing philosophy, the figure of Wittgenstein was hardly one to which I was especially drawn. And since I knew—or thought I knew—that Wittgenstein in his early days had been a rigorous positivist whose work had helped set in motion a philosophical movement I had always considered pernicious, I had two very good reasons for *not* being particularly interested in Ludwig Wittgenstein.

After reading Janik and Toulmin, however, I became much more sympathetic towards Wittgenstein. On a personal level, I was struck by the fact that he gave his entire inheritance away following the First World War and chose to live in great simplicity, and that, during the Second World War, he took up the most menial tasks as a hospital porter and orderly. Here, I thought, was a spirit quite different from that of the typical logical positivist. What had the greatest impact in upsetting my initial view of Wittgenstein, however, was the figure of Karl Kraus. From my studies of Voegelin I had learned about Kraus and of his one man crusade against what he perceived to be the moral and spiritual corruption of Viennese culture. And I knew that it was Kraus with whom Voegelin in his early Viennese days seems most intimately to have identified. But this situation seemed to me incongruous. How, I asked myself, could Wittgenstein, allegedly the founder of Viennese-style positivism, be so deeply attracted, as Janik and Toulmin suggested, to the same person as Eric Voegelin, a great enemy of logical positivism who had drawn most of his philosophical inspiration from the great moralists and mystics of the West? Could there be some similarities, I asked myself, in the ideas and attitudes of these two men? Janik and Toulmin's contention that Kraus's writings formed the unwritten half of the *Tractatus* seemed to me overly speculative, but Wittgenstein's affinity with Kraus and his work was apparently an established fact which couldn't be denied.

The picture of the early Wittgenstein which emerged from *Wittgenstein's Vienna* had certainly aroused my curiosity, so when I returned to Princeton in September, one of the first things I did was to go to the university bookstore and buy a copy of the *Tractatus*. I was immediately impressed by the unimposing size of the work, which even when doubled through the addition of the English translation, measured no more than three-quarters of an inch in thickness, and hardly suggested itself as a philosophical work of major proportions. Realizing that this one 80-page book was the only book of Wittgenstein published during his lifetime, and that it had almost by itself set in motion one of the most powerful philosophical movements of the inter-war period, I often said to myself in mock-seriousness that I had better not open it, or if so only with the utmost caution, lest it explode or touch off an uncontrollable conflagration.

Janik and Toulmin, to be sure, had placed great doubts in my mind concerning the view of Wittgenstein as a positivist, though as I sat down to read the *Tractatus*, I was still under the lingering impression that here before me was a positivist tract written by a man whose only reality was physics, mathematics, and engineering. "What the hell does an engineer know?", I would often say to myself, expecting to encounter a Carnap/Neurath/Ayer style of polemic against all ethical, aesthetic, and religious thought. And this essentially negative attitude persisted for some time as I delved deeper and deeper into the work. Forces, however, had been set in motion which would radically change my basic viewpoint. Janik and Toulmin's contention that the *Tractatus* had been fundamentally misunderstood by the logical positivists, and that the real message and climax of the work was to be found in the last 10 pages, certainly weighed heavily. In addition, I was struck very early in my reading by what might be described as the musical cadence of the work. Not that logical positivists are invariably unmusical, but the musical quality of the writing seemed to create an atmosphere which encouraged the reader to enter a playful frame of mind quite at variance with the spirit I expected from a positivist tract. (One might compare the *Tractatus* in this regard with Ayer's *Language, Truth, and Logic*). But the real decisive turning point came in reflecting on the meaning of the term "world", and of the mystical or higher reality (*das Mystische, Hoeheres*) which lay outside and beyond the world. Positivist readers had apparently thought, like the young Ayer, that Wittgenstein was only joking—putting down metaphysicians, as it were—when he spoke of a reality beyond the world, about which one must be silent. Such passages, where they were taken more seriously by interpreters, had apparently been chalked up to lingering religious or metaphysical impulses which were seen as entirely out of tune with the rest of the work. From Brian McGuinness's article on "The Mysticism of the *Tractatus*", however, I learned that Wittgenstein was quite serious when he wrote about *das Mystische*, and that he had himself apparently undergone a very profound mystical experience sometime before the First World War. With this information, Wittgenstein's use of the term "world" suddenly became clear to me, and I soon broke out into almost uncontrollable laughter which was to reappear intermittently for a period of several months. (I still have trouble maintaining my composure when I consider the *Tractatus* in the light of how it was actually interpreted by positivists). My understanding of Wittgenstein and his early work had completely changed, and I found myself moving more and more from a position of a hostile critic into that of a sympathetic admirer.

My personal Copernican revolution as a *Tractatus* interpreter I would later compare to the following: There was a jig-saw puzzle which many competent people had put together to form a clear and coherent picture. A few of the pieces, however, didn't seem to fit into the picture, and so, were generally ignored or discarded. A radical change, however, was seen to take place when one re-arranged the picture. If one took the existing picture and split it in two, thrust the discarded pieces into the very center of the picture, rejoined the two halves to the new center, and took the resulting whole and turned it completely upside down, an entirely new picture emerged in which all the pieces fit. Everything in the *Tractatus*, I came to realize,—the musical cadence, its logical system of "the world", the say/show itself distinction, the remarks on timelessness, the mystical, silence, etc.—begins to fall into its proper place once the work is seen in its function as a ladder in the mystical ascent along the *via negativa*. Janik and Toulmin, I came to believe, were right in seeing the *Tractatus* as essentially an ethical and culture-critical work whose logical system was instrumentally subordinate to its higher purpose. They failed, however, to realize fully that the ethic upon which the *Tractatus* was built was a mystical or theocentric ethic—i.e. an ethic whose basis was seen to lie in a transcending vision. Ethics and aesthetics, it would seem, were something Janik and Toulmin could live with comfortably and readily accept from Wittgenstein; mysticism and God-consciousness as the basis of such an ethic or aesthetic were something else again.

It was only after I had reached my basic conclusions concerning the meaning of the *Tractatus* that I first came upon Paul Engelmann's memoir of Wittgenstein. In Engelmann's remarks I saw basically confirmed what I had thought, though Engelmann too, I felt, like Janik and Toulmin, seemed a little hesitant to go the whole mystical way with Wittgenstein. Nevertheless, Engelmann's statement that Wittgenstein, in contrast to the logical positivists, "passionately believes that all that really matters in human life is precisely what, in his view, we must be silent about," and his further comment that the logical system of the *Tractatus* outlines the coastline of an island only to get a better view of the boundary of the ocean, seemed to me to capture perfectly the meaning of Wittgenstein's work.

Again and again as I searched through the secondary literature and learned more about Wittgenstein's life and person, I discovered facts previously unintegrated into an overall view of Wittgenstein fitting smoothly into place. The fact that Wittgenstein held St. Augustine in such high regard, that he considered Kierkegaard the greatest thinker of the 19th Century, that he was a great admirer of Tolstoy and Dostoyevsky, that he had early in his studies read and praised William James's *Varieties of Religious Experience*, that as a university professor he gave one of his students a copy of George Fox's *Journal*, and that on a number of occasions he seriously thought of entering a monastery—all these known facts about Wittgenstein's life tended to bolster the ethical and religious view which I had come to form of the *Tractatus*. There was, however, one thing which seemed to speak against my interpretation, namely, the simple fact that it was so radical and ran so counter to the views of the *Tractatus* generally held by Wittgenstein scholars (Janik and Toulmin being partial exceptions). How, I asked, could someone like myself, a graduate student in political philosophy, with only a limited knowledge of logic, and certainly an amateur in the area of modern British thought, come to recognize what had escaped recognition by specialists and people who had studied Wittgenstein for much of their adult lives? Many students of Wittgenstein, I realized, were quite bright—some certainly brighter than myself—and some had even studied under Wittgenstein personally. How, I asked, could something which seemed to me so obvious possibly have escaped them? The answer to my doubts and questions, however, was not long in coming, for the simple fact of the matter was that with few exceptions, writers and commentators on Wittgenstein were not at all familiar with the literature on mysticism and altered states of consciousness, and apparently found it very difficult to empathize with Wittgenstein when he alluded to mystical experience. (It is interesting to note that scholars such as Evelyn Underhill and Alan Watts, who are familiar with the various modes of mystical experience and its symbolization, have had no trouble at all in seeing the *Tractatus* as the product of mystic consciousness). Through natural inclination and through my study of Eric Voegelin, I had come to acquire an understanding of mystical experience, which few commentators on Wittgenstein seemed to possess. It was this fact which gave me confidence in my interpretation despite its extreme radicalness and unorthodoxy, and it was this fact which led me to devote so much space in Section II to the development of the notion of "mystic flight". One of my academic advisers, a specialist in medieval political theory, thought it strange that in an exegetical piece on Wittgenstein, I should spend so much time on a phenomenological description of mystical experience. I replied that for someone like himself, with a strong background in medieval thought, such extended description was unnecessary; for students of philosophy who have been brought up in the positivist and language-analytic traditions, however, the case was quite different.

From the fall of 1974 to the spring of 1975, during which time I researched and composed Sections I and II of the present study, I was literally obsessed with the person of Ludwig Wittgenstein. I saw in him many of my own passions and concerns, and I was haunted by the spectre of his life as I have been haunted by the life of only one other person before. I hoped that my efforts as a *Tractatus* exegete might in some small measure serve to set the record straight and recapture something of the original meaning of a work which Wittgenstein in his own time only lived to see misunderstood. Whether these sections, together with the rest of the present study, accomplish what I had hoped, the reader can decide for himself. Although it has been a number of years since I wrote Sections I and II, and they reflect the general level of development of a graduate student, there is little in them which I would want to change were I writing them today. An exception to this would be the few scattered remarks and innuendos about the European Enlightenment, an intellectual movement which I have since come to have a more ambivalent view of than when I originally wrote these sections.

In Sections III, IV, and V of the present study, I have tried to relate Wittgenstein's post-*Tractatus* work to the purposes and themes of his *Tractatus* period. In trying to form a coherent picture of his thought and development, and in trying to relate my own interpretive efforts to the efforts of others, I have found it helpful in recent days to think in terms of there being three Wittgensteins. There is, first of all, Wittgenstein (T), the author of the *Tractatus*. This is the Wittgenstein who was generally thought to be a positivist. There is then Wittgenstein (O), the philosopher of ordinary language and common sense, whose influence came to dominate British and American philosophy following the Second World War. And finally, there is this mysterious figure lurking in the background of both Wittgenstein (T) and Wittgenstein (O), namely, Wittgenstein (R), the religious personality. There is a good deal of material which has been written on Wittgenstein (T), and one might even say an overabundance of material on Wittgenstein (O). There has also been much written relating the one to the other. By contrast, there is comparatively little that has been written on Wittgenstein (R), and with the exception of Engelmann's comments on the *Tractatus* and James Edwards' more recent *Ethics Without Philosophy*,[1] almost nothing which tries to relate Wittgenstein (R) in any serious or systematic way to the other two Wittgensteins. Throughout the present study I have tried to accomplish this task, and in doing so, have found that the three simple Wittgensteins really combine to form two complex ones, a Wittgenstein (RT) and a Wittgenstein (RO). The first was a prophet, the second a rabbi.

The book is divided into five separate sections, each of which constitutes a semi-independent study of its respective topic. The first section takes up the issue of Viennese positivism and tries to make sense of the famous Carnap-Heidegger dispute over the "nothing". Much of this section is devoted to a careful phenomenological analysis of a type of radical alienation experience that began to attract the interest of philosophers and depth-psychologists in the early decades of this century. The second section then, begins the study of Wittgenstein, and tries to show how his *Tractatus* was based upon a mystic vision and his concern with maintaining the integrity and sacrality of the contents of this vision. Just as Kant wanted to do away with metaphysics in order to make room for faith, so Wittgenstein, it is argued, wanted to do away with metaphysical and theological systems, as well as the violent disputes that are often engaged in by their various adherents, in order to make room for transcendental religious experience and a silent piety in contemplation of such experience. The technique of phenomenological description and personal testimony introduced in the first section, is continued into the second section, where it is used to explain the experience of *ekstasis* or "mystic-flight". A considerable amount of historical material is introduced here in order to draw

1. (University Presses of Florida, Tampa, 1982). Though Edwards' work is the only really thorough attempt to relate Wittgenstein's ethico-religious personality to both phases of his thought, a number of other works take up various moral and religious themes in Wittgenstein, including W. Donald Hudson's *Wittgenstein and Religious Belief* (The MacMillan Press Ltd., London, 1975), Alan Keightley's *Wittgenstein, Grammar, and God* (Epworth Press, London, 1976), and some of the material on Wittgenstein in William Barrett's *The Illusion of Technique* (Doubleday, Garden City, 1979). While all of these works are valuable in one way or another, none of them pay sufficient attention to the experience which Wittgenstein describes as being "*absolutely* safe", an understanding of which, in the view of the present writer, is a *sine qua non* for grasping the full import of the *Tractatus*.

historical parallels to the actual situation in which Wittgenstein found himself as a Central European during the early years of this century. The section concludes with a number of my own criticisms of the Tractarian philosophy.

The third section deals with the transition from the mystic-ecstatic vision of the *Tractatus* to the celebration of the common man and his language that forms the orienting center of Wittgenstein's later philosophical reflections. It is suggested here that a major motive for Wittgenstein's abandonment of the *Tractatus* philosophy was the total misunderstanding of that philosophy by radical positivists. A parallel is drawn here to the shift in ancient Hebrew religion from prophetism to rabbinism. The forth section then, takes up the significance of the mental health metaphors and the quasi-behaviorist account of mind-predicates developed in Wittgenstein's later works, and tries to relate these to Wittgenstein's own fears of insanity, and his concern for the happiness and mental stability of others. A number of criticisms are offered of Wittgenstein's later thought, most of which are closely in tune with the assessments of such critics of Anglo-linguistic philosophy as Gellner, Russell, Kaufmann, and Mundle.

The final section then addresses the idea of linguistic activity constituting a *Spiel* (game or play), and speculates on the play or make-believe nature of human existence and human activities that Wittgenstein may have wanted to express through this term.

My thanks are owed to the following people, who were kind enough to read the manuscript, either whole or in part, and to offer various comments and suggestions: Stratford Caldecott, Malcolm Diamond, Dante Germino, Allen Graubard, Manfred Halpern, George Armstrong Kelley, Peter Lyman, Norman Malcolm, Tilo Schabert, Paul Sigmund, Huston Smith, Dennis Thompson, and Eugene Webb. My thanks are also owed to the late Eric Voegelin and the late Bernard Lonergan, both of whom a number of years before their respective deaths read Section II of the manuscript and were most encouraging in their remarks. A debt of gratitude is also owed to the various librarians and other personnel of the Firestone Library at Princeton and the Speer Library at Princeton Theological Seminary, who were very helpful in assisting me with my research. Finally, I would like to thank Bill Eastman of the State University of New York Press for his continued encouragement and support. Needless to say, none of the people mentioned bear any responsibility for anything I have written.

I

Positivism and Metaphysics: The Vienna Circle and the Dispute Over the Nothing

Now the whole earth had one language and few words. And as men migrated from the east, they found a plain in the land of Shinar and settled there. And they said to one another, "Come, let us shake bricks, and burn them thoroughly." . . . Then they said, "Come, let us build ourselves a city, and a tower with its top in the heavens, and let us make a name for ourselves . . ." And the Lord came down to see the city and the tower, which the sons of man had built. And the Lord said: "Behold they are one people, and they have all one language; and this is only the beginning of what they will do. . . . Come, let us go down, and there confuse their language, that they may not understand one another's speech." So the Lord scattered them abroad from there over the face of all the earth, and they left off building the city. Therefore its name was called Babel, because there the Lord confused the language of all the earth.

Genesis 11:1-9

And Jonah was in the belly of the fish three days and three nights. Then Jonah prayed to the Lord his God from the belly of the fish, saying, "I called to the Lord, out of my distress, and he answered me; out of the belly of Sheol I cried, and thou didst hear my voice. For thou didst cast me into the deep, into the heart of the seas, and the flood was round about me; all thy waves and thy billows passed over me. Then I said, 'I am cast out from thy presence; how shall I again look upon thy holy temple?' The waters closed in over me, the deep was round about me. . . . Yet thou didst bring up my life from the Pit, O Lord my God. When my soul fainted within me, I remembered the Lord; and my prayer came to thee, into thy holy temple."

Jonah 1:9-2:9

He descended into Hell, on the third day he rose again from the dead. He ascended into Heaven and sits at the right hand of God the father Almighty.

(from the Apostles' Creed)

The Vienna Circle

The "Vienna Circle" ("*Wiener Kreis*") was the name adopted by the group of mathematicians and natural science oriented philosophers organized in the late 1920s by Moritz Schlick, then professor of philosophy at the University of Vienna. Numbered among its members were the mathematicians Hans Hahn, Karl Menger, and Kurt Goedel, the sociologist Otto Neurath, and the philosophers Victor Kraft, Friedrich Waismann, Rudolf Carnap and Herbert Feigl.[1] Harnessing the full effect of the faith in science that has accompanied the growth of modern civilization, the group was to lay forth doctrines and ideas whose impact on the intellectual climate, not only of Vienna, but of the entire Western world, was, and to a significant extent still is enormous. At Schlick's instigation, the group held weekly meetings where various topics in the philosophy of science were discussed, but as A.J. Ayer, one of the Circle's later members has remarked, by the early 1930s the group was to take on many of the features (including the issuance of manifestos and the adoption of a uniform ideology) of a radical political party.[2] Schlick's success as an organizer, bringing together men of considerably different temperaments and personalities, seems to have been the result, as members of the Circle have later described,[3] of an unusually kind, unassuming nature. The peculiar messianic ethos which the group developed (and from which Schlick to some extent disassociated himself),[4] was due in large measure to the influence

1. A concise historical account of the Vienna Circle, together with a summary of some of its leading tenets, is given by A.J. Ayer in the introductory essay of his edited work, *Logical Positivism* (The Free Press, N.Y., 1959), pp. 3-28.

2. *Ibid.*, pp. 3-6.

3. Rudolf Carnap writes: "The congenial atmosphere in the Circle meetings was due above all to Schlick's personality, his unfailing kindness, tolerance, and modesty" ("Intellectual Autobiography", in *The Philosophy of Rudolf Carnap*, ed. Paul Arthur Schlipp, Open Court Publishing, La Salle, Ill., 1963, p. 21). Herbert Feigl similarly refers to Schlick's "unassuming character, his great modesty and kindliness" (in *The Legacy of Logical Positivism*, ed. Peter Achinstein and Stephen F. Barker, The John's Hopkins Press, Baltimore, 1969, p. 4).

4. Schlick, for instance, who was away in America at the time of its composition, would have nothing to do with the positivist manifesto, *Die Wissenschaftliche Welt-*

of Otto Neurath, the only member of the group with an interest in history and politics. A decade before the formation of the Circle, Neurath had been an active political revolutionary, taking part in the radical Spartacist government that emerged in Munich amidst the anarchy following Germany's defeat in the First World War. Far from being an orthodox Marxist, however, he seems to have been an early enthusiast of a positivist type doctrine which he called physicalism, and is reputed to have trekked off to Russia in an abortive attempt to convince Stalin (whose hostility towards positivism was conditioned by Lenin's *Materialism and Empirio-Criticism*) of the compatibility of the new physicalism with the spirit of Marxism.[5] Taking his cue from some of the more radical thinkers of the French Enlightenment, Neurath went on to extoll in his writings, in a defiant, self-consciously Promethean spirit, the unlimited capacities of science to solve the problems of human destiny. The "scientific view of the universe (*wissenschaftliche Weltauffassung*)", he proclaimed, would "make it possible for man to attain happiness by definite arrangements of definite methods of conduct (behavior)."[6] Attacking head-on the whole moral, philosophical, and religious tradition of Western society, he wrote further of the new positivism:

> All the adherents of a rigorous empiricism reject anything that smacks of the "absolute", whether the subject matter relates to the world of the *a priori*, or the world of the categorical imperative . . . The representatives of a scientific *Weltauffassung* . . . know only science and the clarification of scientific methods, and this clarification is all that remains of old-fashioned "phi-

auffassung, drawn up by Carnap, Neurath, and Hahn. Herbert Feigl describes the situation as follows:

> In the first flush of enthusiasm of the late 1920's, the Vienna Circle proclaimed its outlook as a philosophy to end all philosophies; as a decisive turn toward a new form of enlightenment. The pamphlet *Wissenschaftliche Weltauffassung: Der Wiener Kreis*, published in 1929, was our declaration of independence from traditional school philosophy. This slender brochure, composed collaboratively by Carnap, Hahn, and Neurath (aided by Waismann and myself), was presented to Schlick upon his return from his visiting appointment at Stanford University. As I remember only too well, Schlick, while appreciative of this token of friendship and admiration, was deeply disturbed by the idea of having originated another "school of thought". . . . he was profoundly convinced that everyone should think for himself. The idea of a united front of philosophical attack was abhorrent to Schlick. (*The Legacy of Logical Positivism, Ibid.*, p. 4).

5. William Bartley, *Wittgenstein* (J.B. Lippincott, N.Y., 1973), p. 4.
6. *The Monist*, October 1931, p. 632.

> losophizing". What can not be regarded as unified science must be accepted as poetry or fiction.
>
> Instead of the priest we find the physiological physician and the sociological organizer. Definite conditions are tested for their effect upon happiness (*Glueckswirkungen*) just as a machine is tested to measure its lifting effect . . . The task demands systematic organization of human effort.
>
> Everywhere we find a growing sense of technical organization, a sense in harmony with the extension of that new scientific conception of the universe (*Weltauffassung*) which forges a powerful weapon by the unification of science.
>
> No matter in what country or continent they may be, those who regard themselves as simple laborers in solving the riddle of life unconsciously join forces whenever they devote time and effort to the clarification of science . . . To predict what will happen and to guide one's actions accordingly is the greatest triumph of earthly striving . . .[7]

And in a similar spirit, concluding an article in *Erkenntnis*, the official journal of the Vienna Circle, he writes:

> If a question can be asked at all, it can also be answered—it is senseless to speak of unsolvable riddles. So on the one hand, the scientific conception of the universe stands in recognition of the boundaries and limitations of human thinking, yet at the same time it contains the proud self-consciousness (which, however, is always controlled) that we find in the words of Protagoras: *Man is the measure of all things.*
>
> Once again we find ourselves, though on a different basis, in a similar frame of mind as that of Hegel, together with whom we can say: *Of the greatness and power of Spirit man cannot think great enough.*
>
> (All emphasis in original)[8]

Neurath's firebrand Prometheanism lent the Viennese movement much of its spiritual dynamism and exerted a considerable influence on the thinking of certain members of the Circle, especially Rudolf Carnap. This same spirit, however, seems to have alienated certain other people, including potential members of the group. Karl Popper, for instance, despite repeated efforts at enlistment, never joined the Vienna Circle, even though his general outlook on philos-

7. *Ibid.*, pp. 619, 622, 623.

8. "Wege der wissenschaftlichen Weltauffassung", *Erkenntnis*, Band I, Heft 2-4, p. 125.

ophy and science stood very near to that of most Circle members. In an article written many years after the Circle had dissolved, Popper speaks of an "anti-metaphysical crusade" which Neurath helped to promote,[9] adding in a footnote to the same article: "One need not believe in the 'scientific' character of psychoanalysis (which, I think, is in a metaphysical phase) in order to diagnose the anti-metaphysical fervour of positivism as a form of father killing."[10] Schlick himself seems to have been aghast when the crusading spirit that took hold of the group culminated in the issuance of the joint manifesto, *Die Wissenschaftliche Weltauffassung.*[11]

If Schlick was the organizer and moderator of the Vienna Circle, Neurath its spark and torchbearer, the chief theoretician of the group was most certainly Rudolf Carnap. As a thinker Carnap combined an anti-metaphysical enthusiasm, spurred to a considerable extent by the personal influence of Neurath and the effects of certain new ideas gathered from Wittgenstein's *Tractatus*, with an extensive background in logic and the philosophy of mathematics. His capacity for rigorous, clear, and sustained analysis was, by anyone's estimate, extraordinary.

One can discern the major thrust of the positivists' attack on metaphysics from an article which Carnap wrote for *Erkenntnis* in 1932—an article which was to become one of the most widely discussed and influential philosophical essays to appear in the interwar period. His "Die Ueberwindung der Metaphysik durch logische Analyse der Sprache"[12] ("The Overcoming of Metaphysics through the Logical Analysis of Language") was an article cogently argued and boldly conceived, representing a direct clash between the aggressive dynamic of the new positivism and the whole Western, particularly German, metaphysical tradition—a tradition epitomized for Carnap in the writings of the most influential metaphysician of the period, Martin Heidegger.

The article begins with an Introduction reminiscent of the opening *bisher*-prelude to Marx's *Manifesto*:

> From the days of the Greek skeptics to the empiricists of the 19th century, there have been many *opponents of metaphysics.* The types of criticisms they have put forth, however, have dif-

9. In *The Philosophy of Rudolf Carnap*, ed. Paul Arthur Schlipp (Open Court Publishing, La Salle, Ill., 1963) p. 201.

10. *Ibid.*, p. 206.

11. See footnote 4.

12. *Erkenntnis*, Band 2, Heft 4, pp. 219-241. An excellent English translation, which has been consulted often in the translations given here, is that of Arthur Pap in Ayer, *op. cit.*, pp. 60-81.

> fered. Many have declared the doctrines of metaphysics to be *false*, since they contradict empirical knowledge. Others have held them only for *uncertain*, since the questions asked go beyond the boundaries of human knowledge. Many anti-metaphysicians have declared the occupation with metaphysical questions to be *unproductive*. (emphasis in original)[13]

But like the present of Marx's *Manifesto* (1848), where, for the first time in all history, a revolutionary class constitutes the majority, the present period for Carnap (1932) begins the dawn of a new age, the age of modern logic, qualitatively different from all hitherto (*bis-her*) existing situations:

> Through the development of *modern logic* it has become possible to give a new and sharper answer to the question of the validity and justification of metaphysics. . . . In the realm of metaphysics (including all value-theory and norm-science) logical analysis leads to the negative conclusion that *the alleged statements in this area are totally meaningless*. Thus is achieved a radical victory over metaphysics, which, from the earlier anti-metaphysical standpoints, was not possible. One can, indeed, find related strains of thought in many earlier reflections—the nominalist type for instance; but the decisive step in carrying through such ideas has only today become possible as advances in logic in the last few decades have provided us with tools of sufficient sharpness. (emphasis in original)[14]

Carnap then goes on to clarify what he means by "meaningless" through the introduction of the concept of the *Scheinsatz* (pseudo-statement). A *Scheinsatz* is any group of words, that, at first glance, looks something like a statement or sentence (*Satz*) but upon closer inspection is revealed to be a meaningless collocation of words which cannot be spoken of as truth-functional.[15] There are, says Carnap, two major types of *Scheinsaetze*: either a word has been used (in what is alleged to be a statement) which has no meaning; or, if each word in the alleged statement, taken individually, is meaningful, the words may have been strung together in a pattern which defies the rules of syntax.[16] A word is meaningful, Carnap contends, if there exists a definite criterion for its application to the empirical world.[17] Directing the reader to the more elaborate treat-

13. *Ibid.*, p. 219.
14. *Ibid.*, p. 220.
15. *Ibid.*
16. *Ibid.*
17. *Ibid.*, p. 222.

ment in Wittgenstein's *Tractatus* and his own larger work, *Der Logische Aufbau der Welt,* Carnap only touches briefly in the article upon the important concepts of truth-conditions, elementary propositions, and—what has become almost synonymous with Viennese positivism—the verification principle. He makes it clear, however, that a statement is only to be held as meaningful if the statement can be related to empirical observations, or more precisely, if the statement is logically derivable from observation or "protocol" statements (*Protokollsaetze*). "The meaning of a statement," says Carnap in an often quoted statement of the logical positivist position, "lies in the method of its verification."[18] And "verification" it is made clear, is to be understood in the sense of (sensory) observational verification.

Employing the technique of sarcasm with considerable skill, Carnap explains through example what he means by the use of a word without a meaning:

> Let us assume as an example that someone formed the new word "googel" and claimed that there were things which were googel and things which were not googel. . . . How, in a concrete case, are we to determine if a thing is googel or not? Now let us assume that the person who uses the word, when asked this question, offers no answer—there are, he says, no empirical indicators of googelness. In such a case we would hold the use of the word for impermissible. If, despite this, he still insists that there are googel things and non-googel things, but for the poor, finite understanding of man it must remain an eternal mystery which things are googel and which not, then we must regard this as empty verbiage. Perhaps he will assure us that he really means something by the word googel. From this, however, we only learn the psychological fact that he connects certain images and feelings with the word. But the word on this account does not acquire meaning.[19]

Commonly used metaphysical terms with a similar meaning as "googel" include, says Carnap, "the Absolute", "the thing-in-itself", "essence", "objective spirit", "Idea", "the Being of beings", "God", "non-being", "Ego", the "not-I", "Emanation", "Manifestation", "the Infinite", "the Unconditional", "being-in-itself", "Being-in-and-for-itself", and the *principium* or *arche*. Concerning the last he has in

18. *Ibid.*, p. 236.

19. *Ibid.*, p. 223. The word translated here as "google" is Carnap's "babig"—a word with as much meaning in German as googel has in English.

mind the pre-Socratic quest for the *arche* (*principium*) of the cosmos: "Various metaphysicians have offered answers to the question, What is the ultimate 'principle of the world', saying, for instance, that it is water, number, form, motion, life, spirit, idea, the unconscious, the deed, the good, and so forth."[20] Since all, however, claim that they intend by such words something that is not determinable by empirical means, all such assertions are without meaning. Carnap singles out the word "God" within this context for special treatment, since, he says, it is commonly used in two distinct senses, one of which is quite meaningful, the other not. One sense is that found in ancient myths where "god" is used to designate one or more "bodily entities that reign, as it is, on Olympus, in the sky or under the earth, and are endowed, to a more or less perfect degree, with power, wisdom, goodness, and fortune."[21] In such cases, talk about gods is perfectly meaningful, though what is said, of course, is false since the statements made do not correspond to empirical reality. If there really were beings of the description given, living on Olympus or under the ground, then the mythological statements about the gods would be true; but true or false, such statements can be verified empirically, and hence, are meaningful. In contrast to the mythological usage, metaphysical statements which employ the word "god" are without sense, since they are supposed to designate something supra-empirical, i.e., something beyond the pale of empirical verifiability. Like "googel", the word "god" in such statements is no more than an empty sound or letter grouping void of meaning. "The definitions that are given for god," says Carnap, "on closer inspection reveal themselves to be pseudo-definitions (*Scheindefinitionen*); they lead either to logically impermissible word-combinations, . . . or to other metaphysical words—e.g., *Urgrund*, the Absolute, the Unconditional, the Autonomous, the Independent, etc."[22]

As examples of pseudo-statements whose component words are all meaningful but whose structure goes against the rules of logical syntax, Carnap offers the following: "Caesar is and", and "Caesar is a prime number".[23] The first of these "rows of words" (*Wortreihe*)—they are, of course, not, properly speaking, statements or sentences —is the more obvious in its senselessness because its component words are strung together in a way that breaks the rules of grammatical syntax. After the subject "Caesar", and the verb form "is", an adjective or a substantive combined with an article must follow;

20. *Ibid.*, p. 224.
21. *Ibid.*, p. 226.
22. *Ibid.*
23. *Ibid.*, p. 227.

but in not doing this, this particular "row of words" breaks one of the syntax rules, and hence, winds up in meaninglessness.[24] The second grouping of words, however, does not go against the rules of syntax (at least the usual grammatical syntax), and, indeed, looks very much like the perfectly meaningful statement, "Caesar is a general." But this only shows that the usual grammatical syntax is not a true representation of the logical syntax. An ideal language, which followed the rules of an elaborately worked out logical syntax, would, Carnap insists, so distinguish "general" and "prime number" that the category of words to which they belong, and the rules governing their combination would not permit such a construction as "Caesar is a prime number".[25] Such a language would divide substantives into several syntactic categories such as "thing", "property of a thing", "relationship of a thing", "number", "property of number", "relationship of number", etc., such that it would be breaking the rules of the syntax of that language to predicate of a thing-word, a property-of-number substantive. The logical syntax for such an ideal language, Carnap explains, is the great task that contemporary logicians have to work on.[26]

Having described the two ways in which an apparent statement can be senseless, Carnap proceeds, in the same sarcastic, mock-pedantic tone, to launch the attack for which all the preparation has been made—the attack on Martin Heidegger's lecture, "Was ist Metaphysik?" ("What is Metaphysics?", hereafter simply the Lecture). Heidegger has been chosen, says Carnap, because he is not only the most influential metaphysician in Germany, but offers in his writing many excellent examples of the pseudo-statements of the kind "Caesar is a prime number", i.e., statements which are consistent with traditional grammatical syntax, but not with a more refined logical syntax.[27] Carnap quotes the following from Heidegger's Lecture:

> What is to be investigated is being only (*das Seiende*) and otherwise—nothing; being by itself, and further—nothing; being simply, and beyond this—nothing. But what about this Nothing? . . . Does the Nothing exist only because the not—i.e., negation—exists? Or is it the other way around? Does negation and the not exist, only because of the Nothing. . . . We contend:

24. *Ibid.*, p. 227.
25. *Ibid.*, pp. 227-8.
26. *Ibid.*, pp. 228.
27. *Ibid.*, p. 229.

> The Nothing is prior to the not and negation. . . . Where do we seek the Nothing? How do we find the Nothing? . . . We know the Nothing. . . . Dread reveals the Nothing. . . . What we dread and why we dread was "really"—Nothing. In fact: the Nothing itself—as such—was there. . . . What about the Nothing? . . . The Nothing itself nothings.

To analyze what Heidegger has written here, Carnap provides the following chart[28] which alleges to explain how nonsense-statements of the Heideggerian sort can arise from everyday language usage:

I. Meaningful Statements of Everyday Language	II. Derivation of Meaninglessness from Meaningful Statements of Everyday Language	III. Logically Correct Language
A. What is outside? Ot(?) Rain is outside. Ot(r)	A. What is outside? Ot(?) Nothing is outside. Ot(no)	A. There is nothing (does not exist anything) which is outside. $\sim(\exists x)\cdot Ot(x)$
B. What about this rain? (i.e., What does the rain do?; or, What more can be said about this rain?) ?(r)	B. "What about this Nothing?" ?(no)	B. None of these forms can even be constructed.
1. We know the rain. k(r)	1. "We seek the Nothing", "We find the Nothing", "We know the Nothing" k(no)	
2. The rain rains. R(r)	2. "The Nothing nothings" No(no)	
	3. "The Nothing exists only because . . ." ex(no)	

28. *Ibid.*, p. 230.

The statements under column I, says Carnap, (i.e., "What is outside?", "Rain is outside", "What about this rain?", "We know the rain", "The rain rains") are statements from everyday language (more or less), all logically and grammatically free from objection. With the exception of II-B3 ("The nothing exists only because . . .") the statements in the second column are all grammatically analogous to the corresponding statements in the first column, though logically quite different. Where trouble begins can be seen in the first question and answer, IIA: What is outside?, Nothing is outside. Such a statement is surely meaningful, as can be seen by the fact that it is translatable into the logically correct form, "There is nothing which is outside", or better, the logical schema, $\sim(\exists x)\cdot Ot(x)$, which might be read, "It is not the case, that there is some x, such that x is outside". As it stands, IIA would not be allowed in a logically perfect language, its lack of logical precision being well illustrated in the ease with which the meaningless sentence IIB ("What about this nothing?") can be derived from it. Negation of an existential condition, which in the logically correct language of IIIA is performed by the logical form of the statement (i.e., $\sim(\exists x) \ldots$) is performed in everyday language by the use of a noun. But as seen in IIB, such a noun, which is really a logical operation, can lead to the construction, through a grammatically unobjectionable operation, of nonsense-statements such as, "What about this Nothing?" Such nonsense-statements cannot arise, however, when the notation of symbolic logic is used (e.g., Ot(?), Ot(no), $\sim(\exists x)\cdot Ot(x)$).[29]

Statement II-B2, says Carnap—"The Nothing nothings"—is a statement of a unique kind, even when viewed from the perspective of the writings of other metaphysicians, or from the rich repertoire of Heidegger's own pseudo-statements. Most metaphysical terms and concepts (e.g., "the thing-in-itself", the Absolute, Being, etc.) are derived from words that were once, in context, quite meaningful, but have been used in a metaphoric way which strips all meaning from them. Here, however, one comes upon one of the rare instances where a metaphysician has used a meaningless word (i.e., the verb *nichten*, "to nothing") that never had a meaning to begin with.[30]

Carnap uses his analysis of Heideggerian metaphysics as the occasion for sharpening the distinction between previous anti-metaphysical positions and the position of logical positivism. Whereas formerly, metaphysical writing was often rejected as fairy tales or fantasies of the imagination, the new rejection of metaphysics is on an entirely different basis. The statements in a fairy tale, like the

29. *Ibid.*, pp. 229-230.
30. *Ibid.*, pp. 232-3.

statements about the gods in mythology, do not, Carnap explains, contradict the rules of logic, only the judgment of experience.[31] Fairy tales are perfectly meaningful, though false; hence, belief in them is false belief or superstition. Metaphysics, of which Heidegger's discussion of "the Nothing" is a good example, is not rejected as superstition, but, being irreconcilable with logical syntax and the empirical modes of science, as meaningless "rows of words" (*Wortreihen*).[32]

Having dealt the *coup de grace* to the most widely read contemporary metaphysician, Carnap then goes on in the article to elaborate his contention that all metaphysicians, not just Heidegger, speak nonsense. Most of the logical fallacies and errors that are to be found in the statements of metaphysicians, he suggests, derive from the misuse of the word "being" (*sein*).[33] "Being" is a particularly dangerous word, says Carnap, because it has two uses which metaphysicians are all too prone to confuse. On the one hand, it can be used as a copula prefixing a predicate of some kind, as in the sentence, "I am hungry"; but it can also be used as a designation for existence, as for instance in such statements of philosophers as "I am."[34] In the latter case, as a designation for existence, the use of the forms of the verb "to be," says Carnap, lead to the erroneous predication of existence as if it were the property of a thing—what Kant long ago showed not to be the case in his refutation of the ontological proof for the existence of God.[35] Developments in modern symbolic logic, Carnap informs the reader, have made such a confusion impossible, since the sign for existence can only be applied to predicates, not objects (e.g., the logical schema allows assertions of the kind, "The book is on the table", where the "is" refers to the predicate "on the table", but not, "The book is", where "is" refers to book). A logically perfect language would not permit the use of the verb "to be" as a predication of existence (e.g., the *sum* of Descartes' *cogito ergo sum*), nor as a substantive of any kind, as in all the talk about "Being" (*das Seiende, das Sein*) which has played such a large role in the history of metaphysics.[36] Heidegger is certainly correct, says Carnap, when, quoting Hegel, he says— "Pure Being and pure Nothing are one and the same."[37]

---

31. *Ibid.*, p. 232.
32. *Ibid.*
33. *Ibid.*, p. 233.
34. *Ibid.*, p. 234.
35. *Ibid.*
36. *Ibid.*
37. *Ibid.*, p. 233.

Carnap concludes his article with some suggestions on why people in so many different epochs, among them outstanding intellectuals, have bothered so much about metaphysics.[38]

> "Even those who agree with our results," he says, "will still feel plagued by something strange: are so many men from a variety of epochs and cultures, among them outstanding minds, really supposed to have expended such effort, indeed passionate fervor, on metaphysics, when it consists of nothing but meaningless strings of words? Is it conceivable that such words could have exerted such an effect on readers up to the present day if they contained not even errors, but really nothing at all?"[39]

The attraction and influence of metaphysics, says Carnap in answer to his own question, is due to the fact that the (pseudo) statements of metaphysics serve as the vehicle for the expression of man's feelings toward life *(Ausdruck des Lebensgefuehl)*.[40] Many men, he says, have the need to express in a concrete way the basic attitude and disposition they feel towards their surroundings, their fellow men, and the tasks of life, and metaphysics is one of the ways in which this is done.[41] As such, metaphysics is a kind of poetry or music. "Metaphysicians," Carnap suggests cryptically, "are musicians without a talent for music."[42]

But metaphysics differs from the various art forms such as poetry, music, and fiction, according to Carnap, in that the latter are appropriate to the task they attempt to achieve, while the former is not. One would normally, he says, not object to the means that someone has chosen to express his particular feelings and attitudes, but the means chosen by the metaphysician are illegitimate because they involve a deception, which is often a self-deception;[43] for the metaphysician makes it appear as if the *Lebensgefuehl* which he tries to express deals with a question of true and false, when actually truth-functionality has nothing to do with what he says. The metaphysician, unlike the lyric poet, "brings in arguments to support his statements; he demands assent to their content, he attacks metaphysicians of another persuasion and seeks in his own treatise

38. Ibid., p. 238.
39. *Ibid.*
40. *Ibid.*, p. 238.
41. *Ibid.*, p. 239.
42. *Ibid.*, p. 240.
43. *Ibid.*

to refute their propositions."[44] Lyric poets know better, and are well aware of the fact that they are dealing with art and not theory.[45]

Carnap's article ends with a reflection on the fact that the most artistically gifted metaphysician, namely, Nietzsche, was also the one who was least guilty of committing the logical fallacies of the kind which abound in Heidegger. "In the work in which he (Nietzsche) brings to the most intense expression what others express through metaphysics or ethics, that is, in *Zarathrustra*, he openly chooses, not the misleading theoretical form, but the form of art—of poetry."[46]

Heidegger's Nothing and the Experience of Radical Derealization-Depersonalization

Carnap's attack on metaphysics—specifically, on Heidegger's metaphysics—was so trenchant, the response it drew from like-minded intellectuals so favorable and enthusiastic, that Heidegger himself in the mid 1930s,[1] in an apparent attempt to take some of the sting out of Carnap's jab, was to begin speaking of the desirability of an *Ueberwindung* of metaphysics. "The question, 'What is Metaphysics?'," wrote Heidegger in the 1943 Postscript to the original Lecture, "is a question that goes beyond metaphysics. It originates in a kind of thinking that has already entered into the *Ueberwindung* of metaphysics. It is in the nature of such transitions that they must, within certain limits, still speak the language of that which they are helping to overcome (*ueberwinden*)."[2] The change, however, like a good deal of Heidegger's thought, seems to have been merely verbal, as he quite obviously had no intention of moving in any direction even remotely near to the logical positivism of the Vienna Circle. The kind of thinking philosophy is concerned with, he explained in the same Postscript, originates in "the experi-

44. *Ibid.*
45. *Ibid.*
46. *Ibid.*

1. H. Spiegelberg, *The Phenomenological Movement* (Martinus Nijoff, The Hague, vol. 1, 1971), p. 290.
2. All quotations from the Lecture (1929), Postscript (1943), and Introduction to the 5th edition (1949) are translated from *Was ist Metaphysik?*, edited by Vittorio Klostermann (Frankfort, 1969).

ence of the truth of Being";[3] and this experience of Being and its truth, it is made clear, does not fall within the domain of logic and mathematical calculation.[4] Heidegger's reply to his logical positivist critics, however, though it reiterates the assertion originally made in the Lecture that metaphysics—or meta-metaphysics, metaphysics-*ueberwunden*—cannot be grasped within the framework of formal logic, does little in the way of clarifying in any direct way the meaning of the Nothing which Carnap had atacked. Just why Heidegger chose to remain so obscure is a question, however, that cannot be taken up here.

Certainly, one of the more striking features of Carnap's attack was its audacity. In one fell swoop he attempted to sweep away, taking relish in the thought, not only Heidegger's metaphysics, but a philosophical enterprize dating back more than two and a half millennia. From a cultural history point of view, one can see such audacity as the by-product of the tremendous practical success of the natural sciences and the enormous prestige that has accrued to the thought modes employed within their domains. As all the members of the Vienna Circle proudly admitted, their thinking was tied closely to modern developments in science and mathematics, along with those in formal logic.[5] Even aside from considerations of practical success and prestige, however, given the clarity and precision of the modes of thought employed within the laboratory sciences, it required little persuasion, especially when the alternative seemed to be the muddled *Wortspielerei* of a Heidegger, to turn many intellectuals away from metaphysics, or even to declare war against it. It is within this context that the extreme audacity of the attack on metaphysics is to be seen.

While the controversy between positivism and metaphysics, like any philosophical dispute, is greatly illuminated by a knowledge of its cultural and historical context, the student of the controversy who wishes to delve deeper must address himself to some of the specific issues raised. Just what, for instance, if anything, could have been meant by Heidegger's lecture on the "Nothing"—a Nothing which nothings and which "science wants to have nothing to do with"?[6] Even if one accepts uncritically Carnap's final suggestion that much of metaphysics is an attempt to express the writer's general attitude toward life, it would be a peculiar attitude indeed, cer-

3. *Ibid.*, p. 48.
4. *Ibid.*, pp. 47-8.
5. On the historical background of logical positivism, see Frederick Copleston, *Contemporary Philosophy* (Newman Press, N.Y., 1956), pp. 26-44.
6. *Was ist Metaphysik*, p. 27.

tainly one worth investigating further, which expressed itself in the form of reflections on a Nothing. Even commentators quite sympathetic to Heidegger, it should be mentioned, have acknowledged difficulty in interpreting the Lecture,[7] and no one could claim, even after the popularization of Sartre's writings, that the meaning of the "Nothing" is self-evident.

Informed by a knowledge of the interest displayed by leading philosophers in Heidegger's time in extreme or abnormal states of mind,[8] a closer examination of the Lecture will reveal that the Nothing which Heidegger talks of is his peculiar way of expressing a radical kind of alienation experience which began to attract attention from psychiatrists and psychopathologists in the last decades of the 19th century under the heading of derealization and depersonalization. The existence of two terms to refer to what most investigators acknowledge as aspects of one and the same experience, and the tendency toward greater reliance on the term depersonalization must be seen as the product of the dominance in the West of ego-psychology[9] a situation which, like Heidegger's obscurity, can only be mentioned here without further consideration. It must be mentioned, however, to explain the adoption for the present analysis (which implicitly rejects the framework of ego-psychology) of the single, hyphenated term, "derealization-depersonalization".

Although ultimately rejecting the suggestion—more it would seem to make Heidegger look like a fool than for the reasons actually advanced—Carnap himself had suspicions that the Nothing of Heidegger's Lecture related to some kind of psychological or psycho-

7. The Heidegger scholar Werner Brock, for instance, apparently seeking to console the doubtful, offers the reassuring description of the problem of the Nothing posed in "Was ist Metaphysik? as "apparently very odd, enigmatic and unusual" (*Existence and Being*, Henry Regnery Company, Ill., 1949), p. 202. Brock does not in his own mind have a really clear idea of what Heidegger meant, but he suggests a comparison both to the Greek understanding of Chaos and to the Hebrew creation myth in *Genesis* (p. 215).

8. E.g., Karl Jaspers in his *Psychologie der Weltanschauungen* (1919), (5th edition, Springer Verlag, Berlin, 1960); and Konstantin Oesterreich, *Die Phaenomenologie des Ich* (Verlag von Johann Ambrosius Barth, Leipzig, 1910). Among earlier philosophers, Nietzsche and William James might be mentioned.

9. For a carefully written and thought-provoking reinterpretation of the derealization-depersonalization experience, drawing heavily from the phenomenology of Husserl and the traditions of the Zen Buddhists, see Bin Kimura, "Zur Phaenomenologie der Depersonalization", *Der Nervenartz*, vol. 34, pp. 391-397. Kimura begins his interpretation with the forthright declaration: [In the interpretation of depersonalization], "the concept of an Ego, which to the present time has been the preoccupation of Western philosophy and psychology, reveals itself to be an *aporia*" (p. 391).

spiritual experience, as can be seen when he voiced the following misgiving:

> In view of the crude logical errors which we find in propositions IIB, we might arrive at the belief that perhaps the word "nothing" in the quoted treatise has a completely different meaning from usual. And such a belief is reinforced when we read further that dread reveals the Nothing and that in dread Nothing itself as such is there. Here it appears as if the word "nothing" is supposed to designate a definite feeling-like essence, pehaps of a religious sort or something that is based on such a feeling.[10]

That the Nothing of the Lecture refers to some kind of extreme experience can be of little doubt if one is willing to discount the obvious logical sophistries as peripheral. The Nothing, we are told in the Lecture, is not a thought or an idea in the mind, something, for instance, that one could imagine sitting in an easy chair. "We can, of course," says Heidegger, "think being as a whole (*das Seiende im Ganzen*) in an 'idea' and then negate in thought what we have imagined and 'think' it negated." "In this way," he continues, "we arrive at the formal concept of the imagined nothing, but never the Nothing itself."[11] This Nothing cannot be comprehended through the normal structures of logic,[12] nor is it accessible to natural science, which is concerned only with beings in their multiplicity (*das Seiende*). The latter turns away from the Nothing as "a horror and a phantasm".[13] Having established the incompatibility of the Nothing with the formal structure of mathematics and logic, and having noted the aversion natural science has for it, Heidegger then says: "If the Nothing itself is still to be inquired about, then it must be already given: *we must be able to encounter it*" (emphasis added).[14] Here the experiential nature of the Nothing comes into view, and is unmistakable further on in the Lecture when Heidegger asserts: "Our search [for the Nothing] . . . can only be proved in its legitimacy by *a fundamental experience of the Nothing*" (emphasis

---

10. Carnap's only reason for rejecting the quoted suggestion is the fact that Heidegger at times definitely does use the word "nothing" in a more usual sense—i.e., as "a logical particle that serves as the expression of a negating existential proposition." ("Ueberwindung," *op. cit.*, p. 231.)

11. *Was ist Metaphysik, op. cit.*, p. 30.

12. *Ibid.*, p. 28.

13. *Ibid.*, p. 27.

14. *Ibid.*, p. 29.

added).[15] Elsewhere in the Lecture he makes reference to an "occurrence" (*Geschehen*) within the inner being (*Dasein*) of man.[16]

The derealization-depersonalization experience may be characterized in the following manner: There is an extreme psychic repulsion and withdrawl from the entire space-time-matter world, including the body and its sensations, and a resulting envelopment of the person in an intense mood of forlornness and dread. The body, the concrete piece of subsisting matter previously distinguished as belonging to, and constitutive of, a "me" or self, suddenly escapes in a process of alienation to become part of the same vast, hostile, unending expanse which is the world. There is the frightful feeling of one's self or ego, including one's connection with the memories of the past, being shattered or obliterated (hence the title "depersonalization"). The alienation of the past destroys all trust in a continuous flow of time, and along with it, all confidence in what will happen in the future. The whole world seems far away, as if seen through inverted binoculars, and, what is worse, it cannot be re-entered or made closer.

Psychoanalytically oriented psychologists describe the experience in the following manner:

> Depersonalization consists of an estrangement of the external and internal world. [The person undergoing depersonalization] has lost the feeling of the reality of inner and outer perceptions and of sensations. Just as the external world appears to him strange, unreal, 'ghostlike', so have his thoughts, his feelings, and the sensations of his own body lost . . . the quality of being real.[17]
>
> To the depersonalized individual the world appears strange, peculiar, foreign, dream-like. Objects appear at times strangely diminished in size, at times flat. Sounds appear to come from a distance.
>
> When an individual is in a state of depersonalization libido is withdrawn not only from the environment, but also from the ego, or, at any rate, from certain of the embodiments of the ego.
>
> . . . subjective life appears to have been robbed of its personal character and removed into the outside world. [Such people] have become strangers to themselves. . . . They experience a fundamental change in their personalities. They do not give

15. *Ibid.*, p. 30.
16. *Ibid.*, p. 31.
17. Herman Nunberg, *Principles of Psychoanalysis*, translated by Madlyn Kahr and Sidney Kahr (International Universities Press, Inc., N.Y. 1955) p. 184.

> themselves wholly to their experiences . . . They meet with an inner opposition to their experiencing of life.
>
> The outer world from which the individual has turned away and withdrawn his libido is only capable of alteration in the direction of the unreal. It no longer possesses the full character of reality. The world appears as a dream, objects as though they belonged to the planet Mars.[18]

An excellent first-hand account by an unidentified man of a sudden and intense manifestation of the experience is given in William James' *Psychology*:

> I was alone, and already a prey to permanent visual trouble, when I was suddenly seized with a visual trouble infinitely more pronounced. Objects grew small and receded to infinite distances—men and things together. I was myself immeasurably far away. I looked about me with terror and astonishment: *the world was escaping from me* . . . I remarked at the same time that my voice was extremely far away from me, that it sounded no longer as if mine . . . In addition to being so distant, objects appeared to me *flat*. When I spoke with anyone, I saw him like an image cut out of paper with no relief . . . Constantly it seemed as if my legs did not belong to me. It was almost as bad with my arms. As for my head, it seemed no longer to exist . . . I appeared to myself to act automatically, by an impulsion foreign to myself . . . I had an ardent desire to see my old world again, to get back to my old self. This desire kept me from killing myself.[19]

The sense of the physical body and the things associated with it as something alien or repulsive is a common feature of the experi-

18. Paul Schilder, *Introduction to a Psychoanalytic Psychiatry*, translated by Bernard Glueck (Nervous and Mental Disease Publishing Co., N.Y., 1928), pp. 32-5. Besides the chapter on "Depersonalization" in this work (pp. 32-38), valuable treatments of the experience are given by Konstantin Oesterreich, "Die Entfremdung der Wahrnehumungswelt und die Depersonalisation in der Psychasthenie", in *Journal fuer Psychologie und Neurologie*, Band VII-VIII (1907), pp. 253-276, 61-97, 141-174, and 220-237; and also by the same author, *Die Phaenomenologie des Ich, op. cit.*, the chapter on "Das Selbstbewusstsein und die Depersonalisation", pp. 306-337; Karl Jaspers, *Allgemeine Psychopathologie* (Springer Verlag, Berlin, 1913), English translation, *General Psychopathology*, H. Hoenic and Marian W. Hamilton translators (University of Chicago Press, 1963) pp. 62-63; T. Weckowicz, "Depersonalization", in *Symptoms of Psychopathology, A Handbook* (John Wiley and Sons, Inc., N.Y., 1970), pp. 151-163. Also the article by James P. Cattel, "Depersonalization Phenomena", in the *American Handbook of Psychiatry*, volume III, pp. 88-100.

19. Volume I, Dover Publications, Inc., N.Y., 1950, pp. 377-378.

ence. Just as saliva or feces, once expelled from the body, is alienated—i.e., no longer accorded the intimacy and identity with the self which it had while within the confines of the body—so the physical body, or certain parts of it such as the legs and arms, is alienated. Frequently this includes, too, the tongue and the sounds it makes, which are seen as part of the same hostile, external world from which the self (psyche) retreats. One's own voice is no longer one's own.

Some accounts which stress the aspect of body and voice alienation are given below:

> Everything appears as through a veil, as if I heard everything through a wall. Things do not look as before, they are somehow altered, they seem strange, two-dimensional. My own voice sounds strange.[20]
>
> I feel funny, I feel I have no body, I am only a head—and yet it draws me down to one side—still my head seems strange, I can't explain it. I hold up my hand and look at it, it does not seem to be my arm. If I try knitting I cannot go on, it does not seem my hands.[21]
>
> Innerly I appear to myself as alien. When I saw myself in the mirror, I did not appear to be me. The face appeared to me different than I expected. I did not have the feeling of identity. My speech too sounded strange to me. The tone seemed to me different.[22]
>
> When I went walking and came upon strange streets and had this sensation, so everything appeared to me strange . . . Indeed, my voice appeared alien, as if I myself was no longer present.[23]
>
> As I sat at home at the dinner table with my parents, everything appeared to me strange. The language of my parents sounded so peculiar as if out of a great distance. Even my own words sounded to me as if those of a stranger.[24]
>
> Everything bodily appeared to me so strange, that I began to doubt its reality. Sometimes I touched the objects around me and myself also in order to convince myself of their and my own bodily existence.[25]

20. Karl Jaspers, *General Psychopathology, op. cit.*, p. 62.

21. Quoted in W. Mayer-Gross, "On depersonalization", *British Journal of Medical Psychology*, Vol, XV, 1935, p. 111.

22. Quoted in Konstantin Oesterreich, "Die Entfremdung der Wahrnehmungswelt und die Depersonalisation in der Psychasthenie", *op. cit.*, p. 260.

23. *Ibid.*, p. 65.

24. *Ibid.*, p. 75.

25. *Ibid.*, p. 74.

> Everything is mechanical and occurs without being known . . . The body, which has no meaning for me, is empty.[26]
>
> The whole universe of space and time, of my own senses, was really an illusion . . . There I was, shut in my own private universe, as it were, with no contact with real people at all. . . . I and all around me were utterly unreal. My soul was finally turned into nothingness . . .
>
> [Analyzing this and similar types of experiences the same author writes]: . . . the ego is not merely cut off; it is also increasingly restricted until it seems to become an almost infinitesimal point of abject misery, disgust, pain and fear. It is very noticeable that the repulsion is not only felt for the outside world; it invades the personality in the form of intense disgust for oneself, horror of one's body, of seeing one's reflection in a mirror and so on. Clothes and personal property associated with oneself become objects of repulsion.[27]

The derealization-depersonalization-type of experience varies considerably, both in degree of intensity, and in duration. In the less extreme variety it may take the form of a pervasive mood of boredom or ennui, a "blah" feeling, but one not connected with physical tiredness, and usually accompanied by acute anxiety feelings:

> I can't get outside my shell or let people or happenings in. . . . I feel detached, everything's blah and I feel I'm sleep-walking.[28]
>
> Participation, interest, and joy in living is what I need above all . . .
> Everything leaves me completely indifferent (*gleichgueltig*) including at times even my own nourishment, to such a degree that I can't overcome myself in order to tend to it. I almost want to say that I no longer have the wish at all to become well, so indifferent have I become towards myself.[29]
>
> The world looks perfectly still, like a postcard. . . . a bus moves along without purpose, it does not feel real . . . Everything in vision is dead, branches of trees are swaying without purpose.[30]

The more extreme variety of the experience, well represented in the first quotation from James, comes suddenly, often without ex-

26. *Ibid.*, p. 91.
27. John Custance, *Wisdom, Madness and Folly: The Philosophy of a Lunatic* (Pellegrini and Cudahy, N.Y., 1952), pp. 73, 78-9.
28. Quoted in James Cattel, *op. cit.*, p. 89.
29. Quoted in Oesterreich, *op. cit.*, p. 82.
30. W. Mayer-Gross, *op. cit.*, p. 111.

pectation, engulfing the person in a wave of panic, fear of losing control, of going insane, of being eternally damned. The extreme or "freak-out" variety of alienation experience is well illustrated in an account given by a young Swiss school girl of an experience she had one day at school:

> One day, while I was in the principal's office, suddenly the room became enormous, illuminated by a dreadful electric light that cast false shadows. Everything was exact, smooth, artificial, extremely tense; the chairs and tables seemed models placed here and there. Pupils and teachers were puppets revolving, without cause, without objective. I recognized nothing, nobody. It was as though reality, attenuated, had slipped away from all these things and these people. Profound dread overwhelmed me, and as though lost, I looked around desperately for help. I heard people talking but did not grasp the meaning of words. The voices were metallic, without warmth or color.[31]

When the experience reaches such a peak, desperate reactions often ensue in a frantic effort to "hold on", to prevent, that is, the whole world, and oneself with it, from slipping away into oblivion. A fixed object—a chair or a tree, for instance—may be violently clutched, perhaps while its name is repeated over and over again. Or there may be an endless and compulsive reciting of memorized lines, songs, prayers, Bible quotes, etc. Anything, even the inflicting of severe bodily pain will be seen as preferable to the freak-out state itself, pain being at least "my" pain, and hence, constitutive of a body-self with orientation in a world:

> I have depression spells and feel I'm going insane. The feeling starts around my waist and swims to my head. I feel very hot inside. The world is unreal and so am I and all my friends. Everything seems so vast and I wonder, 'Where did it all start and where will it all end?' I can combat the feeling by talking or, if alone, by running around the room. When it gets to my head, there's an urge to cry out but I don't. There's a hyper-awareness, not a faint feeling. *There's an urge to hit myself on the head and knock myself out or to have pain, for that feeling would be more real.* (emphasis added)[32]

---

31. From *Autobiography of A Schizophrenic Girl, With an Analytic Interpretation by M. Sechehaye*, translated by G. Rubin-Rabson (Grune and Stratton, N.Y., 1951), p. 7. Quoted in Ben-Ami Scharfstein, *Mystical Experience* (Bobbs-Merril Co., N.Y., 1973), p. 138.
32. Cattel, *op. cit.*, p. 90.

> I held on to my friend's arm in panic; I felt I was lost if he left me for one moment.[33]
>
> All objects appear so new and startling, I say their names over to myself and touch them several times to convince myself they are real. I stamp on the floor and still have a feeling of unreality.[34]

In turning to an analysis of Heidegger's Nothing, one first sees that he associates it with the experience of dread: Does there occur in the inner being of man, Heidegger asks, "a mood in which Dasein is brought face to face with the Nothing?" "This occurrence," he answers, "is not only possible, but really does happen, though only infrequently and for brief instances, in the fundamental mood of dread (*Angst*).[35] Reading this, one familiar with the Kierkegaardian analysis in *The Concept of Dread*,[36] must resist the impulse to conclude that Heidegger is here referring to the dread faced when a man is called to independent action and decision. There is, to be sure, certainly much in the Lecture, as earlier in Heidegger's *Sein und Zeit*, that would tend to support such a conclusion. Heidegger's distinction between dread and fear, for instance, is taken over directly from Kierkegaard's analysis,[37] and while not receiving the emphasis Heidegger gives it, the designation of dread as a "nothing" also has precedent in Kierkegaard.[38] Against such a conclusion,

33. Jaspers, *op. cit.*, p. 63.

34. *Ibid.*, p. 63.

35. *Was ist Metaphysik, op. cit.*, p. 31.

36. Translated by Walter Lowrie, Princeton University Press, Princeton, N.J., 1944.

37. "Dread" in Kierkegaard is distinguished from "fear" in that the latter is directed at a concrete object—e.g., the fear of being run over in the street, of contracting malaria, of losing one's job, of being raped, etc.,—while dread is a kind of fear undirected at a definite object: "One almost never sees the concept dread dealt with in psychology, and I must therefore call attention to the fact that it is different from fear and similar concepts which refer to something definite." (*The Concept of Dread, Ibid.*, p. 38)

And similarly Heidegger in *Was ist Metaphysik*: "Dread is fundamentally different from fear. We are always fearful of this or that definite being that threatens us in this or that particular way . . . Dread-of is always a dread-about—but not about this or that particular thing. The indefiniteness of that of which and about which we dread is not simply the absence of definition, but the fundamental impossibility of defining that of which and about which we dread." (p. 31.).

38. *Cf.* Kierkegaard: "In innocent ignorance there is peace and repose; but at the same time there is something different which is not dissension and strife for there is nothing to strive with. What is it then? Nothing. But what effect does nothing produce. It begets dread. This is the profound secret of innocence, that at the same time it is dread." (*Ibid.*, p. 38).

however, one must take into account the fact that the dread analyzed by Kierkegaard, unlike Heidegger's Nothing, is related primarily to the social world—i.e., the world of public opinion and the crowd—and to the personal ordeal required to break away from it.[39] Heidegger's dread, on the other hand, is involved not merely with disengagement from the social world, but the more radical disengagement from the whole space-time-matter world of *das Seiende*.

---

39. The dread that Kierkegaard describes is what one must endure in taking upon oneself the freedom of making momentous, independent decisions. "Dread is the possibility of freedom." (p. 139) "[Dread] is the alarming possibility of being able." (p. 40). In journeying through the dread of free decision, a person can no longer rely on others to back him up, nor is there any universal and mechanical rule to determine how he is to decide. In the dread of free decision, says Kierkegaard, a man must strip himself of all the socially re-enforced pretensions and illusions he harbors about himself, placing himself through faith in the hands of Divine Providence. "Learning to know dread is an adventure," says Kierkegaard (p. 138), a venture of faith in which a man must free himself from the comforting reassurance of the crowd. And this disengagement, according to Kierkegaard, has cathartic power: "He who sank in the possibility of dread and personal decision has an eye too dizzy to see the measuring rod which Tom, Dick, and Harry hold out as a straw to the drowning man; his ear is closed so that he cannot hear what the market price for men is in his day . . ." (p. 142).

". . . he bids [dread] welcome . . . he shuts himself up with it, he says to the surgeon when a painful operation is about to begin, 'Now I am ready'. Then dread enters into his soul and searches it thoroughly, constraining out of him all the finite and the petty . . ." (p. 142).

"With the help of faith, dread trains the individual to find repose in providence." (p. 144).

While Kierkegaard does not supply the reader with everyday examples of what he means, it would not be difficult to supply situations where something like the dread he has in mind is present—i.e., situations in which a person, confronted with the adventure of possible free decision, no longer concerns himself with what the neighbors or anyone else may think. The teenager who defies his parents or teachers for the first time; the man who opens up a small business or starts an organization consciously accepting the risk of failure and public ridicule; the lover who tells his or her partner that the relationship must be ended (or started up); the individual who involves himself in controversy knowing that his reputation may be damaged because of it; the man who speaks out knowing that what he says may be held opprobrious or evil by those within his peer group; or whenever a person says "no" when it is expected of him to say "yes", or "yes" when he is expected to say "no"—these seem to be decision-situations where something akin to the dread Kierkegaard analyzes would likely be present, though perhaps, as a theologian, he would be more restrictive to situations involving specifically moral or religious conflicts.

Heidegger has taken over the Kierkegaardian understanding of dread in *Sein und Zeit*, developing an extensive vocabulary of his own: Facing the dread of one's own possibility, a person (*Dasein*) frees himself from the temptation (*Versuchung*) of narcotic, passifying (*beruhigend*) submission (*Verfallensein*) to socially accepted standards of what one (*das Man*) is and is not to do. Echoing Kierkegaard, he writes: "Dread reveals in Dasein the *being towards* of its own being-able—that is the *being-*

That a kind of derealization-depersonalization experience is what Heidegger is analyzing under the headings of dread and the Nothing suggests itself when he says: "In dread we say that it is for one unhomelike-and-uncanny (*unheimlich*). All things and we ourselves sink into an indifference (*gleichgueltigkeit*).[40] Here one can see described the beginning of the alienation process, the attentional disengagement from both self and world (ego and environment), and the gradual slipping away of both self and world into an all encompassing mood of anxious indifference. (Certainly no one would describe Kierkegaardian dread, coming in the midst of personal choice and action, as an "indifference".)

The identification of the experience becomes unmistakable, however, when Heidegger says:

> We cannot say what it is before which one feels unhomelike-and-uncanny . . . The indifference into which all things, together with ourselves, sink, is not, however, to be understood to mean that everything simply disappears. Rather in its drawing away (*Wegruecken*) everything turns towards us. This drawing-away of the totality of being (*das Seiende im Ganzen*)—which then crowds around us in dread—threatens us. There is nothing left to hold on to. The only thing that remains as we are overwhelmed in this slipping away of the world of being (*das Seiende*) is this nothing (*dieses "kein"*).[41]
>
> That we often attempt, in the unhomelikeness-and-uncanniness of dread to break the empty silence through an involuntary talk is only proof of the presence of the Nothing.[42]
>
> Dread holds us in suspension because it causes the totality

free for . . . the authenticity of its being as possibility, which it always is." (*Sein und Zeit*, Max Niemeyer Verlag, Tuebingen, 1972, pp. 187-8. Except for the rendering of *Angst* as "dread" the Macquarrie-Robinson translation (Harper and Row Publishers, N.Y., 1962) has been followed almost exactly).

Even in *Sein und Zeit*, however, the analysis of "Was ist Metaphysik?" is anticipated. Going beyond Kierkegaard and the social world, Heidegger makes clear the function of the experience which he calls dread within the context of a fundamental ontology that seeks to comprehend Being and the world—where "world" means the whole universe of space-time rather than just the social world of conformity to *das Man*: "Being in dread opens up primordially and directly the world as world." "In dread what is ready-to-hand in the world sinks away, and so in general does innerworldly being (*das Seiende*). The 'world' can offer nothing more, just as Dasein-with others cannot." (p. 187).

40. Lecture, p. 32. All translations of "Was ist Metaphysik?," particularly these, have been made in close collaboration with the translation of R.F.C. Hull and Alan Crick, in *Existence and Being*, edited by Werner Brock, *op. cit.*

41. *Ibid.*

42. *Ibid.*

> of existent things (*das Seiende im Ganzen*) to slip away. Thus we, existent men in the midst of a world of existents, ourselves slip away. It is not, therefore, in principle unhomelike-and-uncanny for a "you" or a "me", but for a "one" (*einem*). In the trembling of this suspension where there is nothing to hold on to, only pure Da-sein is still there.[43]
>
> In dread there lies a retreat-from . . . and this retreat-from precedes from the Nothing. The Nothing does not attract towards itself; it is in principle repelling. This *re*pulsion from itself is, however, a slipping away and an *ex*pulsion onto the totality of being—as it sinks away. This repelling expulsion onto the totality of being—which is in a process of slipping away—crowds in on Dasein. It is the essence of the Nothing: nihilation. . . . The Nothing itself nothings.[44]
>
> Nihilation is no arbitrary event: as a repelling expulsion onto the totality of being—which is slipping away—it reveals this totality in its complete though up to now hidden alienness (*Befremdlichkeit*) as that which is absolutely other—in contrast to the Nothing that is. . . . Only because the Nothing lying at the core of Dasein is revealed, can the full alienness of the totality of being overwhelm us.[45]

Making allowance for the word-play (most of which can only be partially rendered in English) that typifies the Heideggerian prose style, most of the characteristics of the radical alienation experience (derealization-depersonalization) can be clearly seen in the quoted passages. There is a drawing, sinking, and slipping away of the world (derealization) from psyche (Dasein), which, in its desperate efforts to re-engage reality, can find nothing to hold on to. Expelled onto the infinite, hostile expanse of the space-time-matter world (*das Seiende im Ganzen*), consciousness is repelled, the alien hostility of the world casting it back onto itself—a "self", which, lacking even a body-cathexis, is a trembling, unextended intensity of dread. Since the ego has been annihilated (nothinged), it makes no sense to speak of a "you" or a "me" to which all has become alien, for such would presuppose the self and self-consciousness which no longer exists. As we ourselves slip away and the whole world becomes unhomelike and uncanny (derealized, alien, estranged), we attempt, in our forlornness and dread, to maintain contact with some kind of reality through compulsive, involuntary talk.

Part of the difficulty of interpretation stems from the fact that

---

43. *Ibid.*
44. *Ibid.*, p. 34.
45. *Ibid.*

Heidegger has combined in his analysis the milder forms of derealization-depersonalization with the more extreme. When he talks about the slipping away of the totality of being, of the "you" and of the "me", and when he concludes the analysis with the ominous-looking, "the Nothing nothings", he appears to be describing a more extreme variety of the experience. And when he speaks elsewhere of a "primordial dread" (*urspruengliche Angst*) occurring only in rare moments, he seems to have in mind an experience which is sudden and intense.[46] Yet when he talks of "indifference", particularly in an earlier part of the Lecture where "indifference" is associated with existential boredom,[47] he appears to describe a mood or experience on a much lower order of radicalness and intensity. But that he is alluding in his treatment of the Nothing to the derealization-depersonalization-type of experience, there seems little cause for doubt.

Before leaving Heidegger's Lecture, a brief comment is in order regarding its indictment of science (no doubt the cause of much amusement within the Vienna Circle). When he speaks of science turning away from the Nothing, of wanting to have nothing to do with "a horror and a phantasm", he seems merely to be voicing the simple truth, implicitly or explicitly stated by many prominent thinkers before Heidegger, that the mechanistic bias of 19th century science tended to pass over or discard aspects of human experience which could not be comprehended on its paradigm. While it is not wholly correct in view of the considerable literature on derealization-depersonalization which began to appear in the 1890s to speak of science turning away from the Nothing, there seems to be substantial truth even today, as some investigators have been forced to conclude, to the indictment of science which Heidegger was making (albeit, in his own peculiar idiom) in 1929. The situation in science having, regrettably, changed little from Heidegger's day, a contemporary professor of psychiatry, for example, writing in a recent psychopathology text, offers an assessment of his own scientific discipline not unlike that of Heidegger:

> Depersonalization and derealization phenomena are of great theoretical interest since they are concerned with the core of personal experience. They are linked up with the sense of ultimate reality of the external world and the self and, therefore,

46. *Ibid.*, p. 35.

47. "Profound boredom, thrust hither and thither, in the abyss of Dasein as a silent fog, draws together all, everyone and everything, including itself, into a strange indifference." *Ibid.*, pp. 30-1.

they are of great importance for epistemology, ontology, and other problems of philosophy of mind. Because of the metaphorical language in which they are described and because they belong to a field in which the physical world and the world of symbols overlap, and where mythical thinking interpenetrates reality thinking (Mayer-Gross), depersonalization phenomena offer great difficulty to an experimental attack. For this reason they have been largely ignored by experimentally oriented psychologists.[48]

Freak-Out in a French Town : Sartre and the Nothing

The theme of "Was ist Metaphysik?"—i.e., the Nothing and its encounter—can be brought into sharper relief by a brief look at the writings of a man who was so impressed by Heidegger's Lecture that he went on to write a whole philosophical tome on the Nothing. The man in question, of course, is Jean-Paul Sartre. What is more important for present purposes, however, than Sartre's *Being and Nothingness*—a work which at least approaches Heidegger's work in the turgidness and opacity of its writing style—is the fact that Sartre has given us, in the form of his autobiographical diary/ novel *La Nausée*,[1] an extended account of the very sort of radical alienation experiences that form the basis of all the to-do about the Nothing.

Antoine Roquentin, the lonely, a-social writer of the diary, is plagued by horrible, shattering experiences that show a marked variation in intensity and duration. While a mood of estrangement — of aloneness in one's own private world, of being cut off from the surrounding social and physical world—permeates the whole novel, what is designated by the term Nausea (and what is easily recognized as accute attacks of the derealization-depersonalization experience) occur at definite, peak-instances. A gradual buildup in the feeling of estrangement precedes each attack:

48. T. Weckowicz, "Depersonalization", in *Symptoms of Psycho-Pathology: A Handbook, op. cit.*, p. 163.

1. English translation, *Nausea*, by Lloyd Alexander (New Directions Publishing Corporation, New York, 1964). Quotations reprinted with permission of New Directions.

> I must finally realize that I am subject to these sudden transformations. The thing is that I rarely think: a crowd of small metamorphoses accumulate in me without my noticing it, and then, one fine day, a veritable revolution takes place.[2]

Sartre has apparently chosen the title Nausea to indicate the repulsion and psychic disengagement which characterizes the experience, and images of repelling, disgusting objects are scattered throughout the work—e.g., rotting meat, blood, puss, vomit, mud, excrement, filth, crawling insects, etc. The feeling of repulsion applies to the entire spatio-temporal world, both physical and social, the body included. Physical objects, no longer useable as tools, no longer serving their role as props in a meaningful drama of life, become threatening, repelling. When Antoine Roquentin began to analyze his Nausea, the change in physical objects was what first struck him. The opening of the diary begins:

> The best thing would be to write down events from day to day. Keep a diary to see clearly—let none of the nuances or small happenings escape even though they might seem to mean nothing . . . I must tell how I see this table, this street, the people, my packet of tobacco, since *those* are the things which have changed. I must determine the exact extent and nature of this change.[3]

Two paragraphs later we learn of the repulsion he felt one day upon picking up a muddy rock at the seashore, and the paralyzing-debilitating effect this repulsion had upon him:

> Saturday the children were playing ducks and drakes and, like them, I wanted to throw a stone into the sea. Just at that moment I stopped, dropped the stone and left. . . . I saw something which disgusted me, but I no longer know whether it was the sea or the stone. The stone was flat and dry, especially one side, damp and muddy on the other. I held it by the edges with my fingers wide apart so as not to get them dirty.[4]

And on the following day he comes to realize that the repelling object was the stone:

---

2. *Ibid.*, p. 5.
3. *Ibid.*, p. 1.
4. *Ibid.*, p. 2.

> Now I see: I recall better what I felt the other day at the seashore when I held the pebble. It was a sort of sweetish sickness. How unpleasant it was! It came from the stone . . . a sort of Nausea in the hands.[5]

On other occasions, a glass of beer, a man's hand, and a cheese knife serve as objects of repulsion and the simultaneous psychophysical withdrawl:

> . . . when the Self-Taught Man [an obsequious admirer] came to say good morning to me . . . there was his hand like a fat white worm in my own hand. I dropped it almost immediately and the arm fell back flabbily.[6]
>
> Everywhere, now, there are objects like this glass of beer on the table there. When I see it, I feel like saying: "Enough". . . . I have been *avoiding* looking at this glass of beer for half an hour. I look above, below, right and left; but I don't want to see *it*.[7]
>
> My hand is clutching the handle of the dessert knife. I feel this black wooden handle. My hand holds it. . . . I would rather let this knife alone . . . The knife falls on the plate.[8]

The repulsion and threatening quality which external objects represent is then elaborated:

> Objects are not made to be touched. It is better to slip between them as much as possible. Sometimes you take one of them in your hand and you have to drop it quickly.[9]
>
> Objects should not *touch* because they are not alive. You use them, put them back in place, you live among them; they are useful, nothing more. But they touch me, it is unbearable. I am afraid of being in contact with them as though they were living beasts.[10]

Alienation of the body is also part of Roquentin's Nausea, and he is afraid to look in the mirror for fear that it will reveal a changed self. His face, he tells us, is no longer the same; while not entirely dead, it has lost all radiance, character, aliveness. It is as drab and

---

5. *Ibid.*, pp. 10-11.
6. *Ibid.*, p. 4.
7. *Ibid.*, p. 8.
8. *Ibid.*, p. 122.
9. *Ibid.*, p. 122.
10. *Ibid.*, p. 10.

lifeless as a stone or clod of earth. At best it is on the life-order of a jellyfish:

> There is a white hole in the wall, a mirror. It is a trap. I know I am going to let myself be caught in it. I have. The grey thing [i.e., his face] appears in the mirror. I go over the reflection of my face. Often in these last days I study it. I can understand nothing of this face. . . . I think it is ugly because I have been told so. But it doesn't strike me. At heart, I am even shocked that anyone can attribute qualities of this kind to it, as if you called a clod of earth or a block of stone beautiful or ugly . . . what I see is well below the monkey, on the fringe of the vegetable world, at the level of a jellyfish. It is alive, I can't say it isn't; but this was not the life that Anny [a love from former times] contemplated. . . . I see the insipid flesh blossoming and palpitating with abandon. The eyes . . . are glassy, soft, blind, red-rimmed, they look like fish scales.[11]

During one of the acute attacks of the Nausea—a psychotic episode in the local café—Roquentin experiences his whole head, with the exception of the eyes, as artificial, as a piece of alien matter estranged from the will of a living, acting being:

> I can move my eyes but not my head. The head is all pliable and elastic, as though it had been simply set on my neck; if I turn it, it will fall off.[12]

Since the psychic estrangement pertains to the body as well as all other physical objects, at one point Roquentin is not sure what has really changed, his hands or the objects they contact:

> There is something new about my hands, a certain way of picking up my pipe or fork. Or else it's the fork which now has a certain way of having itself picked up, I don't know.[13]

The disengagement from the social world is equally radical as that from the world of objects. Roquentin is a loner: "I live alone, entirely alone. I never speak to anyone, never: I receive nothing, I give nothing. . . . I have no friends."[14] While somewhat of an exaggeration since he does have some psychic interaction with people, and

11. *Ibid.*, pp. 16–17.
12. *Ibid.*, p. 19.
13. *Ibid.*, p. 4.
14. *Ibid.*, pp. 6, 18.

some know him and talk to him, during the acute phases of the Nausea, he is utterly alone, finding no comfort whatever in social discourse. At such times, others appear changed, living in a world in which he is not. Despite his fear of an impending Nausea attack in the Café Mably, Roquentin can find no solace in the men around him:

> For the first time I am disturbed at being alone. I would like to tell someone what is happening to me before it is too late . . . I know very well that all these bachelors around me can be of no help: it is too late, I can no longer take refuge among them. . . . I can't explain what I see. To anyone. . . . I am quietly slipping into the water's depths, towards fear. . . . I am alone in the midst of these happy, reasonable voices.[15]

Three days later a full-scale freak-out experience occurs in the Railwaymen's Rendezvous Café. After failing to recognize the once familiar waitress, his whole microcosm is thrown into chaos:

> 5:30. Things are bad! Things are very bad: I have it, the filth, the Nausea. And this time it is new: it caught me in a cafe. Until now cafes were my only refuge because they were full of people and well lighted; now there won't even be that any more . . . I felt my shirt rubbing against my breasts and I was surrounded, seized by a slow, coloured mist, and a whirlpool of lights in the smoke [i.e., of the cafe], in the mirrors, in the booths glowing at the back of the cafe . . . I was on the doorstep, I hesitated to go in and then there was a whirlpool, an eddy, a shadow passed across the ceiling and I felt myself pushed forward. . . . Madeleine [the waitress] came over to take off my overcoat . . . I did not recognize her. . . . Madeleine smiled:
>
> "What will you have, Monsieur Antoine?"
>
> Then the Nausea seized me, I dropped to a seat, I no longer knew where I was; I saw the colours spin slowly around me, I wanted to vomit. And since that time, the Nausea has not left me, it holds me. . . . The Nausea is not inside me: I feel it *out there* in the wall, . . . everywhere around me. It makes itself one with the cafe, I am the one who is in *it*.[16]

Here the psychic disengagement, the repulsion and fleeing from the world, is total; the whole spatio-temporal world is experienced as hostile. The Nausea is not, like a physical illness, a property of a

15. *Ibid.*, pp. 8, 9.
16. *Ibid.*, pp. 18–20.

body-enclosed "me", but engulfs everything that exists. Psyche, in desolation, without anything to call its own, is cast into an alien, hostile world which it can neither extricate itself from, nor enter into.

The manner in which the Nausea attack subsides is equally revealing. Roquentin asks the waitress to play his favorite jazz record on the phonograph. Hearing the Negress sing generally has therapeutic value, and in this case it turns out to be of an almost miraculous kind:

> A few seconds more and the Negress will sing . . . If I love this beautiful voice it is . . . because it is the event which so many notes have been preparing from so far away, dying that it might be born. And yet I am troubled; it would take so little to make the record stop: a broken spring, the whim of Cousin Adolph [the acting bartender] . . .
>
> The last chord had died away. In the brief silence which follows I feel strongly that there it is, that *something has happened.*
>
> Silence.
>
> "Some of these days
> You'll miss me honey"
>
> What has just happened is that the Nausea has disappeared. When the voice was heard in the silence, I felt my body harden and the Nausea vanish. . . . My glass of beer [once threatening, repelling] . . . it seems heaped up on the table, it looks dense and indispensable, I want to pick it up and feel the weight of it, I stretch out my hand . . . This movement of my arm has developed like a majestic theme, it has glided along the song of the Negress; I seemed to be dancing.[17]

Roquentin's world is now filled with music. The Nausea has vanished. Psyche has returned to soma ("my body hardened") and from the security and safety of its new-found home, it can reach out and interact with the once hostile environment.

At other times Roquentin tries to escape the Nausea attacks by taking refuge in fixed objects, staring at houses, or frantically clutching a book. But such actions are usually ineffective, or only of short-term value. When the freak-out comes, all is to no avail. Roquentin describes the efforts he made in one such attempt to "hold on" as he sat alone in the local library, anticipating an impending attack:

17. *Ibid.*, p. 22.

The last readers left around one o'clock . . . I felt shrouded in silence. . . . I raised my head: I was alone . . . The inconsistency of inanimate objects! The books were still there, arranged in alphabetical order on the shelves . . . along with the stove, the green lamps, the wide windows, the ladders [i.e., other fixed objects], they dam up the future. As long as you stay between these walls, whatever happens must happen on the right or the left of the stove . . . Thus these objects serve at least to fix the limits of probability.

Today they fix nothing at all: it seemed that their very existence was subject to doubt, that they had the greatest difficulty in passing from one instance to the next. I held the book I was reading tightly in my hands: but the most violent sensations went dead. Nothing seemed true: I felt surrounded by cardboard scenery which could quickly be removed. The world was waiting, holding its breath, making itself small—it was waiting for its convulsion, its Nausea . . .

Frightened, I looked at these unstable beings which, in an hour, in a minute, were perhaps going to crumble; yes, I was there, living in the midst of these books full of knowledge describing the immutable forms of the animal species, explaining that the right quantity of energy is kept integral in the universe; I was there, standing in front of a window whose panes had a definite refraction index. But what feeble barriers! [i.e., natural laws]. I suppose it is out of laziness that the world is the same day after day. Today it seemed to want to change. And then, *anything, anything*, could happen . . .

I seized my overcoat and threw it round my shoulders; I fled. . . . A real panic took hold of me. I didn't know where I was going. I ran along the docks, turned into the deserted streets in the Beauvois district: the houses watched my flight with their mournful eyes. I repeated with anguish: Where shall I go? Where shall I go? *Anything* can happen. Sometimes, my heart pounding, I made a sudden right-about-turn: what was happening behind my back? . . . As long as I could stare at things nothing would happen: I looked at them as much as I could, pavements, houses, gaslights; my eyes went rapidly from one to the other, to catch them unawares, stop them in the midst of their metamorphosis. They didn't look too natural, but I told myself forcibly: this is a gaslight, this is a drinking fountain, and tried to reduce them to their everyday aspect by the power of my gaze.[18]

The quoted passage is a powerful account of the derealization aspect of the more extreme variety of derealization-depersonali-

18. *Ibid.*, pp. 76-8.

zation experience. The state of chaos into which psyche has been thrown, however, is also depersonalizing or ego-annihilating since the estrangement of the environment extends to both the body and the memory images of the past. Just as the body and what happens to it are events that happen to an "it", but not to a "me", so memory images lose the intimacy and possessedness of being "mine". This ego-annihilating aspect of the experience becomes the major theme of the novel as the Nausea attacks are seen by Sartre-Roquentin not as a passing sickness, but as constitutive of his true nature. "The Nausea has not left me," he says at the beginning of the celebrated passage in the park under the chestnut tree, "and I don't believe it will leave me soon: but . . . it is no longer an illness or passing fit: it is I."[19] The Nausea, furthermore, is seen not merely as a revelation of the true nature or essence of one particular man—an "abnormal" or "mentally ill" man perhaps—but of all men in their unique status as human beings, however hard most may try to hide this fact from themselves through the various forms of self-deception.[20] Hu-

19. *Ibid.*, p. 126.

20. This revelation serves as the basis for the novel's attack (which cannot be analyzed further on this occasion) on all those "normal" people (i.e., the French bourgeoisie) who order their lives through custom and habit, taking refuge in such things as the regularities of nature, the laws of science, fixed time-tables, etc. In what might be described as a kind of Satanic Sermon on the Mount, Roquentin lashes out at the citizens of Boulville, wishing upon them, in hatred and vengeance, the same Chaos, the same Hell, which his own psyche has had to bear:

"The Nausea has given me a short breathing spell. But I know it will come back again: it is my normal state. . . . I do not neglect myself, quite the contrary: this morning I took a bath and shaved. Only when I think back over those careful little actions, I cannot understand how I was able to make them: they are so vain. Habit, no doubt, made them for me. . . . Did habit also lead me to this hill? I can't remember how I came any more. Probably up the Escalier Dautry: Did I really climb up its hundred and ten steps one by one? . . .

"I watch the grey shimmerings of Boulville at my feet. . . . These little black men I can just make out in the Rue Boulibet—in an hour I shall be one of them.

"I feel so far away from them, on the top of this hill. It seems as though I belong to another species. They come out of their offices after their day of work, they look at the houses and the squares with satisfaction, they think it is *their* city, a good, solid, bourgeois city. They aren't afraid, they feel at home. . . . They have proof, a hundred times a day, that everything happens mechanically, that the world obeys fixed, unchangeable laws. In a vacuum all bodies fall at the same rate of speed, the public park is closed at 4 p.m. in winter, at 6 p.m. in summer, lead melts at 335 degrees centigrade, the last street car leaves the Hotel de Ville at 11:05 p.m. . . . Idiots. It is repugnant to me to think that I am going to see their thick, self-satisfied faces. They make laws, they write popular novels, they get married, they are fools enough to have children. And all this time, great, vague nature has slipped into their city [i.e., the Nausea], it has infiltrated everywhere, in their house, in their office, in themselves. It doesn't move, it stays quietly and they are full of it inside, they breathe it, and they

man reality (the *Néant* and *pour soi* of *Being and Nothingness*) *is* the Nothing of the freak-out state, Sartre declares in effect, the ego-annihilation of the Nausea revealing the ultimate void in man as it whisks away all the pretensions and illusions which men use to try to convince themselves that they are really something. This aspect of the experience impels Roquentin to declare at the end of his diary, as he leaves to take up new residence in Paris, that Antoine Roquentin has faded away:

> I savor this total oblivion into which I have fallen . . . Who remembers me? Perhaps a heavy young woman in London [i.e., Anny, his former love]. And is it really of *me* that she thinks? . . . I am no more for her than if I had never met her, she has sud-

---

don't see it, they imagine it to be outside, twenty miles from the city. I *see* it, I *see* this nature . . . I know it has no laws: what they take for constancy is only habit and it can change tomorrow.

"What if something were to happen? What if something suddenly started throbbing? Then they would notice it was there and they'd think their hearts were going to burst. Then what good would their dykes, bulwarks, power houses, furnaces and pile drivers be to them? . . . For example, the father of a family might go out for a walk, and, across the street, he'll see something like a red rag, blown towards him by the wind. And when the rag has gotten close to him he'll see that it is a side of rotten meat, grimy with dust, dragging itself along by crawling, skipping, a piece of writhing flesh rolling in the gutter spasmodically shooting out spurts of blood. Or a mother might look at her child's cheek and ask him: "What's that—a pimple?" and see the flesh puff out a little, split, open, and at the bottom of the split an eye, a laughing eye might appear. Or they might feel things gently brushing against their bodies, like the caresses of reeds to swimmers in a river. And they will realize that their clothing has become living things. And someone else might feel something scratching in his mouth. He goes to the mirror, opens his mouth, and his tongue is an enormous, live centipede, rubbing its legs together and scraping its palate. He'd like to spit it out, but the centipede is part of him. . . . And someone might be sleeping in his comfortable bed, in his quiet, warm room and wake up naked in a bluish earth, in a forest of rustling birch trees, rising red and white towards the sky like the smokestacks of Jouxteboulville . . . and birds will fly around these birch trees and pick at them with their beaks and make them bleed. Sperm will flow slowly, gently, from these wounds, sperm mixed with blood, warm and glassy, with little bubbles. Or else nothing like that will happen, there will be no appreciable change, but one morning people will open their blinds and be surprised by a sort of frightful sixth sense, brooding heavily over things and seeming to pause. Nothing more than that: but for the little time it lasts, there will be hundreds of suicides . . . Then you will see other people, suddenly plunged into solitude. Men all alone, completely alone with horrible monstrosities, will run through the streets, pass heavily in front of me, their eyes staring, fleeing their ills yet carrying them with them, open-mouthed, with insect-tongue flapping its wings. Then I'll burst out laughing even though my body may be covered with filthy, infected scabs which blossom into flowers of flesh, violets, buttercups. I'll lean against a wall and when they go by I'll shout: 'What's the matter with your science? What have you done with your humanism? Where is your dignity?'" (*Ibid.*, pp. 157-160).

> denly emptied herself of me, and all other consciousness in the world has also emptied itself of me . . . Antoine Roquentin exists for no one. That amuses me. Just what is Antoine Roquentin? An abstraction. A pale reflection of myself wavers in my consciousness. Antoine Roquentin—and suddenly the "I" pales, pales, and fades out.[21]

Before moving on from Sartre, mention should be made of the reception his own philosophy of the Nothing received at the hands of Viennese positivism. Not long after the publication of *L'Etre et le Néant*, A.J. Ayer, a late joiner of the Vienna Circle, wrote a critique for the literary monthly *Horizon*,[22] which was in many respects a repeat performance of Carnap's *Erkenntnis* article. Though more humble and self-critical, acknowledging for instance, his lack of full confidence in his interpretation, Ayer found in Sartre's *néant* the same nonsense and sophistry as Carnap had found in Heidegger's *Nichts*.

Summarizing first the Sartrean argument on the origin of negation and the nature of self-consciousness, Ayer writes:

> Is negation merely a 'quality of judgements', or is the negative element, *le néant*, part of 'the structure of the real'?
>
> Sartre concludes that *le néant* is the origin of negation, and not the other way round. But where then does he ask, does *le néant* come from? It must be produced by something, he thinks, since, being a Nothing, it itself has no being but 'is been' . . . Its property is 'to make nothing of', but since it is not, it cannot do that even to itself, but has somehow to suffer it.

Ayer continues:

> . . . pursuing this preposterous course of reasoning, Sartre then declares that it is beyond the power of any wholly positive being to produce the Néant. What is required is a being which 'makes

21. *Ibid.*, pp. 169-170. The ego-annihilation aspect of the Nausea—i.e., the radical alienation of the memory chain together with the body and sensory field belonging to and constitutive of an "I" or ego, seems to have been the basis for Sartre's attack, written during the same period in which he was writing *La Nausée*, on the concept of a transcendental-ego ("la Transcendance de L' Ego: Esquisse d'une description phenomenologique", first published in *Recherches Philosophiques*, VII, 1936-7, English translation, *The Transcendence of the Ego: An Existentialist Theory of Consciousness*, by Forrest Williams and Robert Kirkpatrick, Farrar-Straus-Giroux publishers, N.Y., 1957). See especially his remarks on psychasthenia (an older term covering depersonalization and other types of psychic disorders) on pages 98-103.

22. July 1945, vol. 12, no. 67, pp. 12-26.

> nothing of the Nothing in its being', which is, in fact, its own *néant*; and this he finds in the person man.
>
> . . . According to Sartre, every conscious state is necessarily a self-conscious state. . . . Since he assumes that all consciousness is intentional, and therefore in some manner distinct from its object . . . he argues that to be present to oneself implies being, in a certain sense, absent from oneself. One remains oneself, but in so far as self-consciousness involves division, the presence *of* self *to* self, one is not entirely oneself. . . . What is it that divides me from myself? . . . Sartre answers that it is Nothing, the Void, *le Néant.*[23]

Ayer then sets forth his critique of Sartre's Nothing in a section entitled "Looking-glass Logic":

> Sartre's reasoning on the subject of *le néant* seems to me exactly on a par with that of the King in "Alice through the Looking-glass". "I see nobody on the road", said Alice. "I only wish I had such eyes", remarked the King. "To be able to see Nobody! And at that distance too!" And again, if I remember rightly: "Nobody passed me on the road". "He cannot have done that, or he would have been here first." . . . The point is that words like "nothing" and "nobody" are not used as the names of something insubstantial and mysterious: they are not used to *name* anything at all. To say that two objects are separated by nothing is to say that they are *not* separated; and that is all that it amounts to. What Sartre does, however, is to say that, being separated by Nothing, the objects are both united and divided . . . The confusion is then still further increased by the attempt to endow Nothing with an activity, the fruit of which is found in such statements as Heidegger's 'das Nichts nichtet' ['the Nothing nothings'] or Sartre's 'le Néant est neantise' ['the Nothing is nothinged']. For whatever may be the affective value of these statements, I cannot but think that they are literally nonsensical.[24]

The Nothing and the Christian Purgatorial Night

Even if one assumes that the Nothing which Heidegger talks of is somehow connected with a radical derealization-depersonaliza-

23. *Ibid.*, pp. 15-17.
24. *Ibid.*, pp. 18-19.

tion-type of experience, the interpreter of "Was ist Metaphysik?" is still left with a perplexing problem—namely, what could an "encounter with the Nothing" possibly have to do with "metaphysics"? This "Nothing", says Heidegger in the Postscript to the Lecture, prepares man for the experience of "Being"—a term which, as it is increasingly clear from Heidegger's later works, including the Postscript itself (if it were not already at least suspected by the suspicious reader of *Sein und Zeit*), is used by Heidegger in a distinctly theological sense.[1] If the interpreter perseveres through the initial perplexity, however, summoning forth once again some of the resources of imagination, and combining these with a general knowledge of Heidegger's intellectual background, the main "metaphysical" impact of the Lecture begins to come into view.

Heidegger, it must be kept in mind, was raised as a Roman Catholic, and studied for a time, before deciding to pursue an academic career, at the Jesuit theological seminary in Konstance, Germany.[2] His interests in both Christian and Greek thought, the ma-

1. The following description of Heidegger's post-*Sein und Zeit* (or more accurately, post-"Was ist Metaphysik?") writings is offered by Laszlo Versenyi:

". . . The relationship between Being and man that now occupies his thought bears closest resemblance to the God-man relationship that is the subject of theology; the language he now uses is most analogous in its structure to theological language; and his ambiguous passion for Being is most like faith's passion for God." (*Heidegger, Being and Truth*, Yale University Press, New Haven, 1965, p. 164)

Versenyi's personal judgement of Heidegger's shift in concern from the analytic of Dasein in *Sein und Zeit* to the Being of his later works, is summed up well in his remark: "*Holzwege* [roughly: "dead ends"] is an apt title not only for the particular collection of essays it has been chosen for, but indeed, for all of Heidegger's later writings." (*Ibid.*, p. 114). Despite his lack of general sympathy, however, Versenyi's book combines good scholarship with lively, critical, and thought-provoking analysis. Unlike many commentators on Heidegger, he asks the relevant questions. In taking a stand as he does, the reader is at least offered a perspective with which he can agree or disagree, declare if a bull's-eye has been made or the mark missed entirely, and thus always a point of reference. The work is also commendable for its often successful attempt to translate Heidegger's language into a more comprehensible idiom, making use of examples to which the reader can relate, terms drawn from an actual stock of existing words, and a writing style marked by clarity and unpretentious simplicity. Reams of pages have been written on Heidegger that do little more than slavishly reproduce Heidegger's thought through memorized Heideggerese, with little if any critical sense or regard for the meaningfullness of what is being regurgitated. (William Richardson's *Heidegger: Through Phenomenology to Thought* [Martinus Nijoff, The Hague, 1963] is perhaps the most extensive effort of this kind, and understandably, has won for itself an introduction by Heidegger himself.)

2. J.L. Metha, *The Philosophy of Martin Heidegger* (Harper and Row, N.Y., 1971), p. 6; Frederick Copleston, *Contemporary Philosophy* (Newman Press, N.Y., 1956), p. 176.

jor intellectual concerns of Roman Catholic education, continued, however, even after his transition to the Academy, and, as is generally known, his familiarity with classical and medieval writings is extensive. His *Habilitationsschrift*, written when he accepted the position in philosophy at Freiburg, concerned the thought of the medieval philosopher-theologian Duns Scotus.[3] Aquinas and Augustine were among those whom he treated in his early (pre-*Sein und Zeit*) lectures at Freiburg.[4] What is, in regard to his later writings, of considerable biographic and hermeneutical interest—as Karl Loewith has suggested[5]—is the final chapter of his Scotus book.

---

3. *Die Kategorien und Bedeutungslehre des Duns Scotus* (J.C.B. Mohr, Tuebingen, 1916).

4. Karl Loewith, *Heidegger: Denker in Duerftiger Zeit* (Fischer Verlag, 1953), p. 76.

5. *Ibid.*, pp. 19-20. Loewith writes:

"The first mention of the problem of the ontic-ontological difference as developed in *Sein und Zeit*—the difference, that is, between Being and beings—is already to be found in Heidegger's *Habilitationsschrift* on *Die Kategorien und Bedeutungslehre des Duns Scotus*, where it says in the final chapter that a philosophy of the living spirit cannot be satisfied with the "spelling out of reality" (of beings), but must, beyond the totality of the knowable, aim at a breakthrough into true reality and real truth. To this end it is necessary to bring to the fore once again that dimension of the soul which reaches into the "transcendent" and which gave the Christian philosophy of the Middle Ages its orientation—this in contrast to the shallow modern view and its "fleeting expanse" without grounding in the absolute spirit of God and in the (transcendent) "primordial relation of the soul to God." If one replaces "true reality" and "real truth" with "truth of Being" and "being of truth"; the dimension of the "life of the soul" which reaches into the transcendent with "*Ek-sistenz*"; "God" with "Being"; and the self-loss of contemporary man in "the substantive expanse of the sense- perceivable world" with fallenness in the world (*Verfallen an die Welt*) and abandonment from Being (*Verlassenheit vom Sein*), so one can recognize the late Heidegger already in his *Habilitationsschrift* . . . If, with Heidegger, one agrees that essential thinking always involves just *one* thought, and that with every thinker of stature this essential thought is already present from the beginning, then the analytic of Dasein returning to itself in decision, which rises to its peak in the doubly emphasized "*freedom* towards death", would be only a way-station (*Zwischenstadium*), and Heidegger's "turn" (*Kehre*) towards self-giving Being a re-turn (*Rueckkehr*) to his theological beginnings."

If the interpretation of "Was ist Metaphysik?" presented here is correct, then this *Zwischenstadium* is taken up by the Purgatory of the Dark Night, the Night in which Dasein (ego-centered existence), lost to the seductions of the world, is annihilated, thus attuning the purgated "Da" to the call of Being, preparing the way for the ultimate disclosure of God in the mystic union. In view of the declaration made at the very beginning of the fragmentary character of *Sein und Zeit* (i.e., "Erste Haelfte"), perhaps one should speak neither of a "Kehre" nor a "Rueckkehr", but of a two-decade long masquerade, a masquerade in which the masquerader—tired of composing overtures for the benefit of the secular intelligentsia, and ashamed of having allowed himself to be taken in by the Horst Wessel choir—casts off his mask to return

There, as a young academic philosopher, he makes plain his disdain for most modern thinking and his belief that the "essential calling" of philosophy—more in tune with the orientation of men in the Middle Ages—is to aim at a "break-through into true reality and real truth" (*wahre Wirklichkeit und wirkliche Wahrheit*).[6] In contrast to the modern form of life (*Lebensform*) which loses itself in the fleeting expanse (*fluechtige Breite*) of sense-perceivable reality (*sinnliche Wirklichkeit*), the medieval *Weltanschauung*, says Heidegger, knew a "dimension of the life of the soul that reaches into the Transcendent."[7] In a passage whose assertion of the priority of metaphysics over logic is reminiscent of "Was ist Metaphysik?",[8] Heidegger writes:

> One cannot see logic and its problems at all in the right light if the connection (*Zusammenhang*) out of which they are interpreted is not a trans-logical connection. *Philosophy cannot in the long run do without its essential optic*—METAPHYSICS. For the theory of truth this means the task of a final metaphysical-teleological interpretation of consciousness.[9]
>
> (emphasis in original)

Such a "metaphysical-teleological interpretation of consciousness", the reader learns, so desperately lacking in modern thought, was universal among medieval thinkers who knew the inner being of man (*inneren Daseins*) as "anchored in the transcendent, primordial relationship (*Urverhaeltnis*) of the soul to God".[10] In one of the footnotes to the chapter, suggestive of just such an interpretation of consciousness (and the theory of truth based upon it), Heidegger states his intention to explore at some future time the relevance of the mysticism of Meister Eckhart:

> [From the standpoint of the fundamental correlation between subject and object . . . and] in connection with . . . the metaphysics of the truth-problem, I hope at some other time to be able to

the repentant sinner, explaining to all who will listen that he really was a God-fearing man after all.

6. *Op. cit.*, p. 236.

7. *Ibid.*, p. 240.

8. Compare for instance: "The Nothing is the origin of negation and not the other way around. When the power of reason within the field of questioning after Being and the Nothing is broken, the fate of the dominance of 'logic' within philosophy is thereby set. The idea of 'logic' itself dissolves in the whirl of a more primordial questioning" ("Was ist Metaphysik?", p. 36).

9. *Die Kategorien und Bedeutungslehre des Duns Scotus, op. cit.*, p. 235.

10. *Ibid.*, p. 239.

> show how the mysticism of Eckhart derives its philosophical meaning and significance.[11]

Knowing Heidegger's background in, and affinity for, Christian philosophical-theological thought, and more specifically, for the medieval and medieval-mystic tradition, it is not surprising to find that the Nothing analyzed in "Was ist Metaphysik?" is virtually the same experience, similarly or identically interpreted, as the experience treated in medieval writings under the title of the Dark Night of the Soul.[12] The similarity between Heidegger's Nothing and the Dark Night experience, together with an understanding of the relationship of such experiences to "metaphysics" ("Being", "Transcendence") will come into clear view after a brief look at some of the medieval writings, in particular, those of John of the Cross. John's *The Dark Night of the Soul* originally fixed the term, and presents the most extensive analysis of the Dark Night phenomenon.[13]

The horror-laden dread that characterizes the Dark Night[14] is set forth by John in unmistakable terms:

> Few there are who walk along this road because it is so narrow, dark, and terrible.[15]
>
> [In the Dark Night] disturbance and horror seize upon [the soul] . . . This consternation is a greater suffering than any other torment in this life.[16]
>
> Sometimes this experience is so vivid that it seems to the

11. *Ibid.*, pp. 231-2.

12. That Heidegger gives no credit in the Lecture to the medieval analysis (except perhaps in the vague reference to "the clear night of the Nothing of dread", p. 34) should not be surprising coming from someone who claimed that his own philosophical concern with Being was without historical precedent in the 2½ millennia from Anaximander to Nietzsche.

13. All of John's works can be found in the one volume English translation sponsored by the Carmelite Order: *The Collected Works of St. John of the Cross*, translated by Kieran Kavanaugh, O.C.D., and Otilio Rodriguez, O.C.D, Institute of Carmelite Studies, Washington, D.C., 1973. All page references, whether to *The Dark Night* or *The Ascent of Mount Carmel* are to this volume.

14. John actually uses the term Dark Night (or just Night) in a variety of ways, speaking of religious faith, for instance, as a Night because in faith one must have trust in a God who is unseen. The monastic practice of mortification of the sensual appetite is also called a Night, more specifically, the Dark Night of sense. The Dark Night which forms the most important subject matter of John's analysis, however, and which seems to have been the basic meaning of the term, is what he calls the Dark Night of the spirit. This is the experience treated here.

15. *The Dark Night of the Soul, op. cit.*, p. 320.

16. *Ibid.*, p. 385.

> soul that it sees hell and perdition open before it. These are the ones who go down to hell alive (*Ps*. 55:16).[17]
>
> David describes this suffering and affliction—although it is truly beyond all description—when he says: The sighs of death encircle me, the sorrows of hell surround me, in my tribulation I cried out (*Ps*. 18:5-7).[18]

John frequently identifies the Dark Night as Hell, and as in the above quotation, he draws upon the testimony of the Hebrew prophets to describe what this Hell is like. Elsewhere, for instance, he writes:

> the soul . . . feels terrible annihilation in its very substance . . . as though it were approaching its end. This experience is expressed in David's cry: "Save me Lord for the waters have come in even unto my soul: I am stuck in the mire of the deep, and there is nowhere to stand; I have come unto the depth of the sea, and the tempest has overwhelmed me. I have labored in crying out, my throat has become hoarse, my eyes have failed . . . (*Ps*. 69:2-4)[19]
>
> The [Dark Night] so disentangles and dissolves the spiritual substance . . . that the soul at the sight of its miseries feels that it is melting away and being undone by a cruel spiritual death: it feels as if it were swallowed by a beast and being digested in the dark belly, and it suffers an anguish comparable to Jonah's when in the belly of the whale. (*Jon*. 2: 1-3)[20]

Here, in a concrete, sensuous idiom, one can recognize most of the features that characterize the more radical variety of derealization-depersonalization-type experience. There is an intense and irresistible repulsion from the entire external spatio-temporal world, including the body ("the waters have come in even unto my soul"); the ego or self, once co-extensive with a body, is radically annihilated ("the soul . . . feels terrible annihilation in its very substance", it "feels that it is melting away and being undone by a cruel spiritual death", "it feels as if it were swallowed by a beast and being digested"); psyche, cast into an alien, hostile world ("the dark belly of a beast", "the mire of the deep"), engulfed in a state of forlornness and dread ("I have come unto the depth of the sea, and the tempest has overwhelmed me") searches frantically—and unsuccessfully —

---

17. *Ibid.*, p. 339.
18. *Ibid.*, p. 338.
19. *Ibid.*, p. 339.
20. *Ibid.*, p. 337.

for something to hold on to, ("I am stuck in the mire of the deep and there is nowhere to stand"); the voice and the visual field are no longer the same, they have become alienated, estranged ("my throat has become hoarse, my eyes have failed").

The frantic and unsuccessful efforts of the psyche, in its complete loneliness, to secure itself somewhere within an alien, derealized-depersonalized universe, is even more pronounced in a description of St. Teresa of Avila, who, like John, was a leading figure in the Carmelite reform movement of the period (Spain, 16th century):

> [the soul] feels an extraordinary loneliness, finds no companionship in any earthly creature. . . . She is like a person suspended in mid-air, who can neither touch the earth, nor mount to heaven. She burns with a consuming thirst, and cannot reach water.[21]

The Dark Night experience, however—which John says he has chosen to write about for the benefit of those who have gone through it and not understood its significance[22]—is not an unredemptive horror. It has, in fact, purgative or cathartic significance, though to understand John's analysis on this score, one must keep in mind the Augustinian psychological framework in which it is set. Man in the Augustinian tradition, is a being divided by two loves, "the love of self (*amor sui*), even to the contempt of God", and "the love of God (*amor Dei*), even to the contempt of self."[23] These loves represent the two masters which no man can simultaneously serve. In keeping with this tradition, sometimes substituting the dualism love-of-God/love-of-creature (creatures meaning all which is less than God) for the *amor Dei*/*amor sui* distinction, John writes, for instance:

> It is the common knowledge of experience that when the will is attached to an object, it esteems that object higher than any other, even though another, not as pleasing, may deserve higher admiration. And if a man desires pleasure from both objects, he is necessarily offensive to the more deserving.

---

21. Quoted in Evelyn Underhill, *Mysticism* (E.P. Dutton and Co., N.Y., 1961) p. 395.
Cf. Heidegger's description of the Nothing in the Lecture: "We are suspended (*schweben*) in dread. More precisely, dread holds us in suspension because it causes the totality of existent beings to slip away. . . . In the trembling of this suspension . . . there is nothing to hold on to . . ." (p. 32).

22. *The Dark Night of the Soul, op. cit.* p. 382.

23. *The City of God,* Bk 14, 28.

> Since love of God and attachment to creatures are contraries, they cannot coexist in the same will.[24]

Love in the Augustinian context is structured by two complimentary components: desire and attraction. The *amor Dei*, for instance, comprises both a desire-for on the part of the lover (man)—specifically, the desire of man to know God—together with an attraction-by on the part of the loved object (God)—specifically, the divine call of grace luring man to know God. This call of grace, like the gentle pull of the Golden Cord in Plato's *Laws* (644e), is seen as an ever-present reality within psyche (the soul), though in John's analysis, "ever-present" would have to be qualified, for the Hell of the Dark Night experience is seen as the condition arising from a total withdrawl of divine grace when psyche is cut off from the teleological-metaphysical component of divine attraction. The Dark Night thus represents the state of the soul (psyche) in total estrangement from the *amor Dei*. Alone, in total abandonment from God, thrown back on his own resources, man becomes Hell—a *chaos tes psyches*—because ultimately, cut off from God, the self as self according to the Christian mystic tradition is a horror filled nothingness. In the Hell of the Dark Night (the Chaos of the freak-out state) the self, thrown back on itself, discovers its-self as a nothingness in complete aloneness (alienation), excommunicated from the world, the society of men, even from its own body.[25]

But Hell does not prevail, says John, for the Dark Night experience, though it may seem otherwise to those who are going through it,[26] is not a permanent condition. Hell becomes Purgatory, not only because of its ultimate transiency, but also because of the wonderous cathartic power associated with its capacity to destroy the *amor sui*. (It was the destruction of the *amor sui* that served as the basis for the rigors of the monastic life, and it was to explain to fellow members of his monastic order how a man goes about mortifying — "making dead"—self-love that John took up the writing of *The Dark Night of the Soul*). In the preoccupation with loving a self—i.e., the consuming psycho-volitional involvement in the pleasures

---

24. *The Ascent of Mount Carmel, op. cit.*, pp. 82, 85.

25. *Cf.* the Zen-Buddhist influenced analysis of Ben Kimura, "Zur Phaenomenologie der Depersonalisation", *op. cit.*, allowing what he calls "das Sich-Actualisieren des Ich als eines Ganzen" (p. 397) to be seen as a process dependent on what he describes as the Zen Buddhist's "formloses also nie objectivierbares allerursprunglichestes Ich" (p. 391).

26. *The Dark Night of The Soul, Ibid.*, p. 343.

and delights of the body (the body of a self), material possessions (the possessions of a self), public reputation (the reputation of a self)—the human "desire-for" communion with God must by necessity recede into the background, together with the capacity to hear and respond to the call of grace. The process of "making dead" the self which a man loves begins for John, as for other monastics, in the practice of extreme sensual denial, through fasting, Spartan living, sexual abstention, etc. Once habituated over a prolonged period, such practices offer the promise of liberating a man from enslavement to sensual desires. But equally, if not more important, is the mortification of that aspect of the *amor sui* which manifests itself in pride and the desire for public acclaim. This is accomplished, according to John, through constant self-accusation, both publically before one's peers (interpersonal confession) and privately before God (private prayer and contrition). "Try to act with contempt of yourself and desire that all others do likewise", John counsels; "try to think lowly and contemptuously of yourself and desire that all others do the same."[27] Nevertheless, John explains, even the most conscientious person, making the most arduous demands upon himself, can never through self-accusation and self-denial alone bring about the complete destruction of the *amor sui*. There will always be in one's volitional disposition, even after years of dedicated effort, a certain residue of egoic self-love. Austerity, prayer, self-accusation, and self-denial can at best bring about "a certain reformation and bridling of the appetites rather than a purgation."[28] Total purgation, the total destruction of the *amor sui* and the corresponding shift in one's psycho-volitional orientation to the love of God, is only possible through the Dark Night experience:

> Without this purgation [in the Dark Night] the soul would be wholly unable to experience the satisfaction . . . of spiritual delight. Only one attachment of one particular object to which the spirit is actually or habitually bound is enough to hinder the experience or perception of the delicate and intimate delight of the spirit of love which contains eminently in itself all delights . . .
> . . . the spirit [i.e., a man's soul] must be simple, pure, and naked as to all natural affections, actual and habitual, in order to be able to freely communicate in fullness of spirit with the divine wisdom.[29]

27. *Ibid.*, p. 103.
28. *Ibid.*, p. 333.
29. *Ibid.*, p. 346.

What the Dark Night experience does, according to John's interpretation, is serve as a kind of radical aversion therapy, the ultimate *therapeia tes psyches*. In revealing the true essence of the self which one attempts to love in the *amor sui* as the supreme horror of Hell, the Dark Night offers experiential confirmation of the mystical teaching that the self is ultimately "Nothing"—a term used again and again by John and other mystics[30]—and, hence, that it is an unreliable love-object. The shattering of the ego, the dissolution of the soul that occurs in the Dark Night experience (depersonalization), is the frightful, but most thorough and lasting way of condi-

30. The poem affixed to the front of *The Ascent of Mount Carmel*, which serves as the basis of commentary for both it and *The Dark Night of the Soul*, includes the following lines:

To reach satisfaction in all
desire its possession in nothing.
To come to the knowledge of all
desire the knowledge of nothing.
To come to possess all
desire the possession of nothing.
To arrive at being all
desire to be nothing.
In this nakedness the spirit
finds its rest, for when it
covets nothing, nothing
raises it up, and nothing
weighs it down, because it is
in the center of its humility.

(p. 67).

John Tauler, the 14 century German mystic, who also wrote on the Dark Night experience, speaks of the experience as casting man back on his own "Nichts":

". . . A man is beside himself . . . his senses fail him, which means he loses all support. Everything that was formerly his slips away and he sinks totally into his own stark nothingness (*Nichts*). And were he not maintained by the loving power of God, he would necessarily become, as he truly believes, stark nothingness (*Nichts*). A man will appear to himself as the vilest and lowest of creatures, as destined for death, weak, irrational, and more wicked than the divil or Lucifer . . ." (*Johannes Tauler: Predigten*, herausgegeben von Dr. George Hofmann, Freiburg, 1961, p. 509).

But Tauler, like John, counsels men to seek this Nothing—i.e., to so humble themselves in the process of self-crucifixion that they become one with this Nothing:

". . . the more a man humbles himself, the more he is raised."

". . . if you want to rise to the highest state of being, if you want to be God's disciple and true witness to the highest degree possible, then you must treat yourself and acknowledge yourself before God as the lowliest and of least account. . . . If you direct all your energy to the task of becoming lowly and of no account (*vernichtet*), so it will happen that you will in truth be raised . . . Only by the lowest humility can you achieve this. Oh bretheren, how great the man who can do this and in such a way that he arrives at his own nothingness (*Nichts*) and in truth acknowledges himself lowly before God!" (pp. 509, 151-152)

tioning a man to realize that he cannot rest in himself. Within the monastic context, the experience thus serves as the paroxysmal culmination of the process of self-mortification (ego-annihilation).[31] It

---

31. The medieval understanding of the Dark Night is summarized by Evelyn Underhill in the following words:

> "[The Dark Night] is the last painful break with the life of illusion, the tearing away of the self from that World of Becoming in which all its natural affections and desires are rooted, to which its intellect and senses correspond, and the thrusting of it into the World of Being."
>
> (*Mysticism, op. cit.*, p. 480).

The anonymous author of the *Theologia Germanica*, describing the Dark Night-type experience as a true repentance and expiation for sin, describes the purgative process in the following manner:

> "*How a righteous Man in this present Time is brought into Hell, and there cannot be comforted, and how he is taken out of Hell and carried into Heaven, and there cannot be troubled.*"

"Christ's soul must needs descend into hell, before it ascended into heaven. So much also the soul of man. But mark ye in what manner this commeth to pass. When a man truly perceiveth and considereth himself, who and what he is, and findeth himself utterly vile and wicked, and unworthy of all the comfort and kindness that he hath ever received from God, or from the creatures, he falleth into such a deep abasement and despising of himself, that he thinketh himself unworthy that the earth should bear him, and it seemeth to him reasonable that all creatures in heaven and earth should rise up against him and avenge their Creator on him, and should punish and torment him; and that he were unworthy even of that. And it seemeth to him that he shall be eternally lost and damned, and a footstool to all the devils in hell, and that this is right and just (and all too little compared to his sins which he so often and in so many ways hath committed against God his Creator). And therefore also he will not and dare not desire any consolation or release, either from God or from any creature that is in heaven or on earth; but he is willing to be unconsoled and unreleased, and he doth not grieve over his condemnation and sufferings; for they are right and just, and not contrary to God, but according to the will of God. Therefore they are right in his eyes, and he hath nothing to say against them. Nothing grieveth him but his own guilt and wickedness; for that is not right and is contrary to God, and for that cause he is grieved and troubled in spirit.

"This is what is meant by true repentance for sin. And he who in this present time entereth into this hell, entereth afterward into the Kingdom of Heaven, and obtaineth a foretaste thereof which excelleth all the delight and joy which he ever hath had or could have in this present time from temporal things. But whilst a man is thus in hell, none may console him, neither God nor the creature, as it is written, 'In hell there is no redemption.' (*Ps.* 49.8) Of this state hath one said, 'Let me perish, let me die! I live without hope; from within and from without I am condemned, let no one pray that I may be released.'

"Now God hath not forsaken a man in this hell, but He is laying His hand upon him, that the man may not desire nor regard anything but the Eternal Good only, and

is the crucifixion, death, and descent into Hell, which, in trembling and in faith, a man must endure before he can experience the miracle of resurrection, rebirth, and ascent into Heaven.[32] On the purgative value of the Dark Night John writes:

---

may come to know that this is so noble and passing good, that none can search out or express its bliss, consolation and joy, peace, rest and satisfaction. And then, when the man neither careth for, nor seeketh, nor desireth, anything but the Eternal Good alone, and seeketh not himself, nor his own things, but the honour of God only, he is made a partaker of all manner of joy, bliss, peace, rest and consolation, and so the man is henceforth in the Kingdom of Heaven." (*Theologia Germanica*, translated by Susanna Winkworth, Stuart and Watkins, London, 1966, pp. 50-1).

32. On the descent into Hell passage of the Nicene creed, see the discussion in Anton T. Boisen, *The Exploration of the Inner World: A Study of Mental Disorder and Religious Experience* (Willet, Clark and Co., Chicago, 1936), pp. 125-141.

The purgative-cathartic value which Dark Night-type experiences sometimes have is attested to by modern psychologists and psychopathologists. Karl Jaspers, for instance, drawing upon his clinical experience, writes of the purgative value of what he calls the "Absolute Nihilism in Psychosis":

"In a [certain] type of psychosis one can observe the *movement* of nihilism. In nihilism [i.e. as an intellectual belief] a man still remains capable of going on (*lebensfaehig*) so long as a point to hold on to still remains. The most fearsome shock enters however, when what has all along been taken for granted (*Selbstverstaendlichkeiten*) is yanked from under his feet—and thus, while seeking something to grasp, it cannot be found.

"Psychologically, nihilism is unavoidable if one's life is to be brought to self-consciousness. Everything that is dead and finalized must first be put in question, must be drawn into the witches' kettle of nihilism if a new form of life is to emerge. Nihilism is not to be escaped by dodging around it: it is to be experienced—which is possible only under conditions of inner forlornness—if it is to be overcome." (From *Psychologie der Weltanschauungen*, Springer-Verlag, Berlin, 1960, pp. 301, 303).

Similarly R.D. Laing speaks of the psychotic process as a potential breakthrough rather than (or in addition to) a breakdown:

"Psychotic experience goes beyond the horizon's of our common, that is, our communal, sense. What regions of experience does this lead to? It entails a loss of the usual foundations of the 'sense' of the world that we share with one another . . . But most radical of all, the very ontological foundations are shaken. The being of phenomena shifts . . . There are no supports, nothing to cling to, except perhaps some fragments from the wreck, a few memories, names, sounds, one or two objects that retain a link with a world long lost . . .

"[Yet] madness need not be all breakdown. It may also be breakthrough. It is potentially liberation and renewal as well as enslavement and existential death. . . .

"True insanity entails in one way or another the dissolution of the normal ego, that false-self competently adjusted to our alienated social reality; the emergence of the 'inner' archetypal mediators of divine power, and through this death a rebirth, and the eventual re-establishment of a new kind of ego-functioning, the ego now being the servant of the divine, no longer its betrayer.

"The fountain of the divine has not played itself out, the flame still shines, the river still flows, the spring still bubbles forth, the light has not faded. But between *us* and It, there is a veil which is more like fifty feet of solid concrete. *Deus absconditus.*

> [The Dark Night] strikes in order to renew the soul and divinize it—by stripping it of the habitual affections and properties of the old man to which it is strongly united, attached, and conformed; it so disentangles and dissolves the spiritual substance . . . that the soul . . . feels that it is melting away and being undone by a cruel spiritual death . . . It is fitting that the soul be in this sepulcher of the dark death in order that it attain the spiritual resurrection for which it hopes.[33]
>
> [The Dark Night] annihilates, empties and consumes all the affections and imperfect habits the soul contracted throughout this life.[34]
>
> In this dark purgation . . . God so weans and recollects the appetites that they cannot find satisfaction in any of their objects, and recollecting them in Himself, He strengthens the soul and gives it the capacity for this strong union of love [i.e., communion with God], which He begins to accord by means of this purgation. In this union the soul will love God intensely with all its strength and all its sensory and spiritual appetites. Such love is impossible if these appetites are scattered by satisfaction in other things.[35]

"Intellectually, emotionally, interpersonally, organizationally, intuitively, theoretically, we have to blast our way through the solid wall, even if at the risk of chaos, madness and death. For from *this* side of the wall, this is the risk. There are no assurances, no guarantees . . ." (*The Politics of Experience*, Ballentine Books, N.Y., 1967, pp. 132, 133, 144, 145, 143).

And even an ego-psychologist like Erickson, brought up in a tradition where "becoming like a little child" is recognized only in the pejorative sense of "regression", is forced to observe:

"On facing therapy . . . while the depth of regression and the danger of acting out must, of course guide our diagnostic decisions, it is important to recognize, from the start, a mechanism present in such turn for the worse: I would call it the 'rock-bottom attitude'. This consists of a quasi-deliberate giving in on the part of the patient to the pull of regression, a radical search for the rock-bottom, i.e., both the ultimate limit of regression and the only firm foundation for a renewed progression. . . . the recovery of our patients sometimes coincides with the discovery of previously hidden artistic gifts . . ." ("The Problem of Ego-Identity", *Journal of the American Psychoanalytic Association*, vol. 4, 1956, p. 89).

But ingrained ideology gets the better of the observer, who remarks in a subsequent sentence, bringing to light with almost comic clarity some of the problems with ego-psychology:

"The element of deliberateness added here to 'true' regression is often expressed in an all-pervasive mockery which characterizes the initial therapeutic contact with these patients, and by that strange air of sado-masochistic satisfaction, which makes it often hard to see and harder to believe, that their self-deprecation and their willingness to 'let the ego die' harbors a devasting sincerity." (*Ibid.*, p. 89).

33. *The Dark Night of the Soul*, p. 337.

34. *Ibid.*, p. 339.

35. *Ibid.*, p. 353.

As can be readily discerned from these passages, the purgative effect of the Dark Night serves two functions simultaneously: (a) through the annihilation of the egoic-self it destroys the basis of the *amor sui*, and (b) with the destruction of the *amor sui*, man's love for God and God's love for man is allowed to achieve its full fruition. This fruition is symbolized by John as the completed ascent up Mt. Carmel, and is effected when the desire for God, purged in the Dark Night of all admixture with competing desires related to a self, compliments the attraction by God (the call of grace), so that, in a single event, man ascends to God, and God descends to man. At its peak, this process may culminate in what is the highest goal of the monastic-contemplative life, the *unio mystica*, the miraculous uniting of God and man in the Beatific Vision of Heaven:

> When [a man] is brought to nothing, the highest degree of humility, the spiritual union between his soul and God will be effected. This union is the most noble and sublime state attainable in this life.[36]

The similarity between the Dark Night of the Christian mystics and the Nothing of Heidegger should now be apparent, together with the "metaphysical" significance of both. In John's analysis, the Dark Night experience brings about the purgative destruction of the *amor sui*—i.e., of the love which manifests itself in the consuming attachment to the penultimate "things of the world"; in "Was ist Metaphysik?", the Nothing—if a person lets himself go into it, if he projects himself into its purgative power ("*das Sich-loslassen in das Nichts*," "*die Hineingehaltenheit in das Nichts*")[37]—frees a man from the idols of the world to which he had previously clung ("*das Freiwerden von den Goetzen die jeder hat zu denen er sich wegzuschleichen pflegt*"),[38] frees a man from his loss to the world of beings ("*das Sichverlieren an das Seiende*").[39] And just as the Dark Night, in annihilating the ego-centric self, opens up the way for the miraculous infusion of divine grace, so the Nothing, according to Heidegger, shatters the ego-centric Dasein, leaving only the pure "Da" as the site of divine Transcendence[40]—the "site of the truth of Being"

36. *Ibid.*, p. 125.

37. "Was ist Metaphysik?", *op. cit.*, pp. 42, 32.

38. *Ibid.*, p. 42.

39. *Ibid.*, p. 36.

40. The Purgatorial Night of the Nothing would thus provide the transition from the Dasein analysis of *Sein und Zeit* to the philosophy of Being developed in Heidegger's later works (a transition which was, no doubt, to a considerable extent planned

as Heidegger terms it in his Introduction to the 5th edition of the Lecture (1949):

> Dread holds us in suspension because it causes the totality of existent beings (*das Seiende im Ganzen*) to slip away. Thus we, existing men in the midst of a world of existents, ourselves slip away. It is not therefore, in principle, unhomelike-and-uncanny for a "you" or a "me", but for a one (*einem*). In the trembling of this suspension where there is nothing to hold on to, only pure Da-sein is still there (da).[41]
>
> Dasein means: projection into the Nothing. Projecting itself into the Nothing, Dasein indeed is beyond the world of beings. This being-beyond the world of beings we call Transcendence.[42]
>
> Dread will bequeath the experience of Being as the other to all beings (*zu allem Seienden*) provided that we do not . . . run away from the silent voice that attunes us to the horrors of the abyss . . .[43]
>
> The clear courage for essential dread guarantees the possibility, pregnant with mystery, of the experience of Being.[44]
>
> Dasein designates that which is first to be experienced as —and correspondingly thought of as—a place, as the site of the truth of Being.[45]

---

from the very conception *of Sein und Zeit*. In the annihilation of the subjective, egocentric (as opposed to theocentric) Dasein, and its fallenness (*Verfallenheit*) to the comforting (*beruhigend*) seductions of the ways and opinions of men (*das Man*), the way is open for Dasein to become the site—the Da—of the objective disclosure of Being, the revelation of God.

41. "Was ist Metaphysik?", *op. cit.*, p. 34.

42. *Ibid.*, p. 35.

43. Postscript, *Ibid.*, p. 46. This passage has a distinctly Kierkegaardian ring, reminiscent of the "fear and trembling" in total despair which a man must endure, according to Kierkegaard, in order to become an authentic Christian.

No doubt Kierkegaard knew in his own personal life something of the Dark Night, but Heidegger's Nothing would seem to be patterned more on the medieval analysis than on the Kiekegaardian. The reason for saying this is that "fear and trembling", "dread", etc., are in Kierkegaard related to concrete crises and events—e.g., moral conflicts, conflicts between faith and reason, the agony of momentous, independent decisions, etc.—while the Nothing of "Was is Metaphysik?" does not seem to be connected with any crisis of this kind. Heidegger's Nothing alludes to the slipping away of reality as a whole, not specifically to the slipping away of moral and religious supports. The experiences of which Kierkegaard and the medieval mystics write, however, should not be too sharply distinguished, and Heidegger has obviously drawn heavily, both in *Sein und Zeit* and in the Lecture, from Kierkegaard's writings.

44. Postscript, *Ibid.*, p. 47.

45. Introduction to "Was ist Metaphysik?", *Ibid.*, p. 14.

Who's On First?

Looking back, from the vantage point of the foregoing analysis, to Carnap's original criticism of Heidegger and the Nothing, we find that on the level of existential communication the two famous philosophers have done no better than Abbott and Costello:

ABBOTT: (playing the part of Dexter Broadhurst, manager of the world-famous St. Louis Wolves baseball team): What do you want to do?

COSTELLO: (playing the part of Sebastian Dinwiddie, an inquisitive peanut vendor): Look Mr. Broadhurst—I love baseball!

DEXTER: Well, we all love baseball.

SEBASTIAN: When we get to St. Louis, will you tell me the guys' names on the team so when I go to see them in that St. Louis ball park, I'll be able to know those fellows?

DEXTER: All right. But you know, strange as it may seem they give ball players nowadays very peculiar names.

SEBASTIAN: Funny names?

DEXTER: Nicknames. Nicknames.

SEBASTIAN: Not—not as funny as my name—Sebastian Dinwiddie.

DEXTER: Oh yes, yes, yes!

SEBASTIAN: Funnier than that?

DEXTER: Oh, absolutely. Yes.

DEXTER: Now on the St. Louis team we have Who's on first, What's on second, I Don't Know is on third—

SEBASTIAN: That's what I want to find out. I want you to tell me the names of the fellows on the St. Louis team.

DEXTER: I'm telling you. Who's on first, What's on second, I Don't Know is on third—

SEBASTIAN: Well then, who's playin' first?

DEXTER: Yes.

SEBASTIAN: I mean the fellow's name on first base.

DEXTER: Who.

SEBASTIAN: The fellow playin' first base for St. Louis.

DEXTER: Who.

SEBASTIAN: The guy on first base.

DEXTER: Who is on first here.

SEBASTIAN: Well, what are you askin' me for?

DEXTER: I'm not asking you—I'm telling you. *Who is on first.*

SEBASTIAN: I'm asking you—who's on first?

DEXTER: That's the man's name!

SEBASTIAN: That's who's name?

DEXTER: Yes.

SEBASTIAN: Well, go ahead and tell me.

DEXTER: Who.

SEBASTIAN: The guy on first.

DEXTER: Who.

SEBASTIAN: The first baseman.

DEXTER: Who is on first.

SEBASTIAN: Have you got a first baseman on first?

DEXTER: Certainly.

SEBASTIAN: Then who's playing first?

DEXTER: Certainly.

SEBASTIAN: Then who's playing first?

DEXTER: Absolutely.

SEBASTIAN: When you pay off the first baseman every month, who gets the money?

DEXTER: Every dollar of it. And why not, the man's entitled to it.

SEBASTIAN: Who is?

DEXTER: Yes.

SEBASTIAN: So who gets it?

DEXTER: Why shouldn't he? Sometimes his wife comes down and collects it.

SEBASTIAN: Who's wife?

DEXTER: Yes. After all the man earns it.

SEBASTIAN: Who does?

DEXTER: Absolutely.

SEBASTIAN: Well all I'm trying to find out is what's the guy's name on first base.

DEXTER: Oh, no, no. What is on Second Base.

SEBASTIAN: I'm not asking you who's on second.

DEXTER: Who's on first.

SEBASTIAN: That's what I'm trying to find out.

DEXTER: Well, don't change the players around.

SEBASTIAN: I'm not changing nobody. . . . You got an outfield?

DEXTER: Oh, sure.

SEBASTIAN: The left fielder's name?

DEXTER: Why.

SEBASTIAN: I don't know, I just thought I'd ask.

DEXTER: Well, I just thought I'd tell you.

SEBASTIAN: Then tell me who's playing left field.

DEXTER: Who's playing first.

SEBASTIAN: Stay out of the infield.

DEXTER: Don't mention any names out here.

SEBASTIAN: I want to know what's the fellow's name in left field.

DEXTER: What is on second.

SEBASTIAN: I'm not asking you who's on second.

DEXTER: Who is on first.

SEBASTIAN: I don't know.

DEXTER: Now take it easy, take it easy.

SEBASTIAN: And the left fielder's name?

DEXTER: Why.

SEBASTIAN: Because.

DEXTER: Oh, he's Center Field.[1]

---

1. *Who's on First? Verbal and Visual Gems from the Films of Abbott and Costello*, Richard J. Anobile, editor (Avon Books, 1972), pp. 220-233 (abridged).

II

Metaphysics as Profanation: Wittgenstein Reconsidered

Gott ist so ueber alles, dass man nichts sprechen kann; drum betest du ihm auch mit Schweigen besser an.
(God is so much above all, that one can say nothing. You worship him better, therefore, through silence.)

Angelus Silesius, *Cherubinischer Wandersmann*

And I saw into that which was without end, and things which cannot be uttered, and of the greatness and infiniteness of the love of God, which cannot be expressed by words.

George Fox, *Journal*

But the Lord is in his holy temple; let all the earth keep silence before him.

Habakkuk 2:20

You shall not make for yourself a graven image, or any likeness of anything that is in heaven above, or that is in the earth beneath . . . You shall not bow down to them or serve them. . . .

Exodus 20:4-5

Now the word of the Lord came to Jonah the son of Amitai, saying, "Arise, go to Nineveh that great city, and cry against it; for their wickedness has come up before me."

Jonah 1:1-2

The Philistine and the Prophet

The firebrand, debunking spirit that characterized Carnap's treatment of Heideggerian and other metaphysics in his *Erkenntnis* article (1932) stands in the starkest contrast to the attitude of compromise and co-existence which characterized his treatment of metaphysics in an earlier, larger work, *Der logische Aufbau der Welt* (1928).[1] While the 1932 article, in the spirit of a conquistador, audaciously declared all utterances of a metaphysical kind to be senseless pseudo-statements, the earlier work, by contrast, "proposes" (*vorschlagen*), for purposes of reaching an "agreement" (*Einigung*) with all parties concerned, over a "suitable delineation of the meaning of the term 'knowledge'," that only empirical (sense-perceivable) and formal-mathematical statements be included under such a heading.[2]

Realms of reality ("spheres of life") that do not fit the conceptual framework of physical science—realms which in "Ueberwindung" and other later articles were either thrown out altogether or consigned to the intellectually and scientifically disreputable category of "emotion" or "feeling"—were in *Aufbau* treated with the greatest respect. There, "love", "poetry", "art", even "mystic enrapture" (*mystische Versenkung*) and "faith based on religious revelation" (*Glauben auf Grund religioeser Offenbarung*), were declared to be spheres of life (*Lebenssphaere*) just like any other, and although outside the domain of science, were seen to be of unquestionable importance and worth.[3] Science, understood as a system of conceptual knowledge, was depicted as only one plane within a three-dimensional area of life, a plane which, though unbounded within its domain, is yet cognizant of itself as only one domain among many:

1. *Der logische Aufbau der Welt*, printed together with *Scheinprobleme in der Philosophie*, by Felix Meiner Verlag, Hamburg, 1928, 1961. English translation by Rolf A. George, *The Logical Structure of the World* (University of California Press, Berkeley, 1967).

2. *Ibid.*, German edition, p. 257 (All references to this edition.).

3. *Ibid.*, p. 257.

> Science, the system of conceptual knowledge, has no limits, but that should not be taken to mean that there is nothing outside of science, that science is all-encompassing. The totality of life (*das Gesamtgebeit des Lebens*) still has many dimensions outside of science, but within its dimension, science knows no limit. An unlimited plane in space can serve as an analogy: it does not include the entire space, though nevertheless, is unlimited and without a border, in contrast to a triangle within this plane.[4]

Even the proposed restriction of the term "knowledge" to include only that which fits the conceptual scheme of the physical sciences is advanced in a non-aggressive spirit. It is presented as a means of furthering the harmonious co-existence of the various spheres of life by eliminating the needless confusion that can result from their intermingling, and the resulting discord between men with interests in different spheres:

> [The proposed restriction] should, indeed, be more favorable to the peaceful relations between the various spheres of life if two so heterogeneous spheres of life [as empirical science and religious intuition] are not designated by the same name [i.e., "knowledge"]. It is only through this confusion that disputes and contradictions emerge, which are completely impossible as long as the complete heterogeneity of the spheres is clearly seen and stressed.[5]

One of his more striking departures from *Aufbau*, if Carnap's additional remarks (1957) to the English translation of the "Ueberwindung" article are taken into account, is in the status of Henri Bergson, the man who, before the rise of Heidegger, was the most influential metaphysician in Europe. In *Aufbau* Bergson is treated as a respected philosopher, whose opposing views on the use of the term "science" deserve serious consideration,[6] and whose views on the nature of metaphysics is even quoted at one point to illustrate an area of agreement between the two philosophers.[7] In the English version of "Ueberwindung",[8] however, Bergson has lost his status

4. *Ibid.*, pp. 253-254.
5. *Ibid.*, p. 258.
6. *Ibid.*, p. 259.
7. *Ibid.*, p. 258.
8. Translated by Arthur Pap as "The Elimination of Metaphysics Through Logical Analysis of Language", in A. J. Ayer, editor, *Logical Postivism* (The Free Press, N.Y., 1959), pp. 60-81.

in Carnap's eyes as a thinker deserving serious regard. His writing, like that of Heidegger and all other metaphysicians, is to be seen as so much nonsense with at best an emotive meaning.[9]

The change in attitude with regard to metaphysics can be seen even when *Aufbau* is compared to Carnap's *Scheinprobleme in der Philosophie,* [10] a shorter work written only two years after the completion of *Aufbau.*[11] It was in *Scheinprobleme* that Carnap introduced for the first time his universal "meaning criterium" (*Kriterium des Sinnes*).[12] In the spirit of a revolutionary, it boldly declared all utterances that do not fit its *Kriterium des Sinnes* to be complete nonsense.[13] The striking change which this represented from his *Aufbau* position, as Carnap himself explains in the "Forward" to the Second Edition of that work, was largely the result of Wittgenstein's *Tractatus,* which he and other members of the Vienna Circle had studied together in the first half of 1927. Carnap describes this as follows:

> The pamphlet *Scheinprobleme in der Philosophie* . . . was first written in the Spring of 1927, at the end of my first year in Vienna. It shows, therefore, a stronger influence of the Vienna discussions and Wittgenstein's book.
>
> [The] condemnation [in *Scheinprobleme*] of all theses about metaphysical reality, which I sharply distinguish from empirical reality, is more radical than that in *Aufbau,* where such theses are only excluded from the domain of science. My more radical outlook was influenced by Wittgenstein's view that metaphysical statements, while in principle unverifiable, are therefore senseless. This view was accepted by the majority of the members of the Vienna Circle and other empiricists.[14]

The *Tractatus* directly, and through its influence on other members of the Vienna Circle indirectly, was thus the cause of Carnap's

---

9. *Ibid.*, pp. 80-81.

10. *Scheinprobleme* and *Aufbau* appeared as separate volumes (both in 1928), though they were combined in 1961 as one book.

11. Note, although first appearing in 1928, *Aufbau* was written between 1922 and 1925; *Scheinprobleme* was completed in the Spring of 1927.

12. *Scheinprobleme* (see *Aufbau, op. cit.*) p. 317.

13. The new spirit is captured in the opening of the second section, where the *Tractatus* is obviously drawn upon heavily: "Reinigung der Erkenntnistheorie von Scheinproblemen/ das Kriterium des Sinnes". "Der Sinn einer Aussage besteht darin, dass sie einen (denkbaren, nicht notwendig auch bestehenden) Sachverhalt zum Ausdruck bringt. Bringt eine (vermeintliche) Aussage keinen (denkbaren) Sachverhalt zum Ausdruck, so hat sie keinen Sinn, ist nur scheinbar eine Aussage" (p. 317).

14. *Aufbau*, pp. XIV-XV.

change in attitude regarding the legitimacy of metaphysics. In his "Intellectual Autobiography",[15] Carnap is equally explicit in stressing the radicalizing impact which the *Tractatus* had upon him. He had, he says, at an early age, come under the influence of "anti-metaphysical scientists and philosophers", but it was only as a result of Wittgenstein that his anti-metaphysical leanings became "strengthened and became more definite and more radical."[16] Wittgenstein was the man to whom he was indebted for the "insight that many philosophical sentences, especially in traditional metaphysics, are pseudo-sentences, devoid of cognitive content".[17] Wittgenstein, he says, was "the philosopher who, besides Russell and Frege, had the greatest influence on my life."[18]

Quite naturally Carnap assumed that the author of the *Tractatus* was a man who shared an Enlightenment-*Weltanschauung* much like his own. The man whose writings had inspired him to give up his live-and-let-live attitude towards metaphysics, to abandon the model of a multi-dimensional universe, and to take up the cause of revolutionary positivism against the "pseudo- problems" of metaphysicians, must, Carnap thought, be a man who holds the same general attitude towards religion and metaphysics as he himself. He must, that is, view anything that smacks of religion or metaphysics with ridiculing condescension, seeing in such the reflection of a primitive stage in human development which the progress of enlightenment and science would gradually overcome. Or so Carnap thought. In the summer of 1927, Carnap actually got the opportunity to meet the man who had exerted the radicalizing effect upon his attitude towards metaphysics. Through the efforts of Schlick, who had been meeting regularly with Wittgenstein on a private basis, Wittgenstein consented to meet additionally with Carnap and a younger member of the Vienna Circle, Friedrich Waismann. Carnap describes the man whom he met at that first meeting in the following manner:

> When I met Wittgenstein, I saw that Schlick's warnings [i.e., about engaging Wittgenstein in heated questioning of the kind typical at meetings of the Circle] were fully justified. But his behavior was not caused by any arrogance. In general, he was of a

15. "Intellectual Autobiography", in Paul Arthur Schlipp, editor, *The Philosophy of Rudolf Carnap* (Library of Living Philosophers, Open Court Publishing Co., La Salle, Ill., 1963), pp. 3-84.
16. *Ibid.*, p. 25.
17. *Ibid.*
18. *Ibid.*

> sympathetic temperament and very kind, but he was hypersensitive and easily irritated. Whatever he said was always interesting and stimulating, and the way in which he expressed it was often fascinating. His point of view and his attitude toward people and problems, even theoretical problems, were much more similar to those of a creative artist than to those of a scientist, one might almost say, similar to those of a religious prophet or a seer. When he started to formulate his view of some specific philosophical problem, we often felt the internal struggle that occurred in him at that very moment, a struggle by which he tried to penetrate from darkness to light under an intense and painful strain, which was even visible on his most expressive face. When finally, sometimes after a prolonged arduous effort, his answer came forth, his statement stood before us like a newly created piece of art or a divine revelation.[19]

Creative artists, religious prophets and seers are obviously not the kinds of people whose attitudes and points of view tend to be shared by anti-metaphysical scientists and philosophers, and as Carnap goes on to remark, it was soon to become apparent that between Wittgenstein and himself there lay the most fundamental difference in world-views. With incredible irony, the man whose book had radicalized Carnap against metaphysics, seemed to have a fundamentally different outlook on the subject. Carnap continues:

> Schlick and I . . . had no love for metaphysics or metaphysical theology . . .[20]
>
> Once when Wittgenstein talked about religion, the contrast between his and Schlick's position became strikingly apparent. Both agreed of course, in the view that the doctrines of religion, in their various forms had no theoretical content. But Wittgenstein rejected Schlick's view that religion belonged to the childhood phase of humanity and would slowly disappear in the course of cultural development. When Schlick, on another occasion, made a critical remark about a metaphysical statement by a classical philosopher (I think it was Schopenhauer), Wittgenstein surprisingly turned against Schlick and defended the philosopher and his work.[21]

Although Carnap says that he was usually in agreement with the various things Wittgenstein said at the meetings, he was con-

---

19. "Intellectual Autobiography", *Ibid.*, p. 25.
20. *Ibid.*, p. 27.
21. *Ibid.*, pp. 26-27.

scious too of a difference, more disturbing to Wittgenstein than to himself, on a much deeper level. This difference was apparently so great that a point was finally reached where Wittgenstein could no longer continue with the discussions, which had proceeded at regular intervals from the time of the first meeting. In the beginning of 1929, Wittgenstein let it be known, through Schlick, that he no longer wanted to meet with either Carnap or Herbert Feigl (another member of the Circle who had sometimes joined the discussions).[22] "Although the difference in our attitudes and personalities expressed itself only on certain occasions," Carnap explains, "I understood very well that Wittgenstein felt it all the time and unlike me, was disturbed by it."[23] "I sometimes had the impression that the deliberately rational and unemotional attitude of the scientist and likewise any idea which had the flavor of 'enlightenment' were repugnant to Wittgenstein."[24]

During the meetings, Wittgenstein would, at times, rather than discuss logic and mathematics, read aloud poems from the Bengali poet and spiritual leader Rabindranath Tagore.[25] Very possibly it was occurrences of this kind which gave Carnap cause to speak of an anti-Enlightenment attitude in Wittgenstein. Elsewhere in his "Autobiography", Carnap charges that Wittgenstein sometimes viewed science and mathematics "with an attitude of indifference and sometimes even with contempt."[26]

---

22. *Ibid.*, p. 27.

23. *Ibid.*, p. 27.

24. *Ibid.*, p. 26. Although Schlick, on the articulate level, shared the same basic world-view as Carnap, in contrast to the latter, Wittgenstein found in him a man of high culture (See *Wittgenstein und der Wiener Kreis*, below, p. 5).

Schlick, according to both Carnap and Feigl, found in Wittgenstein an irresistible charismatic force. Carnap writes: "Schlick himself was very strongly influenced by Wittgenstein both philosophically and personally. During the subsequent years, I had the impression that he sometimes abandoned his usually cool and critical attitude and accepted certain views and positions of Wittgenstein's without being able to defend them by rational arguments in the discussions of our Circle" ("Autobiography", p. 27). And Feigl: ". . . so deeply impressed was Schlick with Wittgenstein's genius that he attributed to him profound philosophical insights which he had formulated much more lucidly long before he succumbed to Wittgenstein's almost hypnotic spell." ("The Origin and Spirit of Logical Positivism", in *The Legacy of Logical Positivism*, edited by Peter Achinstein and Stephen F. Barker, Johns Hopkins Press, Baltimore, Md. 1969, p. 4).

Schlick's inability to distinguish his own ideas from those of Wittgenstein would suggest a personal situation in which his own being was apparently so given up to the charismatic power that Wittgenstein exerted, that his sense of selfhood was considerably diminished.

---

25. *Wittgenstein und der Wiener Kreis* (edited by B. F. McGuinness, Basil Blackwell, 1967), p. 15.

26. "Autobiography", *op. cit.*, p. 28.

The realization that the author of the work which had turned him into an active anti-metaphysician, was a man who, in reality, harbored a positive attitude of some kind towards metaphysics and religion, must have filled Carnap with a deeply disturbing uneasiness. In searching for an explanation of why the author of the *Tractatus* did not share his own Enlightenment-*Weltanschauung*, Carnap turned to psychoanalysis. He had read Freud, and was apparently much impressed by the *Future of an Illusion* conception of God as a substitute father.[27] Freud, of course, had tried to explain in *The Future of an Illusion* why it was that so many of his contemporaries, in an age of science, still clung so passionately to their doctrinal religious beliefs, and in answer, offered the now famous pyschoanalytic explanation of religious beliefs as the product of wish-fulfillments. Desiring to re-establish the sense of safety and security lost in childhood, men invent, says Freud, an all-powerful and all-knowing father. Freud had been particularly struck by the psychic conflicts unleashed in people when their religious beliefs were subjected to rational analysis and criticism, and it was in terms of just such a conflict that Carnap tried to explain Wittgenstein's apparent ambivalence to metaphysics:

> . . . there was a strong inner conflict in Wittgenstein between his emotional life and his intellectual thinking. His intellect, working with great intensity and penetrating power, had recognized that many statements in the field of religion and metaphysics did not, strictly speaking, say anything. In his characteristic absolute honesty with himself, he did not try to shut his eyes to this insight. But this result was extremely painful for him emotionally, as if he were compelled to admit a weakness in a beloved person . . . I had the impression that his ambivalence with respect to metaphysics was only a special aspect of a more basic internal conflict in his personality from which he suffered deeply and painfully.[28]

This, to be sure, is a vulgar application of psychoanalytic theory, and might have been avoided by a clearer state of mind. It is absurd on the simplest common-sense basis. One is supposed to believe that a man who not only held a certain view, but was the actual author and originator of that view—i.e., the view that metaphysical and religious propositions are non-sensical—was a man in whom this same view evoked the most powerful emotional opposition. Darwin, one is asked to believe, was really a Biblical fundamental-

27. *Ibid.*, p. 8.
28. *Ibid.*, p. 27.

ist. That a man in whom metaphysical propositions are "beloved" should be the creator of a system of logic in which such propositions are shown to be nonsense begs the question of how anyone so in conflict with his creation could have brought himself to create it in the first place—i.e., how anyone emotionally tied to metaphysical propositions could possibly have summoned forth the "great intensity and penetrating power" needed to analyze their nonsensicalness.

While the venture in psychoanalysis did nothing to help understand Wittgenstein—one might even call it a "desperate effort to evade the problem"[29]—the meetings with Wittgenstein at least induced Carnap to re-read and reconsider passages in the *Tractatus* which he and other members of the Vienna Circle had too lightly passed over:

> Earlier, when we were reading Wittgenstein's book in the Circle, I had erroneously believed that his attitude toward metaphysics was similar to ours. I had not paid sufficient attention to the statements in his book about the mystical because his feelings and thoughts in this area were too divergent from mine. Only personal contact with him helped me to see more clearly his attitude at this point.[30]

Ironically, before the meetings with Wittgenstein, it was only Otto Neurath who paid much attention to the mystical passages in the *Tractatus*, apparently taking them quite seriously, and objecting strenuously to them.[31] Carnap came to recognize that these passages meant much more to Wittgenstein than he had originally thought, though there is no indication in the "Autobiography" that he was able to discover (or interested in discovering) any connection between these and the rest of the *Tractatus*. Other members of the Vienna Circle such as A.J. Ayer, went on thinking of the *Tractatus* as a radical statement of the logical positivist position,[32] even if, like Carnap, they now believed that a few passages revealed a cer-

---

29. This is Freud's characterization of Tertullian's *credo quia absurdum*. See *The Future of an Illusion*, W. D. Robson-Scott translation (Doubleday and Company, Garden City, N.Y., 1964), p. 42.

30. "Autobiography", p. 27.

31. *Ibid.*

32. Ayer begins the Preface (1935) to his *Language, Truth and Logic*, with the declaration, "The views which are put foward in this treatise derive from the doctrines of Bertrand Russell and Wittgenstein, which are themselves the logical outcome of the empiricism of Berkeley and David Hume." (Dover Publications, N.Y., p. 31.).

tain "ambivalence with respect to metaphysics" on the part of their author.

The actual situation was far different.

The Tractatus : *Preliminary Characterization*

On the occasion of Wittgenstein's death, Bertrand Russell was to remark,[1] without recourse to psychoanalysis, that his one-time student (and teacher) was "more or less of a mystic"—a statement which, if intended to mean a person who has known at least one high level religious experience, was no doubt correct. Russell was misleading, however, when to this he added: "which shows itself here and there in the *Tractatus*". For, far from being, as both Russell and Carnap thought, an unintegrated work, a treatise on logic with mystic themes sprinkled "here and there" (or perhaps only in the last few pages), the *Tractatus* is in its entirety, so conceived from the very first lines, an explication and interpretation of an experience of mystic flight.[2]

1. *Mind*, Volume LX, July 1951, p. 297.

2. This is the focus of the rest of the Section. The present interpretation of the *Tractatus* first crystalized upon reading Brian F. McGuinness's article in the *Philosophical Review* (vol. 27, 1966, pp. 305-328), "The Mysticism of the *Tractatus*". Professor McGuinness is convinced, on the basis of the "Lecture on Ethics", biographical information, and internal evidence in the *Notebooks* and the *Tractatus*, that Wittgenstein, at some time before he completed the *Notebooks*, had some kind of mystic experience (p. 326). It is also suggested, on the basis of an account by Erich Heller ("Encounter", vol. 72, 1959, p. 42) that the occasion for at least one such experience was the performance of the play *Die Kreuzelschreiber* by the Austrian dramatist Ludwig Anzengruber, but no date is given for the performance. The scene which Professor McGuinness describes, however,—with the recurring lines, "Nothing can happen to you"—together with the account of a religious awakening, brings immediately to mind the story of Wittgenstein's change in attitude towards religion as told by Wittgenstein to his friend Norman Malcolm (*A Memoir*, p. 70). Since this was in Vienna, "at about the age of 21", it would have been around 1910 or early 1911. If the interpretation of the *Tractatus* offered here is correct, it is very possible that a mystic-type experience around this time—"a time of painful seeking and of final awakening to clarity about his vocation" (von Wright, "Ludwig Wittgenstein, A Biographical Sketch", *Philosophical Review*, vol. 64, 1955, p. 530)—moved Wittgenstein to take up the study of logic in the first place. The tools of modern logic may well have seemed to Wittgenstein as the best way to establish and secure, against profanation and debasement, the *ganz andere* nature of such an experience and of the translogical Reality which it reveals. In any event, if the say/show-itself interpretation presented here is

Mystic Flight : Theophanic Encounter

Mystic (or ecstatic) flight is a term used to designate a type of religious experience that is recounted in the religious literature and oral traditions of virtually all cultures in all periods of history.[1] While the Biblical prophets and medieval mystics, the gurus of the East and the shamans of archaic cultures constitute perhaps the most familiar cases, such experiences are by no means confined to "extraordinary" or exotic peoples. As Abraham Maslow describes, summarizing the findings of his study of mystic experiences among Americans in the early 1960s:

> They are not restricted to far-out people, i.e. to monks, saints, or yogis, Zen Buddhists, orientals, or people in any special state of grace. It is not something that happens in the Far East, in special places, or to specially trained or chosen people. It's available in the midst of life to everyday people in everyday occupations.[2]

---

correct, Wittgenstein must have had the profoundest religious experience long before 1914, when he dictated the notes on logic to G.E. Moore.

The present interpretation takes issue with the McGuinness article in seeing the "absolute safety" experience as the most important of the three experiences described in the "Lecture", at least in so far as *Tractatus* interpretation is concerned. The centrality that has been accorded here to an understanding of mystic experience for an understanding of the *Tractatus* is, of course, also quite alien to anything in the McGuinnes article. It would certainly be a great aid to future students of the *Tractatus* if Professor McGuinness included the "Lecture on Ethics" in future editions of his translation.

---

1. Of the many books on mystical experience among the religions of the world, the following have especially influenced the present writer's views: Mircea Eliade, *The Two and the One* (Harper and Row, N.Y., 1962, especially Chapter 1, pp. 19-77); Aldous Huxley, *The Perennial Philosophy* (Harper and Row, N.Y., 1970); Rufus Jones, *Studies in Mystical Religion* (Macmillan and Co., London, 1909); and Evelyn Underhill, *Mysticism: A Study in the Nature and Development of Man's Spiritual Consciousness* (E.P. Dutton and Co., N.Y., 1961).

2. "Lessons from Peak-Experiences", *Journal of Humanistic Psychology*, vol. 2, 1962, p. 12. For the conclusion of the study alluded to in this article, see by the same author, *Religions, Values, and Peak-Experiences* (The Viking Press, N.Y., 1970). The most extensive survey of mystical experience among Americans is that of Andrew Greeley and William McCready conducted under the auspices of the National Opinion Research Center. The results of the survey are explained in "Are We a Nation of Mystics", *The New York Times Magazine* (January 25, 1975, pp. 81-90). Other accounts of mystic experiences among "ordinary" people can be found in William James's classic, *The Varieties of Religious Experience* (Collier Books, N.Y., 1961);

The mystic-flight experience may be divided for analytic purposes into two components or aspects. First, there is a radical shift in attention (the attending consciousness) away from the body to which it was previously attached as its unshakable spatio-temporal anchoring. The self or sense of "me" becomes disembodied and delocalized. "In this position the individual experiences his self as being more or less divorced or detached from his body. The body is felt more as one object among other objects in the world than as the core of the individual's own being."[3]

This self-disembodiment (ego loss) is accompanied by a feeling of freedom or liberation from the sense of weighted-downness[4] with which embodied existence is characterized. Thus begins the second aspect of the experience: a sudden, enormous intensification of attention (consciousness), simultaneous with its redirection into, and absorption by, an "outside" or "beyond" of the space-time-matter world in which the body remains. Consciousness, no longer anchored in the world, peeks into the world as through a keyhole. The experience is pregnant with both emotion and meaning. It is a "break-through", "ascent", or "flight" of the soul attaining in its culmination the mystery, wonder, and awe of a theophanic Encounter, of a miraculous union between God and man.

It is just in the miraculousness of the attention shift (disattention of consciousness), that an experience of this kind imprints itself as something *sui generis*; in relation to events in the world of objects in space and time (i.e., the world to which the attending consciousness had adhered before it shifted, expanded, and was drawn "up" and "out of") it stands as *ganz andere*.[5] The transcendent realm, the

---

Marghanita Laski's *Ecstasy: A Study of Some Secular and Religious Experiences* (Indiana University Press, Bloomington, 1961); and Richard M. Bucke, *Cosmic Consciousness: A Study in the Evolution of the Human Mind* (E.P. Dutton and Co., N.Y., 1960, pp. 298-363).

3. R.D. Laing, *The Divided Self, An Existential Study in Sanity and Madness* (Penguin Books, Baltimore, Md., 1955), p. 69.

4. The term is borrowed from Theodore Rozak, *Where the Wasteland Ends: Politics and Transcendence in Post-Industrial Society*. (Doubleday and Co., Garden City, N.Y., 1972), p. 392.

5. The term *ganz andere* was popularized in this century by Rudolf Otto, whose book *Das Heilige* (*The Sacred*, translated into English under the unfortunate title, *The Idea of the Holy*, Oxford University Press, 1950) has become a standard work in the philosophy of religion and religious experience. The analysis of the mystic flight experience given here is similar to that of Otto:

> Ecstasy . . . is characterized by two features: by the exclusion of attention and by the extreme intensification (*Hoechstspannung*) of attention . . . Ecstasy is then

"beyond" which is ascended to, is, in its purity, something "outside of" and "wholly other than", the mundane world of space and time. It is the kingdom of God which is not of this world, a Nirvana transcending the world of logic and multiplicity.[6]

The ego-loss or disembodiment of the self in the mystical experience is well represented in the following passage from the 14th century German mystic, Henry Suso:

> When the good and faithful servant enters into the joy of his Lord, he is inebriated by the riches of the house of God; for he feels, in an ineffable degree, that which is felt by an inebriated man. He forgets himself, he is no longer conscious of his selfhood; he disappears and loses himself in God, and becomes one spirit with Him as a drop of water which is drowned in a great quantity of wine. . . . What is that other power, if it be not that by means of his union with the Divine Personality, there is given to man a divine strength and a divine power that he may accomplish all which pertains to his blessedness and omit all which is contrary thereto? And thus it is that . . . a man comes forth from his selfhood.[7]

The shift in the attending consciousness away from the body finds expression here as the losing of one's self-consciousness in God; the immense intensification of consciousness as the giving of "a divine strength and a divine power". The additional elements of redi-

---

[characterized by] (a) the extreme intensification of attention and consciousness together with the necessarily accompanying condition whereby the consciousness of self is diminished, at times to the point of extinction . . . And ecstasy is characterized by (b) the moment . . . where all attention is gathered and collected from its attachment to penultimates to find its rest in loving attachment to its transcendental object. As such, it is the concentrative fixing of attention (*Starrwerden der Aufmerksamkeit*) upon its object. As Meister Eckhart says, "the fixation (*Verstarrtsein*) of the soul in God." (*Das Ganz Andere*, Leopold Kloz Verlag, Gotha, 1929, pp. 70-71).

6. On Nirvana in this regard Walter Stace writes, commenting on certain Buddhist texts: "Buddha refuses to accept the alternatives posed by the logician's 'either-or'. The laws of logic . . . are no doubt valid for the space-time world, the world of samsara, but they have no application to the mystical experience of Nirvana. Mystical experience is . . . 'beyond logic', just as it is beyond space and time" (*The Teaching of the Mystics,* New American Library, New York, 1960, pp. 76-77). *Cf.* Meister Eckhart: "As long as one clings to time, space, number, and quantity, he is on the wrong track and God is strange and far away" (Sermon 25, in *Meister Eckhart*, Raymond B. Blakney translation, Harper and Row, N.Y., 1941, p. 213).

7. From *Buchlein von der Wahrheit*, chapter iv, quoted in Evelyn Underhill, *Mysticism, op. cit.*, pp. 424-425.

rection and ascent, and their connection with the disengagement of the self (soul, consciousness) from its weighted-downness in a body, can be seen in the following account from the Roman Catholic saint, Catherine of Siena:

> Oftentimes, through the perfect union which the soul has made with [God], she is raised from the earth almost as if the heavy body became light. But this does not mean that the heaviness of the body is taken away, but that the union of the soul with [God] is more perfect than the union of the body with the soul; wherefore the strength of the spirit, united with [God], raises the weight of the body from the earth.[8]

The absorption of consciousness away from its former dwelling, its flash-entrance into a non-multiplicitous, transcendent realm, is so spectacular and emotion-laden, the realm itself so wonderous and mystery-laden, that a declaration of the ontological distance from the events and things of the everyday world, i.e., a declaration of being *ganz andere*, is very often seen as the only adequate way of expressing the experience. Such a method of theological symbolization was known in Latin Christendom as the *via negativa* or "negative way" (negative theology). By ennumerating all the categories and concepts of earthly things, and the nature of God in relation to them as *ganz andere*, the *via negativa* stood, first of all, as the most appropriate manner of expressing the pureness of the divine nature; and second, as a meditative aid whereby all the realms of being less than God might be contemplated and transcended in an effort to reach (and renew) the peak of the mystic flight.

In Christian literature, one of the earliest expressions of the nature of the theophanic experience as *ganz andere* is to be found in Book 7, Section 10, of Augustine's *Confessions*:

> Being admonished . . . to return to myself, I entered into my own depths, with You as guide; and I was able to do it because You were my helper. I entered, and with the eye of my soul, such as it was, I saw Your unchangeable light shining over that same eye of my soul, over my mind. It was not the light of everyday that the eye of flesh can see, nor some greater light of the same order, such as might be if the brightness of our daily light should be seen shining with a more intense brightness and fill-

8. Quoted in Underhill, *Ibid.*, p. 365. For the sake of clarity, the first-person personification of the "Divine Voice" which is found in the original has been altered to read simply "God".

ing all things with its greatness. Your Light was not that, but other, altogether other, than all such lights.[9]

This "wholly otherness" is then expressed in the *via negativa* ascent of Section 17 of the same Book:

> I was now studying the ground of my admiration for the beauty of bodies, whether celestial or of earth, and on what authority I might rightly judge of things mutable and say: "This ought to be so, that not so." Enquiring then what was the source of my judgement, when I did so judge, I had discovered the immutable and true eternity of truth above my changing mind. Thus by stages I passed from bodies to the soul which uses the body for its perceiving, and from this to the soul's inner power, to which the body's senses present external things, as indeed the beasts are able; and from there I passed on to the reasoning power, to which is referred for judgement what is received from the body's senses. This too realised that it was mutable in me and rose to its own understanding. It withdrew my thought from its habitual way, abstracting from the confused crowds of fantasms that it might find what light suffused it, when with utter certainty it cried aloud that the immutable was to be preferred to the mutable, and how it had come to know the immutable itself; for if it had not come to some knowledge of the immutable, it could not have known it as certainly preferable to the mutable. Thus in the thrust of a trembling glance my mind arrived at That Which Is.[10]

The immutable "That Which Is", revealing itself to man in a theophanic Encounter, is thus to be distinguished from everything less than it. It is beyond objects, either of the earth or sky, beyond the human body or embodied-self (soul within a body), beyond internal space-time consciousness ("the soul's inner power to which the body's senses present external things"), even beyond the human faculty of reason. Subsuming God under the category of immutability derives of course from the long tradition in Greek philosophy holding permanence higher than change. In what was to become the classic expression of the *via negativa* in Christian literature, however, i.e., in Chapter 5 of Pseudo-Dionysius's *Theologia Mystica*, even this attribute as a predicate of the *ganz andere* is denied:

9. F.J. Sheed translation, Sheed and Ward, N.Y., 1943, pp. 149-150. This and related passages from the *Confessions* are taken up in a short section of Otto's *Das Ganz Andere*, "Das Ganz Andere bei Augustin", pp. 34-36.

10. Sheed translation, *Ibid.*, pp. 149-150.

> Neither is He standing, nor moving, nor at rest; neither has He power nor is power, nor is light; neither does he live nor is he life; neither is he essence, nor eternity nor time; nor is He subject to intelligible contact . . . nor can any affirmation or negation be applied to Him, for although we may affirm or deny the things below Him, we can neither affirm nor deny Him, inasmuch as . . . [He] transcends all affirmation, and the simple pre-eminence of His absolute nature is outside of every negation—free from every limitation and beyond them all.[11]

The Symbolization of the Mystic Peak: Unbefittingness, Inadequacy, Profanation

In view of the *ganz andere* nature of the mystical experience, for many who have it, especially when it comes unexpectedly and in an intense form, the possibility or adequacy of describing it through *any* means, if not denied, is affirmed only with grave reservations. In some cases the experiencer may see himself set off from non-experiencers by an unbridgeable communication gap; or, alternately —what is related to this, but initially more immediate—the experiencer may radically divide his own life into a "Before" of darkness and existential death and an "After" of illumination and re-birth.

11. From the Shrine of Wisdom translation, Fintry, Brook, England, 1923. Pseudo-Dionysius's treatment of ecstasy is taken up in Walter Voelker's *Kontemplation und Ekstase bei Pseudo-Dionysius Areopagita* (Franz Steiner Verlag, Wiesbaden, 1958, Kapitel III). Voelker describes the understanding of ecstasy in Pseudo-Dionysius in the following manner:

> . . . we learn from the use of ἔκστασις that it is a standing outside of self (*ein Heraustreten aus dem Ich*) and a complete deliverance over to God (*ein voelliges Sich-Gott-Ueberantworten*). (p. 203)
>
> In broadest outline Dionysius understands by ecstasy standing outside of oneself so that he can say of inebriation : νοῦ καὶ φρενῶν ἔκστασις [an ecstasy of mind and spirit] . . . The inebriation of God . . . means just the exceeding of all goods, that being-drawn-beyond (*Hinausgeruecktsein*) everything earthly. (p. 202)
>
> It is always God who performs the decisive step; . . . the divine love breaks into the being of man and draws it up towards itself. (p. 199)
>
> On earth divine things are only accessible in a veiled form . . . In ecstasy alone does the veil thrown up by human nature fall away, and with this is tied the view of Truth. (p. 205)
>
> . . . ecstasy [stands] beyond the two theological forms [i.e., the positive and the negative] leaving all discursive proceedings fundamentally behind it. (p. 214)

Since such experiences typically occur for the first time no earlier than late adolescence or early adulthood—i.e., when a person has already assimilated his culture's language—the language which the experiencer has learned will typically be associated with all that happened in the "Before" period, and will thus be seen as incapable of expressing the radically *ganz andere* event that has broken his biography into a Before and an After. Seeking a way to express and communicate what has made one a "new" man, a person will often search for a new language—a search which for many ends in the acceptance of the theological idiom of some established religion. In such a manner a convert is born with a passionate adherence to the new theological idiom (whichever it may be) beyond anything typical of those born into the religion. To the extent that the experience is seen as expressible at all, it is so only in the theological and ritual language of the new religion. In ordinary language—language drawn from the pre-conversion period of darkness—the experience is inexpressible. It may even be seen as a great impropriety or profanation to make the attempt. Considerations of this kind may have been at work in the following account of a mystic-conversion experience taken from William James's *Varieties of Religious Experience.* The account comes from one Alphonse Ratisbonne, a 19th century French "free-thinker", who, as a result of the experience, under the influence of a proselytizing friend, became a Roman Catholic convert:

> Coming out of the cafe I met the carriage of Monsieur B. . . . [who] attended to some duty at the church of San Andrea delle Fratte. Instead of waiting in the carriage, I entered the church myself to look at it. The church of San Andrea was poor, small, and empty; I believe that I found myself there almost alone. No work of art attracted my attention; and I passed my eyes mechanically over its interior without being arrested by any particular thought. I can only remember an entirely black dog which went trotting and turning before me as I mused. In an instant the dog had disappeared, the whole church had vanished, I no longer saw anything . . . or more truly I saw, O my God, one thing alone.
>
> Heavens, how can I speak of it? Oh no! human words cannot attain to express the inexpressible. Any discription, however sublime it might be, could be but a profanation of the unspeakable truth.
>
> I did not know where I was: I did not know whether I was Alphonse or another. I only felt myself changed and believed myself another me; I looked for myself in myself and did not find myself. In the bottom of my soul I felt an explosion of the most

> ardent joy; I could not speak; I had no wish to reveal what had happened . . . All I can say is that in an instant the bandage had fallen from my eyes; and not one bandage only, but the whole manifold of bandages in which I had been brought up. One after another they rapidly disappeared, even as the mud and ice disappear under the rays of the burning sun.[1]

Even when the mystic-ecstatic experience is not, as it is in this case, involved in a conversion or world-view shift, the problems of symbolic expression are by no means eliminated. Since the experience involves the wrenching of consciousness away from its attentional attachments to objects of sense perception, and since any account of the experience will, by necessity, make use of imagery drawn from such objects, the very contrast between the two will often be expressed as an inadequacy of the account given. This is perhaps the most common reservation people have in describing such an experience. It is well represented in another account from James by a man he identifies only as a Swiss hiker:

> I was in perfect health; we were on our sixth day of tramping, and in good training . . . I felt neither fatigue, hunger, nor thirst, and my state of mind was equally healthy . . . I was subject to no anxiety, either near or remote, for we had a good guide, and there was not a shadow of uncertainty about the road we should follow. I can best describe the condition in which I was by calling it a state of equilibrium. When all at once I experienced a feeling of being raised above myself, I felt the presence of God —I tell of the thing just as I was conscious of it—as if his goodness and his power were penetrating me altogether. The throb of emotion was so violent that I could barely tell the boys to pass on and not wait for me. I then sat down on a stone, unable to stand any longer, and my eyes overflowed with tears. I thanked God that in the course of my life he had taught me to know him, that he sustained my life and took pity both on the insignificant creature and on the sinner that I was. I begged him ardently that my life might be consecrated to the doing of his will . . . Then, slowly, the ecstasy left my heart; that is, I felt that God had withdrawn the communion which he had granted, and I was able to walk on, but very slowly, so strongly was I still possessed

1. pp. 186-187. Wittgenstein, it might be noted here, had the greatest respect for William James, and strongly encouraged some of his students to read the *Varieties*. Drury, for instance, says: "Wittgenstein had a great admiration for James, and *The Varieties of Religious Experience* was one of the few books he insisted I must read." ("Ludwig Wittgenstein: A Symposium", in K.T. Fann, *Wittgenstein, The Man and His Philosophy*, Dell Publishers, N.Y., 1967, p. 68).

> by the interior emotion . . . The state of ecstasy may have lasted four or five minutes, although it seemed at the time to last much longer . . . The impression had been so profound that in climbing slowly the slope I asked myself if it were possible that Moses on Sinai could have had a more intimate communion with God. I think it well to add that in this ecstasy of mine God had neither form, color, odor, nor taste; moreover that the feeling of his presence was accompanied with no determinate localization. It was rather as if my personality had been transformed by the presence of a *spiritual spirit.* But the more I seek words to express this intimate intercourse, the more I feel the impossibility of describing the thing by any of our usual images.[2]

Thus no imagery or mode of symbolic communication is really adequate to express the experience. Ironically, this recognition can sometimes lead, especially for someone brought up in an inherited religious tradition, to a rejection and critique of the language of traditional theology. In such cases, the inherited theological symbols, previously conformed to uncritically, come to be associated with the darkness world of the "Before", which now stands in contrast to the new Truth of the revelatory experience. It is from just such a situation, where inherited religion and new revelatory insight are juxtaposed, that the prophet-iconoclast emerges. The paradigmatic instance of such a figure, at least in the Western civilizational orbit, was Xenophanes of Colophon, who deserves perhaps special mention in the present context since the cultural situation of his time was remarkably similar to that in which many people in modern Western societies have found themselves in the wake of the Scientific Revolution.[3]

Writing in the last half of the 6th century B.C. and the first two decades of the 5th, Xenophanes addressed a Greek world in which the traditional Olympian religion was being increasingly undermined by the new physical theories stemming from Ionia. Xenophanes himself was to become the most inspired of all the debunkers of the gods, but his inspiration did not derive from the new physics. Its source, rather, lay in a new theological insight concerning the nature of the divine:

---

2. pp. 70-71.

3. The interpretation of Xenophanes given here follows Olof Gigon, *Der Ursprung der Griechischen Philosophie* (Schwabe and Co., Basel, 1968, sections xx-xxii), and Werner Jaeger, *The Theology of the Early Greek Philosophers* (Oxford University Press, N.Y., 1967, chapter 3).

> One god, the greatest among gods and men, neither in form like unto mortals nor in thought.[4]

Proclaiming this new Truth of the one God, unlike unto mortals, Xenophanes launched an attack on the anthropomorphic representations of the traditional gods of Homer and Hesiod. While it is not possible on the basis of the fragments that remain to determine the exact nature of the experience that gave rise to such a radical proclamation, with great plausibility Olof Gigon suggests, based on his developmental analysis of the Xenophanic fragments within their historical setting, that Xenophanes must have undergone the profoundest conversion-type experience while among the mystical-philosophical community of Pythagoreans in Southern Italy.[5] It was from the standpoint of this new insight, says Gigon, that the Olympian gods were attacked.

The brunt of Xenophanes attack concerned the "befittingness" of representing the "one god, the greatest among gods and men" in the manner of a mere mortal, i.e., in anthropomorphic form. Such representations, he held, did not befit the sublimity of the divine essence,[6] and with ridiculing sarcasm he declared:

> But mortals deem that the gods are begotten as they are, and have clothes like theirs, and a voice and form.[7]
>
> The Ethiopians make their gods black and snub-nosed; the Thracians say theirs have blue eyes and red hair.[8]
>
> Yes, and if oxen and horses or lions had hands, and could paint with their hands, and produce works of art as men do, horses would paint the forms of the gods like horses, and oxen like oxen, and make their bodies in the image of their several kinds.[9]

---

4. 21B23 (Diels-Kranz), in John Burnet, *Early Greek Philosophy*, (Adam and Charles Black, 1968), p. 132.

5. Gigon, *op. cit.*, p. 159. Gigon writes: "In Southern Italy an enormous impression was made upon him by Pythagoreanism, one so decisive that perhaps one must almost speak of a conversion if this concept has any meaning in antiquity. The new teaching concerning God and the soul won him over completely and brought forth a group of poems in which, under the influence of Pythagoreanism, he attacked Homer and Hesiod most sharply."

6. Jaeger, *op. cit.*, p. 49.

7. 21B14, in Burnet, *Ibid.*, p. 131.

8. 21B16, *Ibid.*

9. 21B15, *Ibid.*

Xenophanes was also the first Greek thinker to declare movement as unbefitting the sublimity of what is divine—a thought we have seen re-echoed in Augustine:

> And he abideth ever in the selfsame place, moving not at all; nor doth it befit him to go about now hither now thither.[10]

"In Xenophanes," says Werner Jaeger, "we find a new motif, which is the actual source of his theology. It is nothing that rests on logical proof . . . but springs from an immediate sense of awe at the sublimity of the Divine. It is a feeling of reverence that leads Xenophanes to deny all the finite shortcomings and limitations laid upon the gods by traditional religion. The word ἐπιπρέπει [it is (not) befitting] which Xenophanes uses . . . reveals the criterion on which his entire criticism of anthropomorphism is based . . ."[11]

Jaeger, however, at the end of his chapter on Xenophanes, leaves the reader with the impression that the "utter sublimity" of Xenophanes' God is a postulated sublimity, arrived at by the recognition that any lesser God, such as the anthropomorphic gods of Homer, could not stand up against the skeptical attack of the new Ionian philosophy of nature:

> Xenophanes . . . was an enlightened man with an alert sense for the natural causes of all phenomena. But above all he was profoundly impressed by the way in which philosophy was disturbing the old religion, and it was this that made him insist upon a new and purer conception of the divine nature.[12]

Thus a desperate effort to "save religion" is suggested as the motivating center of Xenophanes' writings, and a more sublime, super-human, postulated God as the result. Such an interpretation, however, does not take account of the great self-assurance with which Xenophanes attacks the gods of Homer, proclaiming his "one God the greatest among gods and men". He may indeed have found the Homeric gods susceptible to skeptical criticism, and personally sought something beyond such criticism, but it is hardly likely that he would have gone about ridiculing other people's gods unless he actually found something that could be set in their place. A postulated God is something very weak indeed to set against a tradition of centuries, and inspires few iconoclasts. The source of the sublimity

10. 21B26, *Ibid.*, p. 131.
11. *The Theology of the Early Greek Philosophers, op. cit.*, p. 49.
12. *Ibid.*, p. 54.

of Xenophanes' God and of the self-assurance with which he set it against Homer and Hesiod is much more likely as Gigon suggests —i.e., the result of some kind of profound religious-experience.

Concern over the "befittingness" of theological symbols as that shown by Xenophanes, has historically served as the source of some of the greatest religious controversies. It was at the heart of the Hebrew prophets' attack on the idols of the neighboring peoples, of Christianity's attack on the state-instituted religious cults of Rome, and later, of the Puritan attack on the sacraments of the Roman Catholic Church. This concern, intimately related to the mystical experience itself, became injected with more passion in the Judeo-Christian civilizational orbit as the concern over befittingness intensified into the charge of profanation and idolatry.

At the peak of mystic ecstasy, the divine Encounter takes on not only the negative characteristic of being "wholly other", but possesses, too, the positive characteristic, giving birth to the negative, of being an encounter with absolute sacredness. It is, in Rudolf Otto's terminology, an encounter with the *mysterium tremendum.*[13] If the experience is to be talked about at all, the first requirement of any attempt to represent it thus becomes the demand that it not be treated in a manner befitting something profane. The treating of the Sacred as if it were something less than sacred—i.e., as if it were profane—is what is meant by profanation. It is the "degradation or vulgarization of [what is] worthy of being held in reverence or respect" (Oxford English Dictionary). And when, to the absence of reverence and respect is added the inability or refusal to distinguish between human representational activity and the divine action in the sacred Encounter, to the charge of profanation is added the additional charge of idolatry and will-worship. It is quite common, of course, when accusations of this kind are hurled against followers of rival religions, that neither side has a sensitive understanding for —nor is interested in acquiring one—the meaning which specific rites and symbols have (or may have) in the lives of their opponents. Thus, the Christians denounce the polytheists as idolators, and the polytheists reply in turn by denouncing the Christians as atheists.

In Hebrew Scriptures, one of the most well-known attacks on profanation and idolatry is found in Second Isaiah:

> I am Yahweh, that is my name;
> my glory I give to no other,
> nor my praise to graven images.

---

13. *The Idea of the Holy, op. cit.*, pp. 12-24.

> (42:8)
>
> The carpenter stretches a line, he marks it out with a pencil; he fashions it with planes, and marks it with a compass; he shapes it into the figure of a man, with the beauty of a man, to dwell in a house. He cuts down cedars . . . it becomes fuel for a man; he takes a part of it and warms himself . . . the rest of it he makes into a god, his idol; and falls down to it and worships it; he prays to it and says, "Deliver me, for thou art my god!"
>
> (44:13-17, RSV)

To the unspeakable majesty and sacrality of Yahweh, the God who has revealed himself to the prophets of Israel, the representations of the neighboring polytheistic cultures are profaning idols. They are the products of a human hand, made of the same lifeless material as the wood one throws into the fire, and in a form indistinguishable from that of an ordinary human.

Similarly for Augustine, the gods instituted by a decadent Rome (and by his backward extrapolation, those instituted by a not-so-decadent Rome) can only profane the majesty of the God whose kingdom is not of Caesar's world. The *civitas Dei*, the wholly other "That Which Is" revealed to man only by a miraculous gift of grace, is not at the disposal of imperial conquerors, driven by lust for power, who would like to transform the *civitas terrena* into their own private empire.

And for the English Puritans, the will of God in dispensing his grace is not something that conforms to a human time-table, in a humanly performed ritual of transubstantiation. God is something *ganz andere*, and the divine election to be the recipient of God's grace is not something the recipient himself can control through participation or non-participation in any ritual.

The Theophanic Encounter and the Rejection of Metaphysics

Metaphysics, understood to include all intellectual arguments and speculations about the nature and existence of God, of ultimate Being, the Absolute, etc., has historically encountered opposition from two quite different sources. The more familiar opponent since the Age of Enlightenment has been the empirical skeptic, the man for whom sense-perceivable objects exhaust all that can be said to be real. For the skeptic, all metaphysical assertions, all assertions about a reality beyond what is known through the senses, are nothing but idle and groundless speculation. This attitude is represented very well by David Hume, who was rightly seen by Carnap and the members of the Vienna Circle as one of their philosophical forefathers. With delightfully refreshing wit, his *An Inquiry Concerning Human Understanding* offers counsel as to what a man should and should not spend his time on:

> It seems to me, that the only objects of the abstract sciences or of demonstration, are quantity and number . . . All other enquiries of men regard only matter of fact and existence, and these are evidently incapable of demonstration . . . When we run over libraries, persuaded of these principles, what havoc must we make? If we take in our hand any volume of divinity or school metaphysics, for instance; let us ask, Does it contain any abstract reasoning concerning quantity or number? No. Does it contain any experimental reasoning concerning matter of fact and existence? No. Commit it then to the flames, for it can contain nothing but sophistry and illusion.[1]

But metaphysics can find opposition from an entirely different source. The very categories used by metaphysicians—categories such as substance, attributes, Prime Mover, being, act, potency, etc.—as well as the manner of demonstration by which metaphysicians sometimes claim to arrive at truths about God or a higher Reality, may stir the opposition of men of highly developed mystic-spiritual sensitivities to an even greater degree than the empirical skeptic. When the theological emphasis falls on insight, personal revelation, and divine grace as the way of knowing God—i.e., on spiritual experience—metaphysical argumentation may be seen as a great impediment in a man's search for God. The God who reveals himself to man in a divine Encounter is not arrived at through argument or demonstration. From such a theological standpoint, to speak of God in the manner of metaphysical demonstration, or to make God the subject of fanciful speculation, may be seen not as (as in Hume) intellect offending sophistry, but—what is far worse—as God-debasing profanation or impropriety.

1. Quoted by Carnap in *Philosophy and Logical Syntax* (Kegan Paul, Trench, Trubner and Co., London, 1935), pp. 35–36. The quotation is from *An Inquiry Concerning Human Understanding* (Library of Liberal Arts edition, N.Y., 1955), pp. 171, 173.

Augustine can once again serve as an example. At the end of the Fourth Book of his *Confessions* (Section 16), Augustine describes how he had been introduced at the age of twenty to Aristotle's book on the *Ten Categories.* He had, apparently, anticipated learning great things from the book, for, as he describes, whenever his teachers at Carthage would mention it,

> Their cheeks would swell with self-importance, so that the title alone was enough to make me stand agape, as though I were poised over some wonderful divine mystery.[2]

But the book offered for Augustine no divine mystery. What did strike him, however, though only in retrospect, was how grossly inadequate Aristotle's categories were for comprehending the "other, altogether other", whose *ganz andere* nature he later describes in the mystic ascent of Book 7, Section 10. On his early study of Aristotle he remarks:

> What profit did this study bring me? None. In fact it made difficulties for me, because I thought that everything that existed could be reduced to these ten categories, and I therefore attempted to understand you, my God, in all your wonderful and immutable simplicity, in these same terms, as though you too were substance—and greatness and beauty were your attributes in the same way that a body has attributes . . .[3]

The categories of Aristotle were thus seen by Augustine as impediments in his earlier search for God, and as wholly inadequate for describing the God whom he actually found—or who found him. The inadequacy and impropriety of metaphysical categories, at least the categories of "being" and "existence," finds even stronger assertion in Pseudo-Dionysius. For the author of the *Theologia Mystica,* the God who erotically unites with the purgated soul in the ecstasy of mystical union, is only to be represented, in relation to things of a profane, spatio-temporal world, by a "beyond", "super", or similar type of symbolism. Even so abstract a metaphysical category as "being" is seen as belonging to the world of profane things, and thus, no more befitting the *ganz andere* wonder of the Sacred than wood icons or anthropomorphic gods:

---

2. R.S. Pine-Coffin translation (Penguin Books, Baltimore, Md.), p. 87
3. *Ibid.,* p. 88.

> Let this be my prayer; but do thou, dear Timothy, in the diligent exercise of mystical contemplation, leave behind the senses and the operations of the intellect, and all things sensible and intellectual, and all things in the world of being and non-being, that thou mayest arise by unknowing towards the union, as far as is attainable, with Him who transcends all being and all knowledge.
>
> But these things are not to be disclosed to the uninitiated by whom I mean those attached to the objects of human thought, and who believe there is no super-essential Reality beyond, and who imagine that by their own understanding they know Him. . . . And if the principles of the divine Mysteries are beyond the understanding of these, what is to be said of others still more incapable there of who describe [God] by characteristics drawn from the lowest order of beings.[4]

Criticism of metaphysics for reasons in tune with Augustine and Pseudo-Dionysius began to proliferate in the 17th century as many men, repulsed by the religious wars and doctrinal disputes of the period, came to see the only hope of liberation from factional rivalries to lie in the inner assurance of personal religious experience. Metaphysics, identified with the argumentations and demonstrations of late Scholasticism, came to be seen by such men as the same wrong-way to God as the bloody wars and acrimonious disputes they saw about them.

Robert Barclay, for instance, whose *An Apology for the True Christian Divinity* (1675) became the chief theoretical work of the Quaker movement, accused Scholastic metaphysics of being one of the destroyers of true Christianity, which, for him and other Quakers, centered around a man's attention to the Inner Light of God's grace. Against those who think they can reach God through argument and demonstration, Barclay writes:

> What I have written [here in the *Apology*] comes more from my heart than from my head; what I have heard with the ears of my soul, and seen with my inward eyes . . . and what hath been inwardly manifested to me of the things of God, that do I declare.[5]
>
> I confess myself to be not only no imitator and admirer of the schoolmen, but an opposer and despiser of them as such, by

4. *Theologia Mystica,* chapter 1, Shrine of Wisdom translation.
5. *An Apology for the True Christian Divinity,* "Unto the Friendly Reader [who] wisheth Salvation", (Friends Book Store, Phila., no date), p. 9.

whose labor I judge the Christian religion to be so far from being bettered that it is destroyed.[6]

Sharing a view similar to Barclay's, though not a Quaker, was the Christian Platonist John Smith, who taught at Cambridge in the 1630s and 1640s. Smith stressed, in addition to the diversionary effect of metaphysics in leading men away from God, the additional danger of pride and conceit that often accompanied the mastery of metaphysical demonstrations and arguments. Opposing those who felt they had come to know God through mastery of demonstration, he charged:

> We have many grave and reverend idolaters that worship truth only in the image of their own wits; that could never adore it so much as they seem to do, were it anything else but such a form of belief as their own wandering speculations had at last met together in . . .[7]
>
> What are all our most sublime speculations of the Deity, that are not impregnated with true goodness, but insipid things, that have no taste for life in them that do but swell, like empty froth, in the souls of men! They do not feed men's souls, but only puff them up, and fill them with pride, arrogance, contempt, and tyranny towards those that cannot well understand their subtile curiosities: as those philosophers that Cicero complains of in his times—who made their knowledge only a matter of ostentation, venditate and set off themselves, but never caring to square and govern their lives by it . . . These indeed are those silly souls that are 'ever learning, but never come to knowledge of the truth' . . . jejune and barren speculations may be hovering and fluttering up and down about divinity, but they cannot settle or fix themselves upon it, . . . they cannot behold the lovely face of it.[8]

Specifically aimed at the Scholastic metaphysics, Smith also proclaimed, in words quoted by Barclay in the *Apology* in support of his own Proposition Concerning Immediate Revelation,[9] that,

> It is but a thin, airy, knowledge that is got by mere speculation, which is ushered in by syllogisms and demonstrations.

---

6. *Ibid.*, pp. 9-10.
7. *The Natural Truth of Christianity*, (Alexander Gardner, Publishers, London, 1855), p. 6.
8. *Ibid.*, pp. 5-6.
9. The Proposition begins: "The testimony of the Spirit is that alone by which the true knowledge of God hath been, is, and can be only revealed", *Apology*, p. 13.

> To seek our divinity merely in books and writings, is to seek the living among the dead; we do but in vain seek God many times in these, where His truth too often is not so much enshrined as entombed—no; *intra te quaere Deum,* seek for God within thine own soul: He is best discerned as Plotinus phraseth it, by an intellectual touch of Him.[10]

The Plotinian soul, in its cathartic, duality-transcending union with God, is not moved by a knowledge of syllogisms. Thus the School metaphysics was seen by Smith as the same detour on the path to God that Aristotle's *Categories* had represented for Augustine. And its effect was more pernicious than someone like Hume would ever suggest, because to this diversionary influence was added the additional factor of moral and spiritual pride.[11]

The century in which Smith and Barclay lived was also the century of Pascal, from whom we have the clearest and certainly most well-known instance in the Western tradition of an attack on metaphysics proceeding directly from a mystical religious experience. In his posthumously published account of the ecstatic encounter on the night of November 23, 1654, Pascal describes how the metaphysical demonstrations and "proofs" of Descartes and the Scholastics melted into irrelevance:

> From about half past ten in the evening until about half past midnight
>
> FIRE
>
> God of Abraham, God of Issac, God of Jacob
> not of the philosophers and the scholars
> Certainty, certainty: emotion, joy, peace
> God of Jesus Christ
> *Deum meum et meum vestrum*

10. Smith, *op. cit.*, pp. 2-3; in Barclay, *op. cit.*, p. 33.

11. Against a one-sided caricature of the Scholastics, one might mention that Pseudo-Dionysius was held in the highest regard by Aquinas and other Scholastics, and that the *cognitio Dei experimentalis* was not neglected in Scholastic writing. And even before Barclay, a Thomist like Hooker could acknowledge that "the powers of the mind are wont to stir when that which we infinitely long for presenteth itself above and besides expectation: curious and intricate speculations do hinder, they abate, they quench such inflamed motions of delight and joy as divine graces use to raise when extraordinarily they are present; the mind therefore feeling present joy . . . casteth off those disputes whereunto the intellectual part at other times easily draweth." (*The Laws of Ecclesiastical Polity,* Book V. LXVIII, 3).

Thy God shall be my God
Oblivion of the world and of everything except God.[12]

This experience was recorded by Pascal on a piece of paper (and later on parchment) which was not found until after his death. Its guiding significance for his whole life, however, was felt to be so great, that, following a not uncommon practice of his time, he sewed the paper to the lining of his clothing so that he would always be reminded of it whatever he did.[13] So intimate and private was the experience that he was not known to have disclosed it to anyone in his lifetime. What is most important for present purposes is the contrasting juxtaposition between the God of the sacred Encounter—the God of Abraham, Issac, and Jacob; the God revealed to Moses in the fire of the Burning Thornbush—and the God of the philosophers and scholars. As a result of the mystic flight—"oblivion to the world and of everything except God"—a breakthrough is achieved revealing a higher-order reality that consigns all metaphysical demonstrations about the nature and existence of God to a shadow-world of lifeless speculation.

Silence

As we have seen in the example of the Swiss hiker, finding the words and images to describe the *ganz andere* nature of the mystical experience can be sensed as an almost insurmountable problem. Since the experience involves the disengagement of consciousness from its attention to a multiplicitous, space-time-matter world, words and images—which by necessity engage consciousness—may be felt as leading one away from the experience, rather than di-

12. Translated by Martin Turnell, in *Pascal,* by Jean Steinmann, (Burns and Oates, London, 1954), p. 80. Though it is not as certain as in this example, the aversion to metaphysical speculation displayed in certain Buddhist writings probably derives from a similar kind of experience. On this point see the discussion in Gustav Mensching, *Das Heilige Schweigen,* "Das antispekulative Schweigen des Buddhismus" (Alfred Toepelmann Verlag, Giessen, 1926), pp. 43-149. Also Walter Stace, *op. cit.,* pp. 76-79.

13. The story surrounding the discovery of the paper and parchment is presented in Emile Cailliet, *Pascal, Genius in the Light of Scripture* (Westminster Press, Phila.), pp. 132-134.

recting one towards it. With this in mind, it is sometimes seen that refraining from words is the first prerequisite for expressing the experience— a view which gains additional support when words are looked upon as the product of a human speech-act, in contrast to the divine action (grace) in the experience. Silence may thus be held as the only manner of symbolization which does not profane, either by suggesting that the experience is an act of human will, or that the Reality revealed through it is like an everyday "thing" in the mundane world.

Again one finds in Pseudo-Dionysius one of the best elucidations. The following segment from the *Theologia Mystica* is simultaneously (a) an explication of a mystic-flight experience, (b) a rudimentary ontology based upon the explicated experience and its Truth as height and measure, and (c) a judgment on the proper use of language:

> The higher we soar in contemplation the more limited become our expressions of that which is purely intelligible; even as now, when plunging into the Darkness which is above the intellect, we pass not merely into brevity of speech, but even *into absolute silence, of thoughts as well as of words* . . . We mount upwards from below to that which is the highest, and according to the degree of transcendence, *so our speech is restrained* until, the entire ascent being accomplished, *we become wholly voiceless,* in as much as we are absorbed in Him who is totally ineffable.[1]
>
> (emphasis added)

In reference to profane things the mystic absorption in God is an *ek-stasis* or "standing outside"; the redirection and intensification of consciousness confers upon all objects and things (even one's own body) the sense of being in some other, far away world—a village seen from a mountain top, or busy street from atop a skyscraper. Since words, images, and concepts, together with the auton-

1. *Theologia Mystica,* chapter III, Shrine of Wisdom translation. See in this connection, Gustav Mensching, *op. cit.,* pp. 134-143. Pseudo-Dionysius's invocation of silence has its roots in neo-Platonic writers. Porphyry, for instance, writes: "For God the spoken word is . . . not adequate, indeed not even the inner word, it is blemished through passions, but we worship him through pure inner silence and pure thoughts." (Quoted in Mensching, *op. cit.,* p. 137). And Plutarch: "When the souls are released, and have passed into the region of the pure, invisible, and changeless, this God will be the guide and king of those who depend on Him and gaze with insatiable longing on the beauty which may not be spoken of by the lips of man" (*De Iside et Osiride,* 78, quoted in Frederick Copleston, *A History of Philosophy, Greece and Rome,* Part II, Image Books, N.Y., 1962, p. 197).

omous will that must go into their formation (an element particularly evident in public disputes) are seen as belonging to this far distant realm, they can never befit the human will transcending, *ganz andere* nature of the sacred Encounter.

Thus the prophet Habakkuk, in castigating the idolaters who worship what they themselves have produced, proclaims:

> The Lord is in his holy temple; let all the earth keep silence before him.
>
> (*Habakkuk,* 2:20)

Out of similar considerations, a mystically based religion such as the Quakers adopted the silent meeting[2] as its main ritual form. Through observance of a silent "waiting upon God", the members of the congregation attempt, in contemplation, to focus their attention away from worldly things in order to re-establish and re-new contact with the transcendence of the Inner Light. Meditative silence and personal attunement to the call of grace were seen by the early Quakers as the only way out of the murderous doctrinal and metaphysical disputes which had traumatized English society in the 17th century. George Fox, the prophet and founder of the Quaker movement,[3] explicitly draws the connection between silence and public controversy in the following epistle:

> Come out of your bustlings, you that are bustling and in strife one against another, whose spirits are not quieted, but are fighting with words . . .
>
> Keep to that God in you, which will lead you up to God, when you are still from your own thoughts and imaginations, . . . desires, . . . motions and will . . .
>
> . . . all you that are in your own wisdom and in your own reason . . . it is a strange life to you to come to be silent, you must come into a new world. Now thou must die in the silence to the fleshly wisdom, knowledge, reason and understanding; so thou comest to feel the power of an endless life, and come to possess it.[4]

2. On the Quaker worship service, see Otto, *The Idea of the Holy, op. cit.,* pp. 210-214, and Menching, *op. cit.,* pp. 89-98.

3. Wittgenstein, it should be mentioned, read Fox with considerable admiration, and once gave a copy of Fox's *Journal* to his friend Norman Malcolm. (*Ludwig Wittgenstein, A Memoir,* Oxford University Press, 1958, p. 71).

4. Quoted in T. Edmund Harvey, *Silence and Worship, A Study in Quaker Experience* (George H. Doran and Co., N.Y., 1924), p. 15.

As indicated here, the emphasis on silence and personal religious experience will be particularly great in socio-historical situations in which religious and metaphysical language has become associated with various rival parties in a public dispute. Fox's counsel to silence was a counsel to turn away from such disputes in complete surrender to the guidance offered by the inner power of divine grace.

Being Absolutely Safe

The mystic-ecstatic experience that forms the radiating core of the *Tractatus,* and the key to its interpretation, was described by Wittgenstein in a lecture on the foundations of ethics which he delivered at the invitation of a Cambridge student group shortly after his return to academic life in 1929. He describes this experience as the experience of being "*absolutely* safe"; it is a "state of mind in which one is inclined to say 'I am safe, nothing can injure me whatever happens'."[1] This experience is offered by Wittgenstein as one of three types which constitute for him personally the terminus of ethical inquiry. By ethical inquiry he understands neither a Weberian-type analysis of postulated norms or values (*wertbeziehende Methode*), nor a demonstration of man's dependence in ethical matters on tradition or revelations of a divine law to men of the past. Ethical inquiry for Wittgenstein is a truth-seeking inquiry (much like the inquiry of Plato's *Republic,* one might say) which delves into "what is really important", "into the meaning of life", "into what makes life worth living".[2] Further on in the Lecture, Wittgenstein links the absolute safety experience to religious literature, equating it with the experience of being "safe in the hands of God".[3]

Being "absolutely safe", or variations on the same theme, can be easily recognized as an expression of the mystic-flight experience in its disengagement of the self or "I" from identity with the body. As a means of interpreting and expressing this aspect of the experience, it suggests itself quite naturally.[4] An embodied self has (in

1. "Wittgenstein's Lecture on Ethics", *Philosophical Review,* v. 74, 1965, p. 8.

2. *Ibid.,* p. 5.

3. *Ibid.,* p. 10.

4. Besides the examples given here, see the summary account of mystic- (peak-) experiences in Maslow, *Religions, Values and Peak-Experiences, op. cit.,* p. 66, number

Laing's words) "a sense of being flesh and blood and bones." It will experience itself as "subject to the dangers that threaten [the] body, the dangers of attack, mutilation, disease, decay, and death."[5] In the mystic-flight experience, however, the self or sense of "I" is disembodied. Ecstatically removed from the body and all objects of the space-time-matter world, it experiences itself as beyond the dangers that accompany existence in such a world.

The connection between *ek-stasis* and the feeling of absolute safety can be well illustrated through the personal testimony of Arthur Koestler. In his autobiography, *The Invisible Writing,* Koestler describes a mystical experience which he had in prison during the Spanish Civil War that eventually led to his break with the materialistic world-view of Marxism. The circumstances surrounding the experience were as follows:

> I was never officially informed that sentence of death had been passed on me. The Franco authorities made ambiguous and contradictory statements, with the apparent intention of confusing the issue . . . On February 19, three officers of the Phalange . . . visited my cell. . . . They informed me that I was or would be (the alternative was left in suspense) sentenced to death for espionage . . . It was my expectation that some night or other I would be taken out of my cell and stood against the cemetery wall. During the first few days after the fall of Malaga, prisoners in that town were taken out in batches and shot at any hour of the day; later on in Seville, things settled down to a more orderly routine, and executions were carried out three or four times a week between midnight and 2 a.m.
>
> The proceedings were as a rule smooth and subdued. The victims were not forewarned . . . On one night, Thursday, April 15, the inmates of cells 39, 41, and 42 on my left and right were marched off, with only my cell No. 40 spared, after the warder had put his key, no doubt, by mistake into my own lock, and then withdrawn it.[6]

Koestler then describes how he was in his cell, trying to pass away the anxious hours, recalling some of the mathematical proofs he had learned as a boy. Euclid's proof especially, the proof that the number of prime numbers is infinite, had always filled him, owing

14. Also, the discussion of security and tranquility in James's *Varieties, op. cit.,* pp. 223, 230-233.

5. R.D. Laing, *The Divided Self, op. cit.,* p. 67. See also Laing's comments on Socrates on the following page.

6. *The Invisible Writing* (The Macmillan Company, N.Y. 1954) pp. 345-347.

to its elegance and simplicity, with a certain aesthetic pleasure. After writing the proof out on the wall of his cell, he began to be stirred by thoughts of the infinite:

> The infinite is a mystical mass shrouded in a haze; and yet it was possible [i.e., through Euclid's proof] to gain some knowledge of it without losing oneself in treacly ambiguities. The significance of this swept over me like a wave. The wave had originated in an articulate verbal insight; but this evaporated at once, leaving in its wake only a wordless essence, a fragrance of eternity, a quiver of the arrow in the blue. I must have stood there for some minutes, entranced, with a wordless awareness that "this is perfect—perfect"; until I noticed some slight mental discomfort nagging at the back of my mind—some trivial circumstance that marred the perfection of the moment. Then I remembered the nature of that irrelevant annoyance: I was, of course in prison and might be shot. But this was immediately answered by a feeling whose verbal translation would be: "So what? is that all? have you got nothing more serious to worry about?"—an answer so spontaneous, fresh and amused as if the intruding annoyance had been the loss of a collar-stud. Then I was floating on my back in a river of peace, under bridges of silence. It came from nowhere and flowed nowhere. Then there was no river and no I, the I had ceased to exist.[7]

He felt absolutely safe because there was no more "I", or rather, no more body-identified "I". The whole body had become like a collar stud, a trivial object far removed from the real self—the self in ecstasy standing outside the world of the body, outside the world of the firing squad. Koestler then describes the ultimacy with which this experience stamped itself:

> When I say "the I had ceased to exist", I refer to a concrete experience that is verbally as incommunicable as the feeling aroused by a piano concerto, yet just as real—only much more real. In fact, its primary mark is the sensation that this state is more real than any other one has experienced before—that for the first time the veil has fallen and one is in touch with "real reality".[8]

The mystic flight as "absolute safety" is equally well illustrated in the initiation rites practiced in certain shamanic societies. The

7. *Ibid.*, pp. 351-352.
8. *Ibid.*, p. 352.

shaman-initiate is, typically, a young man who has been selected out on the basis of unusually great psycho-spiritual sensitivities. In his initiation, older shaman recite to him tales of divine powers—of gods and goddesses—who will mercilessly hack his body to pieces, though without killing him. At the end of the tale, the body comes back to life whole, healthier and purified as a result. One such tale, well illustrating on a pre-philosophic level how the mystic-flight disengagement of the self from the body can be experienced as absolute safety, is presented in Eliade's *Schamanism*:

> There was a Bwili [i.e., shaman] of Lol-narong, whose sister's son came to him and said: "I want you to give me something." The Bwili said: "Have you fulfilled the conditions?" "Yes, I have fulfilled them." . . .
>
> Then he said to his nephew: "Come here, lie down on this leaf," and the youth lay down on it. Then the Bwili made himself a bamboo knife and cutting off one of the young man's arms, placed it on two of the leaves. And he laughed at his nephew and the youth laughed back. Then he cut off the other arm and placed it on the leaves beside the first. And he came back and they both laughed again. Then he cut off his leg from the thigh and laid it along side the arms. And he came and laughed and the youth laughed too. Then he cut off the other leg and laid it beside the first. And he came back and laughed, and saw that his nephew was still laughing. Lastly, he cut off the head, held it out before him. And he laughed, and the head laughed too.
>
> Then he put the head back in its place and took the arms and legs that he had taken off and put them all back in their places.[9]

9. *Schamanism: Archaic Techniques of Ecstasy* (Princeton University Press, 1964) p. 56. The tale was taken by Eliade from an article bearing the incredulous title "Malekula: Flying Tricksters, Ghosts, Gods, and Epileptics". The designation of the shaman as a "flying trickster" comes, not from a scientist's aversion to superstition and tall-tales, but from a literalist-fundamentalist inability to recognize in the schamanic tales, the symbolic expression of an ecstatic experience. To this non-recognition is then added an assertive Philistinism, which, incapable of empathizing with the shamanic experience, safely distances itself from it through the use of psychologizing pejoratives such as "epileptic". An element of ego-defense is clearly present in such designations.

An interpretation of a Tibetian shaman-initiation similar to the interpretation given here is offered by Helmut Hoffmann in his *Symbolik der Tibetischen Religionen und des Schamanismus* (Stuttgart, Hiersemann, 1967, p. 116):

> An initiation is also given in the Lamaistic gCod rite, where a goddess, who has been imagined by the initiate, slices off his head and cuts his body up in pieces. The ritual is . . . a combination of the Buddhist destruction of the ego (in the

Wittgenstein did not say in the Lecture when he first had the experiences described therein, but from autobiographical information disclosed in conversations with Norman Malcolm, the "absolute safety" experience must have occurred for the first time around 1910 or early 1911—which would be not only before the composition of either the *Tractatus* or the *Notebooks,*[10] but before he decided to leave for Cambridge to take up the study of logic under Bertrand Russell. The story Wittgenstein relates to Malcolm is about the change in his attitude towards religion:

> . . . in his youth he had been contemptuous of [religion], but . . . at about the age of twenty-one[11] something had caused a change in him. In Vienna he saw a play that was mediocre drama, but in it one of the characters expressed the thought that no matter what happened in the world, nothing bad could happen to *him—he* was independent of fate and circumstances . . . For the first time [Wittgenstein] saw the possibility of religion.[12]

From this account one must not jump to the conclusion that the "absolute safety" experience described in the Cambridge lecture actually occurred while Wittgenstein was in attendance at the play. Rather than being an occasion for the experience, the thoughts expressed in the play may only have served as a catalyst, perhaps suggesting a new way of looking at things, a clearing away, so to speak, of old cob-webs, and an awakening of a young mind from the slumbers of an inherited tradition (and thus, perhaps, paving the way for a new kind of experience).[13] Or the thought of the play may have had no effect on experiential receptivity at all, but merely served as the vehicle through which a prior experience found articulation. In

---

heightened tantric sense of human sacrifice) with a schamanic presentational form of dismemberment.

10. The *Notebooks,* edited by G.H. von Wright and Miss G.E.M. Anscombe (Harper and Row Publishers, N.Y., 1961) is a large collection of dated notes written by Wittgenstein between 1914-1916, when he was conceiving the *Tractatus*. Many of the notes were incorporated verbatim or near verbatim, into the published work. Wittgenstein had apparently written many similar notes, but his papers were destroyed on his orders in 1950, what is published as the *Notebooks* surviving only because they had been inadvertently stored away from the others.

11. Wittgenstein was born April 26, 1889, his 21st birthday thus falling in 1910.

12. Malcolm, *op. cit.*, p. 70.

13. One thinks in this regard of the effect Ambrose's idea of allegorical interpretation of scripture had on the young Augustine.

such a case, upon hearing the words uttered in the play, Wittgenstein might have said something like, "Wow! I know exactly what he is talking about. *Absolutely* safe! *Nothing* can happen to him." Or alternately, the experience may have come sometime after the play, and the play recalled only in retrospect. Whichever hypothesis is correct, however, the time interval between the play and the first such experience must have been quite short, perhaps a few weeks at the most, one not normally remembering much of a play that was "mediocre drama".[14]

---

14. Although no conclusive statement can be made about the immediate effect upon Wittgenstein of the experience Malcolm relates here, the experience may well have been instrumental in Wittgenstein's decision in 1911 to shift his interest from aerodynamic engineering to philosophy. As previously suggested (footnote 2, p. 69), the tools of modern logic may well have appeared to Wittgenstein as the most promising method of preserving the *ganz andere* nature of the mystical religious experience, and the translogical Beyond which it reveals, against profanation and debasement. Additional evidence for such a conclusion is provided in the sketch drawn of Wittgenstein by his sister Hermine, which suggests that some kind of extraordinary personal experience or state of mind was involved in Wittgenstein's decision to take up the study of philosophy and logic. The relevant part of Hermine's memoir reads as follows:

> After his matura, Ludwig went to the Technische Hochschule in Berlin and then occupied himself extensively with questions and experiments concerning aerodynamics. At this time, or a little later, he was suddenly seized (*ergriff*) so strongly and so completely against his will by philosophy, i.e. by reflections about philosophical problems, that he suffered severly under his double and conflicting calling, and felt inwardly divided. One of several transformations which he was to undergo in his life had come over him and shaken his whole being. At that time he was concerned with writing a philosophical work and finally decided to show the plan of his to a Professor Frege at Jena, who was involved with similar questions. Ludwig found himself in those days to be in a constant, indescribable and almost pathological state of excitement, and I very much feared that Frege, whom I knew to be an old man, would not be able to muster up the patience and understanding to deal with the matter with the required seriousness.

(Quoted in Bernhard Leitner's *The Architecture of Ludwig Wittgenstein*, New York University Press, 1976, p. 18. I have taken the liberty to depart from Leitner's English translation at one point, translating "krankhaften Aufregung" as "pathological state of excitement" rather than "morbid state of excitement", the latter seeming to me an odd combination of words, since "morbid" is usually associated with something gloomy and depressing rather than something exciting).

The World-Symbol of the Tractatus

The *Tractatus*[1] opens with the declaration:

> The world is all that is the case. (1)
> The world is the totality of facts, not of things. (1.1)
> The facts in logical space are the world. (1.13)
> The world breaks up into facts. (1.2)

But a clarification of the term "world" comes only towards the end of the work:

> The meaning of the world must lie outside the world. In the world everything is as it is and happens just as it happens; *in* the world there is no value (and if there were, it would have no value).
>
> If there is value that really has value so it must lie outside of all that happens and is the case. For all that happens and is the case is accidental.
>
> What makes it all non-accidental cannot lie *in* the world, for if it did, this would again be something accidental.
>
> It must lie outside the world (6.41)
>
> The solution to the riddle of life in space and time lies *outside* of space and time. (6.4312)
>
> *How* the world is, is for what is higher a matter of complete indifference. God does not reveal himself *in* the world. (6.432)
> (all emphasis in original)

To these might be added the propositions from the *Notebooks*:

> What do I know about God and the purpose of life? I know that this world exists. . . . That something about the world is problematic—what we call its meaning. That this meaning does not

1. *Tractatus Logico Philosophicus,* with an Introduction by Bertrand Russell, accompanied by a new edition of the English translation of D.F. Pears and B.F. McGuinness (Humanities Press, N.Y., 1961). The translations of the German original given here are, unless otherwise indicated, mostly my own, though they often coincide with, or closely follow those of Pears-McGuinness. The numbers next to each quote refer to the proposition number of each statement as given in the *Tractatus*.

> lie in the world but outside it. . . . We can call the meaning of life—i.e. the meaning of the world, God.
>
> (11. 6. 16)[2]

Carnap and the other members of the Vienna Circle all assumed that the "world" of the *Tractatus* was an ultimate symbol for an all-encompassing reality, which, in the nature of the case, one necessarily stood wholly and totally within. They were able to arrive at such an interpretation only by their refusal to take seriously the "in" and "out" prepositional indices with which the term "world" was surrounded and qualified. Their attitude towards these qualifying correlatives is perhaps well represented in the remarks of Max Black, a more recent commentator. In his Bible commentary style, *A Companion to Wittgenstein's Tractatus*—which is of considerable value as an aid to reading the *Tractatus*—he says in regard to proposition 6.41: "This is irredeemable nonsense . . . How could it be shown that there is 'value' outside of the world? What could at best be shown is that there is no value inside the world."[3]

But the "world" Wittgenstein was delineating in the *Tractatus* was just the world one stands outside of (*ek-stasis*) in the mystic flight, the logical system of the *Tractatus* being a precise delineation of the profane world which is left behind in the transcendental encounter with the Sacred. One might call proposition 6.432—"God does not reveal himself *in* the world"—the *Tractatus* in miniature.

The meaning of the world-symbol may become clearer after a brief look at what it was partially directed against—i.e., Arthur Schopenhauer's *The World as Will and Representation.*[4] In his early years, before conceiving the *Tractatus,* Wittgenstein had been a devotee of Schopenhauer,[5] and specific passages in the *Tractatus,* in-

---

2. Wittgenstein's reflections here bring to mind the following remarks from Reinhold Niebuhr's *The Nature and Destiny of Man* (Charles Scribner's Sons, N.Y., 1964):

> Consciousness is a capacity for surveying the world and determining action from a governing center. . . . The self knows the world, insofar as it knows the world, because it stands outside both itself and the world, which means that it cannot understand itself except as it is understood from beyond itself and the world. The essential homelessness of the human spirit is the ground of all religion; for the self which stands outside itself and the world cannot find the meaning of life in itself or the world.
>
> (volume 1, pp. 13-14)

3. Cornell University Press, Ithaca, N.Y., 1964, p. 370.

4. *The World as Will and Representation,* translated by E.F.J. Payne, Dover Publications, N.Y., 1969.

5. See George von Wright, "A Biographical Sketch", *op. cit.,* p. 530.

cluding the opening lines, seem to have been written in direct opposition to Schopenhauer.

Ekstasis *and* Apatheia

The philosophical system presented in *The World as Will and Representation* begins, in Kantian fashion, by identifying the knowable world with the world of phenomena, or in Schopenhauer's term, representation (*Vorstellung*[1]). The world that I know is representation —i.e., object for a subject. This is the meaning of the opening line, "The world is my representation." But unlike Kant, Schopenhauer wants to assert that there are really two knowable worlds standing in some kind of dynamic relationship with one another. There is an outer-world of material objects, of which the body of each person is a part, and an inner-world, fundamentally different from the outer, sometimes referred to by Schopenhauer as self-consciousness:

> A consciousness of one's own self and a consciousness of other things, are in truth given to us immediately, and the two are given in such a fundamentally different way that no other difference compares with this . . . This is the fact and the problem.[2]

This inner-world is, for Schopenhauer, the world of will and desire. Unlike the world of representation, this world is subject neither to the forms of space, time, and individuation, nor to the principle of sufficient reason (*Satz vom Grund*)—i.e., the law of causality. Schopenhauer thus tends to identify the will with properties of the Kantian thing-in-itself:

> The will as thing-in-itself lies outside the province of the principle of sufficient reason in all its forms. . . . it is free from all *plurality* [*Vielheit,* multiplicity] although its phenomena in time and space are innumerable. It is itself one, yet not as an object is one, for the unity of an object is known only in contrast to possible plurality . . . it is one as that which lies outside time and

1. Perhaps "presentation" is a better English equivalent. "Idea" of the older Haldane-Kemp translation is very misleading.
2. *The World as Will and Representation,* vol. II, p. 192.

> space, outside the *principium individuationis,* that is to say, outside the possibility of plurality.[3]

Unlike Kant's thing-in-itself, however, Schopenhauer often treats the "will" as knowable, and frequently compares knowledge of the will to a lifting of the veil of Maya (illusion):

> Everyone knows only *one* being quite immediately, namely his own will in self-consciousness. . . . there is really *only one being*; the illusion of plurality (Maya) [which results] from the forms of external, objective apprehension, could not penetrate right into the inner, simple consciousness . . .[4]

But in some places Schopenhauer hedges, saying that the will he is talking about, at least the will in so far as it is thing-in-itself, is "not absolutely and completely knowable."[5] Within, however, the inner-world/outer-world conceptual structure that he uses (which is non-Kantian), what he calls the will can be known in two ways. In an inner manner it is known immediately as self-consciousness: I am immediately conscious of myself willing to do various things. In addition, says Schopenhauer, I become aware of my willing by its manifestations in the form of outward, phenomenal movements of my body.

> [The will] constitutes what is most immediate in [a person's] consciousness . . . it becomes known to the individual himself not as a whole, [i.e., not as thing-in-itself], but only in its particular acts.[6]
> Every true act of his will is also at once and inevitably a movement of his body; he cannot actually will the act without at the same time being aware that it appears as a movement of the body . . . The action of the body is nothing but the act of the will objectified—i.e. translated into perception.[7]

The inner-world/outer-world distinction which Schopenhauer uses is essentially that of everyday, common-sense understanding —an "in here" or inner-world of my self-consciousness and will, stands opposed to an "out there," outer-world of matter in motion,

3. *Ibid.*, vol. I, p. 113.
4. *Ibid.*, vol. II, p. 321.
5. *Ibid.*, vol. II, p. 197.
6. *Ibid.*, vol. I, p. 109.
7. *Ibid.*, p. 100.

which is passively observed. (It must be said, however, that the attempt to express such a distinction within the Kantian phenomena/thing-in-itself framework often leads to a clash of conceptual paradigms). The "will" which Schopenhauer talks about also reflects the common-sense viewpoint: it is known immediately in an "inner" way, though its outer manifestations in movements of the body can be perceived in just the same "outer" manner as one perceives the movements of any other object in the (outer) world. But to this conventional understanding, Schopenhauer's "will"-symbol proceeds to acquire three other strata of meaning, all linked together under the same multifaceted term. The first of these additional strata encompasses the forces of nature, seen by Schopenhauer not as the lifeless forces of Newtonian physics, but as powers alive with vitality and purpose:

> I . . . intend every force in nature to be conceived as will . . .[8] [Will] is the innermost essence, the kernel, of every particular thing and also of the whole. It appears in every blindly acting force of nature, and also in the deliberate conduct of man, and the great difference between the two concerns only the degree of the manifestations, not the inner nature of what is manifested.[9]
>
> . . . the force that shoots and vegetates in the plant, indeed the force by which the crystal is formed, the force that turns the magnet to the North Pole . . . the force that appears in the elective affinities of matter as repulsion and attraction, separation and union, and finally even gravitation, which acts so powerfully in all matter, pulling the stone to the earth and the earth to the sun; all these . . . [are] different only in the phenomenon, but the same according to their inner nature . . .[10]

And in determining the inner nature of these physical forces, science, specifically, mathematics and etiology (the science of causes) is completely irrelevant for Schopenhauer:

> Although all mathematics gives us exhaustive knowledge of that which in phenomena is quantity, position, number, in short, spatial and temporal relation; although etiology tells us completely about the regular conditions under which phenomena, with all their determinations appear in time and space . . . we can never with their assistance penetrate into the inner nature of things.[11]

8. *Ibid.,* p. 111.
9. *Ibid.,* p. 110.
10. *Ibid.,* p. 110.
11. *Ibid.,* p. 121.

The second additional meaning encompassed by Schopenhauer's "will"-symbol is the will as survival instinct. In a manner that foreshadows Bergson's concept of an *elan vital,* Schopenhauer sees in various instinctive activities—e.g., the reproduction and nest-building instinct of birds and the instinct spiders have to spin webs and nourish upon the insects caught in these webs—manifestations of a survival instinct or will-to-live. Just how the instinct to survive in animals is related, at one extreme, to the physical forces in nature, and at the other, to human acts of willing, is not, however, self-evidently clear in Schopenhauer.

The third and for Schopenhauer's philosophy most important additional meaning of "will," deals with man's strivings towards self-aggrandizement. Man, in Schopenhauer's view, is by nature ego-centric: "every individual makes himself the center of the world, and considers his own existence and well-being before all else. . . . everyone wants everything for himself, wants to possess, or at least control, everything."[12] With a psychology far from sophisticated, Schopenhauer sees self-centeredness and ego-striving in man as manifestations of the will-to-live, though of a specifically human kind. The human will-to-live for Schopenhauer, differs from the survival instinct in animals in that it is a will which can be willed against. And willing against this will-to-live is critical for Schopenhauer since the selfishness and ego-striving associated with the will-to-live constitute for him the primary source of disharmony between man and man, as well as between man and nature. Schopenhauer devotes the whole second half of *The World as Will and Representation* to an explanation of the two paths through which this disharmony can be overcome—to the paths, that is, of aesthetic contemplation and Stoic-ascetic self-denial. It was this latter formula, of course, that so distanced Schopenhauer from the spirit of his age.

Aesthetic contemplation for Schopenhauer offers the possibility of fusing the inner-world of the self and will with the outer-world of nature. In the contemplation of great beauty, whether natural beauty or a human work of art, it is possible, he believes, for a man to overcome his self-assertive ego-strivings and become one with the world—i.e., one with nature and one with his fellow men. In beholding great beauty, a man "draws nature into himself, so that he feels it to be only an accident of his own being." "In this sense," Schopenhauer goes on (quoting Byron),

> Are not the mountains, waves and skies, a part
> Of me and of my soul, as I of them?[13]

12. *Ibid.,* p. 332.
13. *Ibid.,* p. 181.

Similarly, in contemplating Platonic Ideas (an activity akin to the apprehension of beauty),

> The person who is involved in this perception is no longer an individual, for in such perception the individual has lost himself . . .[14]
>
> [We] devote the whole power of our mind to perception, sink ourselves completely therein, and let our whole consciousness be filled with the calm contemplation of the natural object actually present, whether it be a landscape, a tree, a rock, a crag, a building or anything else. We *lose* ourselves entirely in this object . . . in other words, we forget our individuality, our will . . .[15]

A similar, and presumably more lasting, losing-of-oneself, can be attained, according to Schopenhauer, through a life committed to self-denial and mortification of the appetites and will. It is in this aspect that Schopenhauer's philosophy comes closest to Stoicism and reveals itself as a reaction against the frenzied strivings of his day, and a search for a way out of the boredom[16] and spiritual *ennui* that followed in the wake of material abundance and Enlightenment.[17] Ego-striving, says Schopenhauer, is by its very nature condemned to perpetual failure because every satisfaction or attainment of the goal that the unbridled ego or appetite strives after is followed by the emergence of a new desire, and hence, a new source of dissatisfaction. Under such conditions, "no satisfaction . . . is lasting: . . . it is always merely the starting-point of fresh striving."[18] The only solution for Schopenhauer, the only way to overcome this perpetually unfulfilled striving on a lasting basis, is the permanent mortification of the appetites and deprecation of the self. This involves an ascetic process, a "deliberate breaking of the will by refusing the agreeable and looking for the disagreeable, the volun-

---

14. *Ibid.*, p. 179.

15. *Ibid.*, p. 178.

16. Schopenhauer's analysis of boredom is given in chapter 57 of the First Book, pp. 311-319.

17. Among such strivings, one might mention the frenzied efforts in pursuit of a "career" by those who had lost the consciousness of calling (vocation). Revealingly, the transformation of the course of a man's life into a "career"—i.e., "the ground on which a race is run" (OED)—did not occur in the English language until the beginning of the 19th century. The first use of "career" in this sense in OED is from 1803. For an older manner of symbolizing the course of human life, before the emergence of the "career", see John Bunyan's *The Pilgrim's Progress*.

18. *The World as Will and Representation*, vol. I, *Ibid.*, p. 309.

tarily chosen way of life of penance and self-chastisement, for the constant mortification of the will."[19]

The outcome of such efforts, Schopenhauer professes, is not a sullen or melancholy life, but a life of greater inner tranquility and peace. It is a life in which the inner and outer worlds fuse, just as temporarily they fuse in aesthetic contemplation: "Instead of the constant transition from desire to apprehension and from joy to sorrow; instead of the never-satisfied and never-dying hope that constitutes the life-dream of the man who wills, we see that peace that is higher than all reason, that ocean-like calmness of the spirit, that deep tranquility, that unshakable confidence and serenity."[20] It is a state of *apatheia,* which, together with the moments of self-loss in aesthetic contemplation, form the real heart of Schopenhauer's philosophical system. Such states are described by Schopenhauer as revelations of a higher truth. The fusion of inner and outer that occurs in these states is again and again referred to by him as a lifting of a veil of Maya.[21] Schopenhauer's knowledge of Hindu and Buddhist writings surpassed that of any other German philosopher of his time, and it was Schopenhauer who was perhaps more responsible than anyone else for spreading an interest in Eastern religious writings among the educated German public. The separation (or alienation) between the inner-world of the individual self and the outer-world of nature and other men, is what is revealed as Maya or illusion in the fusion states of *apatheia* and aesthetic contemplation.

Such fusion states confer meaning upon human existence, answering the "riddle of the world" and of human existence within the world. Kant is specifically taken to task on this point for seeing the answer to the riddle only in the unknowable, world-transcending realm of the thing-in-itself—i.e., the Kantian realm of God, freedom, and immortality. Kant, says Schopenhauer, was wrong in thinking that the "solution of this riddle cannot result from a thorough understanding of the world itself, but must be looked for in something quite different from the world."[22]

> I say that the solution to the riddle of the world must come from an understanding of the world itself; and hence that the task of metaphysics is not to pass over experience in which the world exists, but to understand it thoroughly, since inner and outer experience are certainly the principle source of all knowledge. I

19. *Ibid.,* p. 392.
20. *Ibid.,* p. 411.
21. *Ibid.,* pp. 8, 17, 253, 274, 352, 365, 365, 370, 373, 397, 419.
22. *Ibid.,* p. 427.

> say, therefore, that the solution to the riddle of the world is possible only through the proper connection of outer with inner experience.[23]

This is exactly what Wittgenstein sets himself against when in 6.4312 and 6.41 of the *Tractatus* he says, "The solution to the riddle of life in space and time lies *outside* of space and time"; "The meaning of the world must lie outside the world." And the difference between the two formulations shows clearly the difference between the experience which is most central to *The World as Will and Representation* and the more radical experience that forms the radiating core of the *Tractatus,* the difference, that is, between *apatheia* and *ekstasis*.

Although Schopenhauer has appropriated symbols and metaphors drawn from mystical writings—e.g., allusions to an ascent from the cave[24] and a lifting of the veil of Maya—regarding the possibility of the mystic-ecstatic state itself (*ekstasis*), he is strangely incredulous. Though he extols, it is true, the mystical writings of Eckhart, Tauler, Madam Guyon, and the *Theologia Germanica*,[25] it is not the mystic-experiential aspect of these writings that interests him, but only what is said about the ascetic practice of will-mortification. Schelling's "intellectual intuition" (*intellektuelle Anschauung*) he dismisses as "humbug" (*Windbeutelei*)[26], and he even goes so far as to designate "Nirvana" and "re-absorption in Brahman", as "myths and meaningless words".[27] At the one point in the first volume of *The World as Will and Representation* where Schopenhauer does pay lip-service to the ecstatic experience[28] ("that state . . . denoted by the names ecstasy, rapture, illumination, union with God")[29], he evades discussing it, either its possibility or characteristics, claiming—disingenuously, to be sure—that such a state is necessarily incommunicable and outside the only province that interests him, the province of knowledge, i.e., of object for a subject.[30] This is an obvious evasion coming from someone who has

23. *Ibid.*, pp. 427-428.
24. *Ibid.*, p. 419.
25. *Ibid.*, pp. 387, 389.
26. *Ibid.*, p. xxi.
27. *Ibid.*, p. 411.
28. The short paragraph in which this theme is introduced opens on the grumpy concessional note: "If, however, it should be absolutely insisted on that somehow a positive knowledge is to be acquired of what philosophy can express only negatively as the denial of the will . . ." (*Ibid.*, p. 410).
29. *Ibid.*, p. 410.
30. *Ibid.*

spent the better part of a book discussing what is claimed to be thing-in-itself (the will) and hence transcending the object-for-a-subject form. In the second volume of *The World as Will and Representation,* however, Schopenhauer dispenses with all attempts to conceal his skepticism, especially since Schelling (like Hegel and Fichte, an enemy of Schopenhauer) is part of the target: "Regarding the systems that start from intellectual intuition [*intellektuelle Anschauung*], i.e., a kind of ecstasy or clairvoyance . . . , all knowledge so gained must be rejected as subjective, individual, and consequently problematical. Even if it actually existed, it would not be communicable."[31]

What Schopenhauer has done throughout his work is to tear mystic symbols away from their contexts as they have been developed by mystic writers in explication of experiences of *ekstasis,* and apply them to a philosophical system grounded in aesthetic contemplation (note, not artistic creation) and a tranquility state of *apatheia.* He has, through terminological escalation, watered down the meaning of the terms used. The radical disattention of consciousness and *ganz andere* nature of the ecstatic experience, symbolized by Plato as a being dragged-up in an ascent from the cave, and by Hindu writers as a lifting of the veil of Maya from the phenomenal world, is completely lost when these symbols are applied to an aesthetic experience or a serenity-state of *apatheia,* however related such lower level experiences may be to the mystic experience of *ekstasis.*

By the time he was conceiving the *Tractatus,* Wittgenstein had probably come to regard Schopenhauer, at least in his treatment of Hindu and other mystic writings, in a manner similar to that in which he had originally regarded Tagore (though his view of Tagore subsequently changed):

> It seems to me as if all that wisdom has come out of the ice box; I should not be very surprised to learn that he got it all second hand by reading and listening (exactly as so many among us acquire their knowledge of Christian wisdom) rather than from his own genuine *feeling.* Perhaps I do not understand his tone: to me it does not ring like a man who is *seized* by the truth.[32]
>
> (emphasis in original)

---

31. *Ibid.,* vol. II, p. 186.

32. Letter to Paul Engelmann, September 23, 1921, in *Paul Engelmann: Letters from Ludwig Wittgenstein* (Horizon Press, 1967), p. 46 (The English translation found in this work has been altered slightly). Indeed, Schopenhauer's tone is that of a boaster and braggart, i.e., of someone who publically vents his own inflated ego as a substitute for the truth he doesn't have to offer.

Wittgenstein rejected the inner-world/outer-world/fusing-worlds framework of Schopenhauer, replacing it instead with his own, more radical, in-the-world/out-of-the-world paradigm. As Professor Stenius suggests, such a paradigm has many resemblances to the Kantian distinction between phenomena and thing-in-itself.[33] Both Wittgenstein and Kant juxtapose a "world" and a "beyond", though for Kant the distinction was not made in explication of a personal religious experience of *ekstasis,* but the result of an inherited Christian religious tradition that had long distinguished a world from a Kingdom of God.[34] It was only after religious symbols and religious experience had been irreparably torn asunder upon the intellectual rack of Enlightenment—surely the Darkest Age in Western history—that it became necessary to re-establish the tradition on the basis of a postulate of the practical reason. Though a man of exemplary piety, unlike Paul on the road to Damascus, the author of the *Critiques* was not a man *seized* by the truth. His philosophy, however, bore the vestigial imprint of those who were.

God and the World

To sum up:

The "world" symbol of the *Tractatus,* together with its correlative indicies "in" and "out", was intended to express the radical otherness of the God who is miraculously revealed in the mystic Encounter. The "world", as a profane realm, is just what God is wholly other *than,* and it is only on the occasion of the mystic flight that this radical separation is made—a separation in which the profane is clearly distinguished from the Sacred, a "world" from a Kingdom of God, a *civitas terrena* from a *civitas Dei,* a *samsara* from a Nirvana. The sacrality of God is thus established symbolically by a desanctification of all that is less than God.[1]

33. *Wittgenstein's Tractatus* (Basil Blackwell, Oxford, 1960), pp. 214. The last chapter on "Wittgenstein as Kantian Philosopher" is valuable reading.

34. On Kant in this regard, see the comment of Walter Stace in *Religion and the Modern Mind* (J.B. Lippincott Company, N.Y. 1960), pp. 274–275.

1. In the present analysis "reality" will be used to encompass both of Wittgenstein's correlatives, "in-the-world" and "out-of-the-world". This is done despite the fact that Wittgenstein sometimes uses the term *Wirklichkeit* (reality or actuality) in a manner similar to "world" (e.g., "The sum total of reality is the world" 2.063). *Wirklichkeit,* however, is less frequently used than world (*Welt*) and should not give occasion for

The in-the-world of the *Tractatus* is a thoroughly profane realm. It is the world of physical science in which things just happen and are the case, or do not happen and are not the case. Unlike the enchanted Nature of the German Romantics,[2] it is a thoroughly desacralized world, but only because the Sacred has been revealed in its purity, in the radicalness of its world-transcendence.[3]

Of What One Can and Cannot Speak: The Say/Show-Itself Distinction

Concerning the Reality revealed in the theophanic Encounter itself, all the *Tractatus* says is:

> There is of course the unspeakable[1]. It *shows* itself; it is the Mystical.
>
> (6.522)

---

confusion if the two different usages (here and in the *Tractatus*) are kept in mind. The term "being" might have been chosen instead, but its association with speculative philosophy makes it not as well suited to an elucidation of concrete experience, such as that treated in the *Tractatus*.

The contrasting of the reality revealed in the mystical experience with terms that are generally understood as final and all-inclusive—an effort designed to secure terminologically the *ganz andere* nature of what is absolutely Sacred—can even reach the point, as in Buddhist and related Christian mystical writings, where God is declared to be either "nothing" or "void". *Cf.* Otto: "Mysticism continues to its extreme point this contrasting of the numinous object (the numen) as the 'wholly other', with ordinary experience . . . Mysticism concludes by contrasting it with Being itself and all that 'is', and finally actually calls it 'that which is nothing'. By this 'nothing' is meant not only that of which nothing can be predicated, but that which is absolutely and intrinsically other than and opposite of everything that is and can be thought." (*The Idea of the Holy, op. cit.*, p. 29).

2. *Cf.* Schopenhauer's phantasmagoric world of physical nature, above p. 101.

3. Tolstoy, who, along with Augustine, commanded Wittgenstein's profoundest regard (see Engelmann, *op. cit.*, p. 79) makes a similar, equally radical distinction between sacred and profane: "If you speak of what happens in the world, everything in the world is dead and carcasses, and where the carcasses are, there crows gather . . . 'Where?' we may say of the carcass, of the crows, but for what is spiritual there is no space, as there is no time" (from his commentary on Luke 17:37, in *The Four Gospels Harmonized and Translated,* vol. II, Leo Wiener translation, Dana Estes Co., Boston, 1904, p. 109).

---

1. *Unaussprechliches*—also "inexpressible" or "ineffable". Pears-McGuinness's rendering of *sich zeigen* in this context as "manifest itself" conveys the intended meaning

> What one cannot speak about, one must pass over in silence.
> (7)

The last proposition is the concluding line of the *Tractatus,* and as indicated in the Preface, part of the central theme of the work:

> One could sum up the whole import of the book in the following words: what can be said at all can be said clearly; and what one cannot talk about one must pass over in silence.

As we have seen, Pseudo-Dionysius writes:

> The higher we soar in contemplation the more limited become our expressions of that which is purely intelligible . . . we pass not merely into brevity of speech but even into absolute silence, of thoughts as well as of words . . . we mount upwards from below to that which is the highest, and according to the degree of transcendence, so our speech is restrained until the entire ascent being accomplished, we become wholly voiceless, inasmuch as we are absorbed in Him who is totally ineffable.

The *Theologia Mystica* differs from the *Tractatus* in distinguishing a hierarchy of being, but regarding the impropriety of language in dealing with the ascent to the highest level, they proclaim the same message. And ironically, with a true Promethean's instinct for competition from the gods, it was only Otto Neurath among the members of the Vienna Circle who seems to have had a vague understanding of what this message was. When it comes to metaphysics, said Neurath, "one must indeed be silent, but not *about* anything."[2]

If one understands the basis for the invocation of silence as lying in the same experience that gave birth to the in-the-world, out-of-the-world indices, one of the key distinctions running throughout the *Tractatus* becomes readily comprehensible. This is the distinction between what can be said in language and what cannot be said in language, or, alternately stated, between what can be said and what must show itself (*sich zeigen*). Failing to grasp the experiential basis of the work, just about all who have written on the *Tractatus* have failed to grasp the meaning of this distinction. Some commen-

---

much better than "shows itself", but the connection is then lost to other propositions where the latter translation must be used.

2. Quoted in A.J. Ayer, "The Vienna Circle", *The Revolution in Philosophy* "Macmillan and Co., London, 1956) p. 75.

tators, for instance, such as Max Black, have suggested explanations in terms of things none of which offer any resistance to being stated— e.g., the distinction between a language and the semantical rules of that language.[3] Others, such as George Pitcher, think the distinction, at least regarding its meaning, is self-evidently clear, and thus in need of no explanation.[4] While still others, such as G.E.M. Anscombe, find it not so self-evident, but offer an expla-

---

3. *A Companion to Wittgenstein's Tractatus, op. cit.*, p. 191. Black is himself by no means satisfied with this explanation. His attempts to offer a better one, however, were doomed to failure from the start since he rejected as "doubtful" (p. 191) the key "show-itself" proposition 6.522. He also failed to grasp the meaning of solipsism in the *Tractatus* (next subsection) and thereby categorized the use of "show-itself" in 5.62 ("What solipsism *means* is completely correct; only it does not lend itself to being said, but, rather, shows itself") under the same "doubtful" heading as 6.522.

4. Pitcher sums up what to him is self-evident in the following manner:

> An elementary proposition, we know, is a picture of reality. In a picture, a certain situation is depicted. The picture has the same structure as the situation. But I cannot make a picture which depicts the fact that a picture has the same structure as its situation. I can make a picture of a picture, and a picture of its situation, but I cannot, so at least it might seem, make a picture of a picture's having the same structure as its situation. (*The Philosophy of Wittgenstein,* Prentice Hall, Englewood Cliffs, N.J., 1964, p. 153).

He goes on:

> One immediately feels a sense of uneasiness with Wittgenstein's position here, and I think it is in fact untenable. In the course of the *Tractatus,* he has said certain things about the relationship between propositions and situations: that one is a logical picture of the other, that they have the same structure, and so on. *We understand these doctrines,* we weigh their merits and demerits, and no doubt take a stand on them, either accepting or rejecting them. But then at the end we are told that they are all nonsense and that such doctrines cannot be stated, that they merely try to say something that can only be shown and that cannot be said. This evaluation cannot be accepted (p. 155).
>
> (emphasis added)

Actually there is sense to be made of the say/show-itself distinction as Pitcher presents it, but only as an instance of what Wittgenstein calls the "urge to the Mystical". The form or structure that objects share with the pictures that depict them—which, however, is itself non-depictable—is nothing more than the in-the-world property which they possess by virtue of the fact that the consciousness which perceives objects always experiences itself as standing outside what it perceives, even when this "standing outside" is not meditatively pursued to its origin in God. This non-mystical sense of "standing outside", however, can be experienced in its function as an urge to the mystic *ekstasis* only in the wake of the mystical experience itself.

nation that obviously fails to do justice to the importance the distinction has in the *Tractatus*.[5]

5. Miss Anscombe tries to explain the distinction using as an example the pseudo-sentence ("pseudo" on the criteria of the correspondence theory of truth and the picture theory of language given in the *Tractatus*): "'Someone' is not the name of someone." The sentence is given as an example of a meaningful proposition whose meaning does not depend on the correlation or lack of correlation between the words of the proposition and any kind of object. The sentence is intended to make clear the confusion in such a conclusion as: "Everyone hates someone, therefore someone must be hated by everyone".

"'Someone' is not the name of someone"—i.e., "someone" is not a person's name.

(See *An Introduction to Wittgenstein's Tractatus,* University of Pennsylvania Press, Phila., 1971, pp. 85-86)

Needless to say, this hardly sounds like the stuff of which the cardinal problem of philosophy is made. Like most commentators (see also, Eddy Zemach, "Wittgenstein's Philosophy of the Mystical", *Review of Metaphysics,* September, 1964, pp. 38-57), Miss Anscombe could not believe that passages about the mystical had anything to do with mystical experience. Quite logically, she was impelled to criticize Wittgenstein for terminological over-kill: "'Mysticism' is a rather odd name for what Wittgenstein is speaking of; in popular language it suggests extraordinary and unusual experiences, thoughts and visions peculiar to an extraordinary type of individual . . ." (*An Introduction,* pp. 169-170).

In fairness to Miss Anscombe, as well as to Professors Pitcher and Black, it should be mentioned that all of their works were written before the publication of Engelmann's *Memoir*. Very possibly, their understanding of the *Tractatus* has changed considerably.

The commentary by Wittgenstein's friend Paul Engelmann, is one of the few secondary works on the *Tractatus* to grasp what its author was trying to say. Wittgenstein and Engelmann had the most intimate personal friendship during the critical period of the First World War when Wittgenstein was writing and subsequently trying to publish the *Tractatus*. The letters received by Engelmann from Wittgenstein over this period, together with Engelmann's commentary on the *Tractatus* and various topics relating to it and its author, are published together in a paperback volume under the title, *Paul Engelmann: Letters from Ludwig Wittgenstein with a Memoir* (Horizon Press, N.Y., 1968). The designation "Memoir", however, does not adequately describe Engelmann's efforts, which offer a fresh look at the *Tractatus* based on a personal understanding of Wittgenstein at the profoundest level, in addition to a contemporary's understanding of the cultural and historical circumstances from which the work emerged.

Engelmann points out the source of misunderstanding of the *Tractatus* when he says:

> To the ordinary reader, even if versed in philosophy, Wittgenstein's basic thoughts, as stated in the *Tractatus* . . . seem incomprehensible . . . they are incomprehensible owing to the absence of the psychological conditions from which alone such thinking can spring and which must exist, though to a lesser degree, in the reader's mind as well (p. 94).

The reader must indeed be capable, to some degree, of an empathetic re-creation of the experiences explicated in the *Tractatus*. Engelmann's interpretation of the *Tractatus*, however, is flawed by his refusal to carry out the full implications of what he himself describes as the "anti-psychologistic" method of the *Tractatus* (*Memoir*, p. 100)—a refusal which can be seen in the quoted reference to the mystical experience as a certain "psychological" condition.

Similarly, in trying to clear up the view that "certain mystical conclusions" found in the *Tractatus* were a secondary derivative from its views on logic, Engelmann writes:

> logic and mysticism have here sprung from one and the same root, and it could be said with greater justice that Wittgenstein drew certain logical conclusions from his fundamental mystical *attitude* to life and the world (p. 97).
>
> (emphasis added)
>
> What Wittgenstein's life and work shows is the possibility of a new *spiritual attitude* (p. 135).
>
> (emphasis in original)

By associating "spiritual" and "mystical" with "attitude", Engelmann resorts to just what he has said the *Tractatus* was trying to break free of—i.e., psychologism. Engelmann, however, acknowledges at one point that this is what he is doing, or at least, that this is what Wittgenstein would have accused him of doing (see page 135). The world of the *Tractatus* is not a given, standing over against an observer, who then takes a certain (psychological) attitude towards what he sees—perhaps materialistic, perhaps mystical. The *Tractatus* world, rather, comes into clear view only in the mystical experience itself, as the profane contrast to the "out-of" flight.

Engelmann's inability to transcend psychologistic categories is manifest in the confusion of the following:

> *As on the one hand* the unutterable lies in the relation between language and the world ('the outside world') *so on the other hand* does it lie in the relation between language and the world of intuitive values (p. 111).
>
> (emphasis in original)

The distinction made in the first part of the sentence is that common to various ego-psychologies, and similar to what we have seen in Schopenhauer. The distinction is one between an "outside world" which is not part of me, and an "inner world" which is the site of my true being—i.e., of my self, ego, or self-consciousness. But such a distinction is alien to the *Tractatus* (see next subsection) where the "inner world" of ego-psychology shrinks to an extensionless point as it is gobbled up by the "outer world", i.e., as all that was seen to be part of "me", the ego-embodied "I" spatially identified with the private space filled by my feet, hands, legs, arms, torso, head, and eyes, is delivered over to the sciences of the external (outer) world. As a result of this shrinkage of the "I" to an extensionless point (ego-loss), there is no "inner world" in the *Tractatus* that would make sense to talk of an "outer world". The ego of ego-psychology is declared to be a non-entity (5.542). Instead there is only an "in-the-world" and an "out-of-the-world", and a "me" or "I" as an extensionless point bordering between them. The in-the-world realm encompasses the region of spatio-temporal objects, including language, which is passively observed by the eye-point, while the out-of-the-world realm is the mysterious, enchanted realm of the Sacred, where words are singularly out of place.

Just how important the say/show-itself distinction was intended to be is indicated in a letter Wittgenstein wrote to Bertrand Russell after the First World War. Having just read Russell's comments on the unpublished *Tractatus* manuscript, Wittgenstein said the following:

> Now I'm afraid you haven't really got hold of my main contention, to which the whole business of logical propositions is only corollary. The main point is the theory of what can be expressed (*gesagt*) by propositions—i.e. by language (and, what comes to the same, what can be *thought*) and what cannot be expressed by propositions, but only shown (*gezeigt*); which, I believe, is the cardinal problem of philosophy.[6]

For someone reared in the philosophical culture of Kant, Fichte, Schelling, Hegel, Marx, Kierkegaard, and Nietzsche—indeed, for someone who had been a one-time follower of Arthur Schopenhauer—the cardinal problem of philosophy was obviously not a technicality of logic, though even after a subsequent meeting between Wittgenstein and Russell in Holland in 1919, Russell was unable to come to an understanding of what this cardinal problem was. In another letter to Russell (May, 1920) concerning his Introduction to the *Tractatus*, Wittgenstein said that he could not permit the *Tractatus* to be published alongside of what Russell had written because it contained nothing but "superficiality" and "misunderstanding".[7]

Wittgenstein's "cardinal problem" was the Reality revealed in the mystical experience itself and the impossibility of describing it in a non-profaning manner by language drawn from, and sharing the structure of, a logical-multiplicitous world. His critique of language in the *Tractatus* was an attempt to show that language is a profane, inner-worldly medium, and that through such a medium, a message which is sacred cannot be articulated. Moreover—and this is critical for understanding the application of the say/show-itself distinction beyond its use in the passages about mysticism and solipsism (5.61, 6.522)—the profane, in-the-world structure of lan-

---

6. Quoted in G.E.M. Anscombe, *An Introduction to Wittgenstein's Tractatus, op. cit.*, p. 161.

7. The letter is printed in Appendix III of the *Notebooks*, p. 131. A similar characterization is found in a letter Wittgenstein wrote to Engelmann (May 8, 1920): "My book will probably not be printed, as I could not bring myself to have it published with Russell's Introduction, which looks even more impossible in translation than it does in the original." (Engelmann, *op. cit.*, p. 31). Wittgenstein, of course, later reversed this decision.

guage is a property it has only by virtue of its being contrasted to the sacred, transcendent realm in the divine Encounter itself, "profane" and "sacred" being correlative indices on the same order as "in" and "out".

The distinction between what is said in language and what is shown by language emerges from Wittgenstein's picture theory of language. Language for Wittgenstein, by which he has primarily in mind discursive propositions (4.001), is a model or picture of reality.[8] This picture can be either true or false depending on its correspondence or lack of correspondence with the reality which it purports to depict.

> The proposition is a picture of reality.
> The proposition is a model of reality as we imagine it.
>
> (4.01)
>
> In order to tell if the picture is true or false, we must compare it with reality.
>
> (2.223)
>
> The truth or falsehood [of a picture] consists in the correspondence or non-correspondence of its sense [i.e., of what it represents] with reality.
>
> (2.222)

One might think of the proposition as a kind of road map whose truth depends on how accurately it represents (scaled and projected) the paths the roads actually take. At first glance, says Wittgenstein, the proposition as it stands on the page might not look like a picture of anything, but this is only so because one has not taken into consideration the rules of projection by which reality can be depicted in the proposition (4.011, 4.0141)—in the same way that a road map does not look much like a vast system of highways, until one has understood the scale and legend.

Then Wittgenstein says that the proposition or picture has some property in common with the reality which it depicts that only shows itself, i.e., that cannot be said or depicted in language. This is called by him variously "the form of depiction", "the form of representation", "the logical form", and at one place is identified with "logical-mathematical multiplicity" (4.004, 4.041). What the picture-proposition has in common with the reality it depicts could only be said in language, Wittgenstein asserts, if one could station oneself with the language medium (propositions) outside of the world:

8. "Reality" in Wittgenstein's sense of in-the-world (empirical) reality.

A picture has logical form in common with what it depicts.

(2.2)

A picture can depict any reality whose form it has.

(2.171)

The proposition [i.e., picture of reality] cannot represent [or depict] logical form.

(4.121)

The proposition *shows* the logical form of reality.

(4.121)

The proposition can represent (depict) the whole of reality, but it cannot represent what it must have in common with reality in order to be able to represent it—i.e., logical form.

In order to represent the logical form, we would have to be able to station ourselves with the proposition outside of logic, which means, outside of the world.

(4.12)

Russell, missing entirely the point that was being made here, suggested that perhaps there were other languages besides propositional language—logical-technical languages, for instance—that may have a different form or structure than propositions, and thus capable of representing this allegedly non-depictable (unsayable) "logical form" which propositions have in common with the reality they depict.[9] There would thus be no say/show-itself problem. But what Wittgenstein was stating here about the proposition was only an application—a "corollary" as he phrased it in his letter to Russell—of what he had stated at 6.522 when he said that the Mystical was an unspeakable that shows itself (*zeigt sich*), and at 6.432 when he said that God does not reveal himself *in* the world. The "outside of the world" of proposition 4.12 alludes to the realm of the mystical ascent. We cannot place ourselves *with the proposition* outside of the world (outside of logic), because this is just the region where "we pass into absolute silence, of thoughts as well as of words."

What language shares with the reality it depicts that shows or manifests itself but cannot be said, is just its *in*-the-world structure. This structure cannot be described by language because it is a property possessed only by virtue of, and in contrast to, the *out*-of-the-world mystic flight—the flight (i.e., consciousness disattention, intensification, and absorption) into a sacred realm. It *is* this contrast.

This *in*-the-world structure is then identified by Wittgenstein with "logical form" and "mathematical-logical multiplicity" because logic and mathematical multiplicity represent the outer scaffolding

9. *Tractatus*, Introduction, p. xxii.

or framework of the world[10] which, in *ekstasis,* is broken out of. The both/and, either/or framework of consciousness in its attention to a multiplicitous world is transcended in the disattending flight of the mystical experience. In this "flight", logic represents the "/" in the in/out travelogue.[11]

The two types of showing in the *Tractatus* are thus intimately related to one another. There is, first of all, the showing of what lies beyond the world in mystic vision (ethical, aesthetic, religious showing); and secondly, there is the isomorphic showing of the world and its contents, together with language, *in their mutual relationship to what lies beyond the world* (the showing of logical form). Language and the world do not exist by themselves in the *Tractatus,* but are bounded by a translogical, transcendental realm that manifests itself and its beyondness of the world in a heightened state of consciousness—a state of consciousness that also reveals with great clarity the peculiar inner-worldliness and inner-worldly form of all spatio-temporal objects.[12]

---

10. Like Russell and Whitehead, Wittgenstein believed mathematics was reducible to logic. See 6.124, 6.2, 6.22, 5.61.

11. The nature of the mystical *realissimum* as beyond the logical differentiating structure of the attended consciousness is a common theme in mystic literature. We have already seen it, for instance, in Schopenhauer's Hindu-Christian influenced discussion of the thing-in-itself as lying beyond *Vielheit* and the *principium individuationis.* The logic-mathematics transcending nature of the mystical ascent is well illustrated by Meister Eckhart:

> The mind . . . will press through the firmament and press through the heavens to find the breath that spins them. Yet this does not satisfy it. It must press farther into the vortex, into the primal region where the breath has its source. Such a mind knows no time nor number: number does not exist apart from the malady of time. Other root, the mind has none save in eternity. It must surpass all number and break through all multiplicity. Then it will be itself broken through by God.
> (Quoted in Rudolf Otto, *Mysticism East and West,* Macmillan Co., N.Y., 1932, p. 205)

12. A number of commentators have failed to see the intimate relationship between the two types of showing in the *Tractatus,* i.e. the showing of the mystical Beyond and the showing of language and the world in their common relationship to the mystical Beyond. W. Donald Hudson, for instance, although he is well aware that Wittgenstein himself saw unity in the two types of showing, describes Wittgenstein's two uses of the term "showing" as a "purely verbal coincidence." Referring to the two types of unspeakable transcendentals in the *Tractatus,* the ethico-religious and the logical, he writes:

> In its ethico-religious instantiation the transcendental shows itself in art and action [i.e. ethical and religious activity]. . . . But whatever it could mean to say that the highest cannot be spoken but only shown—in art or action—this sense

Besides the in–out prepositional indices then, the world-transcending, "breakthrough" nature of the mystic flight is also symbolized by the ladder of proposition 6.54. Having stated that language, along with logic, is a boundary of the world (5.6), and that only picture-propositions can count as language, Wittgenstein was left, apparently painted into a corner, with the problem of how to explain the propositions of the *Tractatus* itself. Since they were neither picture propositions, nor tautologies—the only types of statements recognized in the *Tractatus* as meaningful—they would seem to have a unique status all their own. Wittgenstein tried to extricate himself from this predicament in what might at first appear to be a frivolous remark:

> My propositions serve as elucidations in the following way: anyone who understands me eventually recognizes them as nonsensical, when he has used them—as steps—to climb up beyond them. (He must, so to speak, throw away the ladder after he has climbed up it.)
>
> He must transcend these propositions, and then he will see the world aright.
>
> (6.54)[13]
>
> What one cannot speak about, one must pass over in silence.
>
> (7)

---

of 'showing' does not seem to be conceivable in anything like the sense in which logical form may be said to show itself in logical implications.

It is difficult to see any similarity between the *way* in which the transcendental is conceived to show itself in the logical and the ethico-religious instantiations respectively.

In both instantiations, the transcendental is indeed said to show itself. But this common feature is a purely verbal coincidence.

It is hard to avoid the conclusion that there is simply *no* similarity between either what is *meant* by the transcendental, or what is *meant* by its showing itself, on the respective interpretations of it which are to be found in the *Tractatus*. Wittgenstein evidently thought that there was some essential connexion on both counts; but we have found it impossible to form any clear idea of what this could be.

(*Wittgenstein and Religious Belief*, The Macmillan Press Ltd., London, 1975, pp. 111, 112).

Although Hudson writes very clearly and has obviously thought a good deal about Wittgenstein's relation to ethics and religion, like almost all commentators except Engelmann, he has failed to understand the radicalness of the ecstatic experience towards which the *Tractatus* points, and thus, has not grasped fully the meaning of either type of showing.

13. Pears McGuinness translation.

These remarks are anything but frivolous. The ascent over the ladder alludes to the mystical ascent;[14] the world that one sees from the height of this ascent, is the world seen from outside the world (*ekstasis*); and the throwing away of the ladder and transcending of the propositions establishes the function of the *Tractatus* as a *via negativa*. And the final statement was perhaps intended as the most serious of all, for in its counsel to silence we can see the reverence of a pious man before the divine *Mysterium*.

The Solipsism of the Tractatus

The say/show-itself distinction is interwoven with another theme of the *Tractatus* which has been no better understood—i.e., the remarks concerning solipsism:

---

14. A ladder naturally suggests itself as a symbol for the mystic flight, and is quite common, not only in the shamanic tales, but in Hebrew, Christian, and Islamic writing as well. See Eliade, *Shamanism, op. cit.*, pp. 487-494. On the necessity to go beyond images and symbols in the meditative ascent to God—i.e., to leave the ladder behind as one climbs up over it—*cf.* the metaphor of the stairs in the following from John of the Cross:

> Since all created things . . . are unproportioned to God's being, all imaginings fashioned out of their similarities are incapable of serving as proximate means toward union with Him. . . . Those who imagine God through some of these figures . . . and think that He is somewhat like them are very far from Him. These considerations, forms, and method of meditation are necessary to beginners that the soul may be enamored and fed through the senses . . . They are suitable as the remote means to union with God, which beginners must ordinarily use . . . Yet these means must not be so used that a person always employs them and never advances, for then he would never achieve his goal, which is unlike the remote means and unproportioned to it—just as none of the steps on a flight of stairs has any resemblance to the goal at the top toward which they are the means. If a man in climbing them does not leave each one behind until there are no more, or if he should want to stay on one of them, he would never reach the level and peaceful room at the top.
>
> Consequently a man who wants to arrive at union with the Supreme Repose and Good in this life, must climb all the steps, which are considerations, forms, and concepts, and leave them behind, since they are dissimilar and unproportioned to the goal toward which they lead.
>
> (*The Ascent of Mount Carmel*, in *The Collected Works of John of the Cross*, translated by Kieran Kavanaugh and Otilio Rodrigues, ICS Publications, Wash. D.C., 1973, p. 138).

> *The boundaries of my language* are the boundaries of my world. (5.6)[1]
>
> Logic fills the world up completely; the boundaries of the world are also the boundaries of logic.
>
> We can in logic, therefore, not say, "In the world there is this and this, but not that."
>
> For that would apparently presuppose that we exclude certain possibilities, and this cannot be the case, for logic would then have to go beyond the boundaries of the world; it would, in other words, have to view these boundaries from the other side as well.
>
> What we cannot think, we cannot think; and we cannot *say* what we cannot think.
>
> (5.61)
>
> This remark gives the key to understanding to what extent solipsism is a truth.
>
> What solipsism *means*, is wholly correct, only it does not permit itself to be *said*; it shows itself.
>
> (5.62)

This "somewhat curious discussion of solipsism", as Russell characterized it,[2] presents interpretive difficulties even if the say/show-itself distinction is clearly understood. Logic and language are the boundaries of the world, which are only broken out of in the logic and language transcending experience of the mystic flight. One cannot *say* what does not exist in the world, because what does not exist *in* the world is the out-of-the-world mystic union, and for expressing this experience, the in-the-world structure of language and logic is not appropriate. Similarly, the out-of-the-world experience cannot be construed in thought, because "thought" (*Gedanke*), in the technical sense of the *Tractatus*, is closely tied to picture-propositions (3.01, 3.1)—i.e., to what can be said in language. But, one must ask, what does all this have to do with solipsism, and is this truth of solipsism which cannot be said, a different kind of unspeakable truth from the divine Encounter in the mystic flight and the inner-worldy structure of all worldly content which it reveals? The answer is contained in the following propositions:

> The thinking, representing subject does not exist. If I were to write a book, *The World as I Found It*, such a book would have to

1. Note, the translation of *Grenze*—which can mean variously, frontier, border, boundary, limit, extremity—has had to be varied in different contexts in order to bring out the intended meaning.

2. *Tractatus* Introduction, xviii. Russell attempted no interpretation, merely repeating in summary fashion what Wittgenstein had said.

contain something about my body, and would have to say which of my body's members were subordinate to my will, and which not, etc.—this being a method of isolating the subject, or rather of showing, that in an important sense no subject exists. It alone could such a book *not* discuss.

(5.631)

The human body, *my* body in particular, is a part of the world among other parts—e.g., among animals, plants, rocks, etc., etc.

(*Notebooks*, 2. 9. 16.)

Where *in* the world is a metaphysical subject to be found?

You say it is just like the eye in relation to the visual field. But you really do *not* see the eye.

And nothing *in the visual field* allows you to conclude that it is seen by an eye.

(5.633)

. . . the soul—the subject, etc.,—as it is conceived in today's superficial psychology, is a non-entity.

(5.5421)

The subject does not belong to the world, but is a border of the world.

(5.632)

The "I" of solipsism shrinks to an extensionless point, and there remains the reality co-ordinate to it.

(5.64)

That the world is *my* world, is shown by the fact that the boundaries of language . . . mean the boundaries of *my* world.

(5.62)

There is really a sense in philosophy in which one can speak non-psychologically about an "I" . . .

The philosophical "I" is not the human being, not the human body, or the human soul of which psychology treats, but the metaphysical subject, the border—not a part—of the world.

(5.641)

Like the claim that metaphysics is nonsense, and much else contained in the *Tractatus*, this looks very much like a Humean argument[3]. Yet it is not trying to show that no self or "I" exists, only that the self or "I" is not to be understood as a body in the world. The true, metaphysical "I" is an extensionless point—a pupil of an eye —on the border of the world. What Wittgenstein is doing here is

3. Hume's famous contention that only phenomena (sensory perceptions) exist, but not anything which could be clearly distinguished from these as a self, is to be found in *A Treatise of Human Nature* (Green-Grose edition, Longmans, Green and Co., London, 1898), p. 534.

denying the reality of the embodied-self, i.e., the ego of ego-psychology and common sense, in the name of the higher reality of the mystic vision.[4] The disembodiment of the self that occurs in the mystical experience is represented as the shrinkage of the "I" or self from its body-identity to a point—a vantage point—from which it views the whole world, including the body which it had previously felt itself *in*.

"The world is my world"—i.e., solipsism—is only another way of saying that the divine Encounter is the most intimately *private* experience. It is the experience symbolized by Plotinus in the concluding line of his *Sixth Ennead* (9.11) as the "flight of the alone to the Alone". The private nature of the world proceeds directly from the private nature of the mystical experience itself because only through such an experience does a logical-multiplicitous "world" come into view as the profane, consciousness-attending contrast to the translogical, transmultiplicitous realm in the divine Encounter. Only in the mystical ascent to God, in the Beatific Vision of the Kingdom of God (to speak in Christian mystical symbols) does a "world" come into being.[5] The "I" which Wittgenstein represents as a point at the border of the world is thus the "I" of the ecstatic soul

---

4. The denial of the reality of the ego—i.e., of the spatially located, enclosed, embodied self—is, of course, a common feature of philosophies and religions that acknowledge mystical experience as ultimate experience revealing a higher (and only properly so-called) reality. As Laing explains: "Most people most of the time experience themselves and others in one or another way that I . . . call *egoic*. That is, centrally or peripherally, they experience the world and themselves in terms of a consistent identity, a me-here over against a you-there, within a framework of certain ground structures of space and time shared with other members of their society . . . All religious and all existential philosophies have agreed that such *egoic experience* is a preliminary illusion, a veil, a film of *maya*—a dream to Heraclitus and to Lao Tzu, the fundamental illusion of all Buddhism, a state of sleep, of death, of socially accepted madness, a womb state to which one has to die, from which one has to be born." (from "The Transcendental Experience", chapter 6, *The Politics of Experience*, Ballantine Books, N.Y., 1967, pp. 137-138).

Dr. Laing's *The Politics of Experience* contains insights of enormous value for all those interested in the sciences of culture—it may well be, in fact, one of the most important works of social science to have come out of the 60s. It cannot be said, however, that the good Doctor himself has been led by these insights into any greater degree of self-awareness, maturation, or wisdom. Apparently thrown off balance by it all, he vacillates about, adolescent-like, unable to make up his mind whether to play the role of left-revolutionary or flipped-out hippie.

5. And it should be mentioned that it is only by virtue of the translogical realm revealed in the mystical ascent that it becomes meaningful to speak of a *totality* of facts (thoughts, propositions), rather than simply an infinity. See propositions 1.1, 3.01, 4.001. Also 6.45: "To view the world *sub specie aeterni* is to view it as a whole—a limited whole."

which has known divine communion in a realm beyond logic and language.[6]

The intimately private nature of the mystical experience was the special concern of the American poet Walt Whitman. In his *Democratic Vistas*, he makes use of a border metaphor for the "I" very similar to Wittgenstein's:

> There is, in sanest hours, a consciousness, a thought that rises, independent, lifted out from all else, calm, like the stars, shining eternal. This is the thought of identity—yours for you, whoever you are, as mine for me. Miracle of miracles, beyond statement, most spiritual and vaguest of earth's dreams, yet hardest basic fact, and only entrance to all facts. In such devout hours, *in the midst of the significant wonders of heaven and earth* (*significant only because of the Me in the center*), creeds, conventions, fall away and become of no account before this simple ideal. Under the luminousness of real vision, it alone takes possession, takes value.[7]
>
> (emphasis added)

Similarly, in the same volume:

> . . . only in the perfect uncontamination and solitariness of individuality may the spirituality of religion positively come forth at all. Only here, and on such terms, the mediation, the devout ecstasy, the soaring flight. Only here, communion with the mysteries, the eternal problems, whence? whither? Alone, and identity, and the mood—and the soul emerges, and all statements, churches, sermons, melt away like vapours. Alone and silent thought and awe, and aspiration—and then the interior consciousness, like a hitherto unseen inscription, in magic ink, beams out its wonderous lines to the sense. Bibles may convey and priests expound, but *it is exclusively for the noiseless operation of one's isolated Self*, to enter the pure veneration, reach the divine levels, and commune with the unutterable.[8]
>
> (emphasis added)

---

6. If one keeps in mind the unspeakable as well as the speakable side of the in/out paradigm, Wittgenstein's pupil-point metaphor resembles to a certain extent Meister Eckhart's often quoted lines: "The eye by which I see God is the same as the eye by which God sees me. My eye and God's eye are one and the same." (From Sermon 23, in *Meister Eckhart*, Raymond B. Blakney translation, Harper Torchbooks, N.Y., 1941, p. 206). The resemblance is more striking in Professor Stace's paraphrase of the passage: "The apex of the soul is like an eye from which one may look in two directions, upward unto the Godhead, and downward into the world." (*The Teaching of the Mystics, op. cit.*, p. 157).

7. *Democratic Vistas* (E.P. Dutton and Co., N.Y., 1930), p. 329.

8. *Ibid.*, p. 333. Whitman's treatment of the mystic experience is similar to Witt-

The intimately private nature of such an experience was the basis of Whitman's personalism—i.e., of his belief that the ultimate unit of human reality was the individual person in his immediacy before God. This immediacy before God, Whitman believed, conferred upon every man, regardless of membership in any race, religion, state, class, or family, an untouchable dignity. It was, in fact, the transgression of this dignity by the social institution of slavery that inspired Whitman and many of his contemporaries in their support of the abolitionist cause.

Whitman's notion of the "person" and Wittgenstein's notion of the solipsistic "I" derive from the same experience, and stress the same privacy, intimacy, and ultimacy. The difference between the two terms, however, cannot be overlooked. That the human encounter with God should be associated with solipsism, rather than personalism, can only be understood when one takes into account the extreme, pathological state of consciousness occlusion that typified late 19th and early 20th century Europe. In a world of battling ideological systems (Hegelian, Marxist, Neo-Thomist, and later National-Socialist) all embraced with equally murderous dogmatism and fanaticism by the chaos-threatened psyches of their adherents, the man who *knows* the Divine Measure really *is* alone. The social world about him is not Whitman's America, where the relative sanity and spiritual vitality of the colonial and frontier experience was still very much alive, but the lunatic world resulting from centuries of cultural disintegration—a world which, not long after Wittgenstein conceived the *Tractatus*, would throw itself into the bloody slaughter of a Great War, and which, not content with one slaughter, would only too willingly hand itself over to the tyrants and madmen bent on leading it into the holocaust of an even greater war.

Existential Yearning: The Urge to the Mystical

A very important theme taken up in the *Tractatus* is what one might designate, staying within Wittgenstein's general terminolog-

genstein's in three important respects: 1) it is a private, person-constituting experience (Wittgenstein's solipsism); 2) it is an experience in which "all statements churches, sermons, melt away" (the nonsense status of metaphysical propositions for Wittgenstein); 3) it is a union with the Sacred whose utterance through language could only be a profanation.

ical framework (or at least not running against it) as existential yearning. The same theme, outside this framework, might be spoken of as the "problem of human existence", or the "problem of the 'givenness' of human existence". Man finds himself in a world, *thrown* into a world in existentialist parlance, but this world that he is *in*, he feels himself not wholly *of*. This feeling of belonging to some other world, of not being fully at home in the world one finds oneself in, gives rise to a powerful yearning, but a yearning *for what* one does not know. All that one knows is that in the depths of one's being, one is something more than chemistry and physics, and that there is some meaning to human existence beyond the senselessness of a biological cycle beginning at birth and ending inevitably in death.

This yearning, at least in modern Western societies, is a near universal phenomena, and, when the yearning takes on the nature of a search, it may be variously designated as a search for the meaning of life, for the ground of being, for God, etc. Quite often, especially for those who have grown up in a religious tradition that places great emphasis on post-mortal existence, the search will be seen as inherently doomed to failure during one's biological lifetime, and the yearning, which remains unsatiated, will serve as a basis for faith in a post-mortal heaven. It was man's existential yearning, coupled with the Christian doctrine of the after-life, that served as the basis for Kant's postulation of the realm of God, freedom, and immortality.

Wittgenstein takes up the theme of existential yearning in its particular relation to the world of natural science—i.e., the "world" proper in the *Tractatus*:

> We feel that even if all *possible* scientific questions have been answered, the problems of life remain completely untouched.
>
> (6.52)
>
> The urge to the Mystical comes from the non-satisfaction of our wishes by science.
>
> *Notebooks* (25. 5. 15.)
>
> The feeling of the world as a limited whole is the mystical feeling.
>
> (6.45)

The phrase "urge to the mystical" (*der Trieb zum Mystischen*) occurs only in the *Notebooks* (immediately before the passage that was to become proposition 6.52 of the *Tractatus*) but it says essentially the same as 6.45: Existential yearning, the feeling that one is *in* the world (the world describable by natural science) but not wholly *of* it,[1] is identified as a mystical feeling, or an urge to the mystical. This might seem like a watering-down in the meaning of terms *à la* Schopenhauer, until one realizes that it is a retrospective interpretation, relating a critical feature of the mystical experience itself. When such an experience occurs, as is so often the case, after a period of intense searching and struggling to find meaning in life, the higher reality which the experience reveals is also revealed as the culmination of that past struggle. It was in cell # 40 that Koestler, the Marxist revolutionary who had so passionately sought to find—or to create—some kind of meaning in his own life, discovered what he was really after:

> Whether the experience [in cell # 40] had lasted for a few minutes or an hour, I never knew. In the beginning it occurred two or even three times a week, then the intervals became longer . . . [These experiences filled] me with a direct certainty that a higher order of reality existed, and that it alone invested existence with meaning.[2]

But only *post facto*, in the wake of the experience, will the struggle of the past be seen as a yearning to know what has now been re-

---

1. No doubt this commonly experienced tension in existence, this being-in-but-not-of whereby a world is constituted as that order which is *not* one's ultimate abode, was intended by Wittgenstein as the departure point for the non-mystic reader of the *Tractatus*, since it is an experience to which most people can relate. The mystic ascent (using somewhat different language than Wittgenstein) reveals this in-but-not-of tension in existence, i.e., this "feeling of the world as a limited whole", as man's estrangement from the ground of his being, from his absolute safety in the hands of God.

2. *The Invisible Writing, op. cit.*, p. 353. Koestler continues:

> I came to call it [i.e., this higher order reality] later on "the reality of the third order". The narrow world of sensory perception constituted the first order; this perceptual world was enveloped by the conceptual world which contained phenomena not directly perceivable, such as gravitation, electro-magnetic fields, and curved space. The second order of reality filled in the gaps and gave meaning to the absurd patchiness of the sensory world.
>
> In the same manner, the third order of reality enveloped, interpenetrated and gave meaning to the second. . . . Just as the conceptual order showed up the illusions and distortions of the senses, so the 'third order' disclosed that time, space and causality, that the isolation, separateness and spatio-temporal limitations of the self were merely optical illusions on the next higher level. If illusions of the first type were taken at face value, then the sun was drowning every night in the sea and a mote in the eye was larger than the moon; and if the conceptual world was mistaken for ultimate reality, the world became an equally absurd tale, told by an idiot or by idiot-electrons which caused little children to be run over by motor cars, and little Andalusian peasants to be shot through heart, mouth and eyes, without rhyme or reason (pp. 353-354).

vealed. The yearnings of existence are thus seen as an "urge to the mystical" only in retrospect, when that yearning has found satiety in the theophany of the mystic flight. Abraham Maslow brings this out very well in his summary of the accounts of the people in his investigation:

> Everyone knows how it feels to want something and not know what. These mystic experiences feel like the ultimate satisfaction of vague, unsatisfied yearnings . . . [People who have such experiences have] the feeling that they had really seen the ultimate truth, the essence of things, the secret of life . . . Alan Watts has described this feeling as 'This is *it*!', as if you had really gotten there, as if ordinary life was a striving and a straining to get some place and this was the arrival, this was *Being There*!; the end of straining and of striving, the achievement of the desire and the hope, the fulfillment of the longing and the yearning.[3]

Wittgenstein objects, however, to yearnings of such kind being called a "problem", because the "answer" takes the form of an experience that does not fit the question-answer form of language—an experience of such ultimate sacrality, that one must pass over it in silence. The question-answer form is appropriate to questions in natural science, but *only* to questions in natural science. The problem of life is not a question with an answer, but the yearning of existence (the urge-towards, *der Trieb-zu*) which is satisfied only in a miraculous Encounter about which it is not fitting to speak:

> When the answer cannot be put into words, neither can the question be put into words. If a question can be framed at all, it is also *possible* to answer it.
>
> (6.5)[4]
>
> The solution to the problem of life is seen with the disappearance of the problem.
>
> Is this not the reason why men, to whom the meaning of life has become clear after prolonged doubt, why these men could not say what this meaning consisted in?
>
> (6.521)
>
> There is of course the unspeakable. It *shows* itself; it is the Mystical.
>
> (6.522)

3. "Lessons from Peak-Experiences", *Journal of Humanistic Psychology*, v. II, p. 10.
4. Pears-McGuinness translation.

By virtue of the mystical experience, not only questions about the meaning of life, but also questions about the existence or non-existence of God are rejected. Since the in-the-world (spatio-temporal) structure of language is not appropriate to the out-of-the-world mystic flight, and since the theophanic sacrality of the experience can be expressed only through silence, it makes no sense to speak of a "question" regarding the revealed God. A God who could be spoken of as existing or non-existing, as a question or hypothesis to be answered affirmatively or negatively, is not the God of the theophanic Encounter:

> Scepticism is *not* irrefutable, but obviously nonsensical when it tries to raise doubts where no questions can be asked.
>
> For doubt can exist only where a question exists, a question only where an answer exists, and an answer only where something *can be said*.
>
> (6.51)[5]

Profanation and Obscurantism: The Judgment on Metaphysics

The opposition to metaphysics in the *Tractatus* is on two grounds, both suggested in the previously quoted summary statement of the Preface:

> What can be said at all can be said clearly; and what one cannot talk about, one must pass over in silence.

The first part is obviously aimed at the obscurantist tradition in 19th century German metaphysics, the tradition that reached its

5. Pears-McGuinness translation. Wittgenstein's remarks on this score are not out of tune with the thoughts of a theologian like Tillich. *Cf.*:

> . . . the question of the existence of God can be neither asked nor answered. If asked, it is a question about that which by its very nature is above existence, and therefore the answer—whether negative or affirmative—implicitly denies the nature of God. It is as atheistic to affirm the existence of God as it is to deny it. . . . As the power of being, God transcends every being and also the totality of beings —the world.
>
> (*Systematic Theology*, volume I, University of Chicago Press, 1951, p. 237).

apex in the works of Hegel. The designation of metaphysical propositions as "nonsense" (*Unsinn*) was obviously made with this tradition in mind:

> Most of the questions and propositions which have been written about philosophical things are not false but nonsensical. We cannot even begin to answer questions of this kind but only show their nonsensicalness.
>
> (4.003)

In this regard, the assessment of the *Tractatus* differed little from the assessment of Wittgenstein's one-time mentor, Arthur Schopenhauer:

> Kant's style bears throughout the stamp of a preeminent mind, genuine strong individuality, and quite exceptional powers of thought... Nevertheless Kant's language is often indistinct, indefinite, inadequate, and sometimes obscure. . . . he who is himself clear to the bottom and knows with perfect distinctness what he thinks and wishes, will never write indistinctly, will never set up wavering and indefinite conceptions. . . . the most injurious result of Kant's occasionally obscure language is, that it acted as *exemplar vitiis imitabile*; indeed, it was misconstrued as a pernicious authorization. The public was compelled to see that what is obscure is not always without significance; consequently, what was without significance took refuge behind obscure language. Fichte was the first to seize this new privilege and use it vigorously; Schelling at least equaled him; and a host of hungry scribblers, without talent and without honesty, soon outbade them both. But the height of audacity, in serving up pure nonsense, in stringing together senseless and extravagant mazes of words, such as had previously only been heard in madhouses, was finally reached in Hegel, and became the instrument of the most barefaced general mystification that has ever taken place, with a result which will appear fabulous to posterity, and will remain as a monument of German stupidity.[1]

But the second ground for the attack on metaphysics—a recognition of what must be passed over in silence—is certainly the more important. It was this concern which raised the whole tone and character of the *Tractatus* above polemics to the level of an oracular decree, though the seriousness of the message, it is true, has been

---

1. *Die Welt als Wille und Vorstellung*, Haldane-Kemp translation (*The World as Will and Idea*, v. 2) Kegan Paul, London, 1891, pp. 20-22.

balanced by a spirit of playfulness. "Wittgenstein," says Paul Engelmann in his *Memoir*, "passionately believes that all that really matters in human life is precisely what, in his view, we must be silent about."[2] The whole logical-linguistic system of the *Tractatus* was developed as an attempt to circumscribe the boundary beyond which profane language may not enter. And the system which outlines this boundary, beginning with the opening, "The world is . . .", is put forth with such oracular assurance precisely because its author has successfully crossed beyond the boundary. He is a shaman, a "one who knows", and when he speaks, he speaks with the authority of a prophet. It was *this* authority, the authority of charisma rather than Wittgenstein's analytic powers (which were at least equaled by Carnap) which held such an irresistible sway over men such as Moritz Schlick.[3]

Language can be seen, as it is in the *Tractatus*, in terms of structured sounds or ink marks on paper. It thus exists within a space-time structured world. Even the mental image of a written word, the image in my mind, for instance, when I recall mentally Wittgenstein's first name as I have seen it written on paper (an act of recollection requiring that I not focus my visual attention, staring into the distance if possible), while not existing in the same space as the soda can which presently sits across from my desk, or the "Mountain Dew" label on its front side, is nevertheless in the same time-matrix. Moreover, the image that I bring into my mind is in some kind of space in that it has parts and I encounter some of the same difficulty in focusing my attention on the mental image as I do on the written word—e.g., I tend to see the letters grouped in Gestalts, so that I have to picture the word as "Lud-wig" and read across from the first group to the second, and the tendency is, even within a Gestalt-group, to have a shifting focal awareness among the three letters comprising the Gestalt. And here is where the contrast between the word and the mystical religious experience enters.

---

2. "When he nevertheless," Engelmann continues, "takes immense pains to delimit the unimportant, it is not the coastline of the island which he is bent on surveying with such meticulous accuracy, but the boundary of the ocean" (*Memoir, op. cit.*, p. 97).

Wittgenstein himself wrote in a letter to Ludwig Ficker: ". . . I wanted [in the Preface] . . . to write: my work consists of two parts: of that presented here and of all that I have *not* written. And just this second part is the really important one . . . I believe that what is just hot air when *many* others today talk, I have established securely in my book through being silent about it . . . I would now recommend you to read the Preface and Conclusion as these express most directly the meaning of the book." (Quoted in Engelmann, *Memoir*, p. 144).

3. See footnote 24, p. 66.

If language is seen in terms of letters and sounds within a multiplicitous, space-time world, then the mystical experience will obviously be seen as something quite beyond language. And this "beyond-language" designation will be re-enforced when additionally, language is viewed as the product of humanly willed activity—as the vibration of vocal chords, as handwriting, as a typed page, etc.—in contrast to the divine action in the experience.

This is essentially the verdict of the *Tractatus*. As propositions (language) are models or pictures of the profane world, so metaphysical propositions are graven images which can only profane the absolute sacrality of the theophanic event and the translogical Reality manifested in it. Before the revealed God, man must keep silent. For an understanding of the passion that lay behind Wittgenstein's invocation of silence one must bear in mind the historical circumstances from which his critique of language arose. Like George Fox, Wittgenstein lived in a time of battling theological and metaphysical belief systems. At the turn of the century, Germany and Austria were, in fact, a microcosmic crucible of all the major ideological battles—theological, metaphysical, and political—which have plagued Europe since the break-up of the medieval world-order. From the Church sphere, rival Catholic and Lutheran religious doctrines still stood against one another as antagonistic enemies, the former holding sway in Austro-Hungary and Southern Germany, the latter throughout the rest of the German speaking world. Only the memory of the bloody religious civil wars and the common enemy of atheism toned down the absolute claims each made to truth, and moderated the hatred with which each attacked the other as heretics or servants of the Anti-Christ. Added to this (by no means settled) dispute, was, then, the whole cacophony of 19th century metaphysical systems, Hegelianism in its various branches being the most influential. Polarizing on the political front into warring camps that would at least equal the hatred and animosity that the Catholics and Lutherans had earlier displayed towards one another, revolutionaries seeking to establish an eschatological Kingdom through their own *praxis*, battled it out with their reactionary opponents who believed that they themselves had already realized the Absolute in their own thinking about thinking, and that it resided from now until eternity in the order of the German state. And in Hapsburg Austria, the monarch still claimed his rule by order of God—a claim undergirded by Jesuit neo-Thomism.

It is no wonder in such a situation that a Viennese such as the legal theorist Hans Kelsen could come to see in the competing moral and religious claims to truth, only the way to anarchy, and would recommend as the only way to peace, a positivist legal theory founded on the principle that all talk about natural law, divine law, justice, or morality was just the rationalization of private interests and preferences.[4] Or similarly, that a man of such humane instincts as Moritz Schlick could open the lead article in the first issue of *Erkenntnis* expressing the hope that through new developments in science and logic, the chaos of conflicting philosophical systems (*das Chaos der Systeme, der Streit der Systeme*)[5] might at last come to an end.

And this is just the situation in which the *Tractatus* was conceived. The metaphysical-theological language in the German speaking world of Wittgenstein's time had become so corrupted and debased by ideological disputes between rival religious, philosophical, and political factions, that men of spiritual sensitivity—men like George Fox more than two centuries earlier—could only turn away from it as a medium of expression and counsel their fellow men to a path of silence. Symbols such as "the Absolute", "God", "Spirit" (*Geist*), "Being" (*Sein*) etc. had become so closely associated with the rationalizations, hatreds, and ideological close-mindedness of those from whose lips and pens they flowed, that they could no longer serve as the vehicle for conveying a sacred truth. Wittgenstein's attitude in this regard is perhaps well represented in a remark made by a German friend of Martin Buber concerning the latter's use of the word "God". Having heard Buber read aloud the Preface to a book he had just completed, the friend turned to him and with steadily increasing passion reproached the philosopher in the following terms:

> How can you bring yourself to say "God" time after time? How can you expect that your readers will take the word in the

---

4. See for instance *The General Theory of Law and State* (Harvard University Press, Cambridge, Mass., 1949), pp. 10-13.

5. *Erkenntnis*, Band I, Heft 1, 1930, p. 5. The hope which positivism held out for humanists like Schlick and Popper is well captured by Leszek Kolakowski:

> [the positivists] represented the humane protest against a world traumatized by bloody clashes in the conviction that the spread of the so-called scientific attitude would be an effective means against the insane acts of ideologists . . . If such an attitude [i.e., that of empirical method] could be successfully propagated, the beneficial effect of scientism would be spontaneously felt in the form of the disappearance of all those disputes to which one could not ascribe a scientific meaning— and as a consequence, the disappearance of the wars, persecutions, and intolerant acts to which such disputes are genetically tied.
> (*Die Philosophie des Positivismus* R. Piper and Co, Munich, 1971, pp. 240-241)

> sense in which you wish it to be taken? What you mean by the name of God is something above all human grasp and comprehension, but in speaking about it you have lowered it to human conceptualization. What word of human speech is so misused, so defiled, so desecrated as this! All the innocent blood that has been shed for it has robbed it of its radiance. All the injustice that it has been used to cover has effaced its features. When I hear the highest called "God", it sometimes seems almost blasphemous.[6]

It is significant that the only time that Wittgenstein is known to have revealed publically, through traditional theological language, the type of experience explicated in the *Tractatus*, was to a group of British undergraduates—i.e., to people distanced from him by virtue of age, culture, and past history. And perhaps equally sig-

---

6. *The Eclipse of God* (Harper and Row, N.Y., 1952) p. 7. Buber's reply (which in general might be characterized more as the gut-reaction of a theologian than a sustained argument) ends with the following declaration—which might just as well have been addressed to Wittgenstein:

> How understandable it is that some suggest we should remain silent about the "last things" for a time in order that the misused words may be redeemed! But they are not redeemed *thus*. We cannot cleanse the word "god" and we cannot make it whole; but, defiled and mutilated as it is, we can raise it from the ground and set it over an hour of great care (pp. 8-9).

Wittgenstein was certainly not alone among his contemporaries in his reluctance to express his personal religious experience through traditional metaphysical and theological idioms. Consider, for instance, the following personal testimony by the classical scholar Jane Harrison, contained in a letter she wrote to Gilbert Murry a couple of years before the outbreak of the First World War:

> . . . Do you remember contending with me on the cliffs and maintaining that there was more in religion than the collective conscience? I think I know now at first hand that there is. Last night I was awake all night with misery and utter loneliness such as often comes upon me now that I have to go about alone—only it was worse than anything I had ever felt—like a black despair . . . I fell asleep at last and woke about six bathed in a most amazing bliss and feeling that all the world was new and in perfect peace. I can't describe it—the 'New Birth' is the best—it was what they all try to describe, and it is what they mean by communion with God. Only it seems senseless to me to give it a name, and yet I do not wonder for it is so personal. . . . I can't put it into psychology yet. What I feel most is that a wall of partitions is broken down and a whole crust of egotism gone, melted away, and that I have got hold of something bigger than me that I am part of. . . . What is it? *I will never call it God—that name is defaced*, but it is wonderful and you were right as always.
>
> (emphasis added, quoted in *Epilegomena to the Study of Greek Religion*, University Books, New Hyde Park, N.Y., p. xii)

nificant, it was an address given not in his native language with all the negative associations a sensitive German might have built up against the inherited theological-metaphysical terminology of his culture, but in English—from Wittgenstein's standpoint, a new language without all the paralyzing associations of his mother tongue. "'Mystical experiences'," says Koestler, "are not nebulous, vague, or maudlin—they only become so when we debase them by verbalization."[7] And debasing is just what one would be doing if one tried to express the experience through the publicly debased language of metaphysics and theology. Wittgenstein's entreaty to silence should thus be seen not merely as an assertion of the sacrality of God, but simultaneously as an indictment of the social-historical debasement of that sacrality in the rival systems of metaphysics and theology.

The main villain in the *Tractatus* would seem to be academic metaphysical systems; but the *Tractatus* critique is equally applicable to theological doctrines, and it is not certain whether Paul Engelmann is talking for himself or his friend at Olmuetz when he says in defense of a "wordless faith": "Any doctrine uttered in words is the source of its own misconstruction by worshippers, disciples and supporters. It is they who have so far without exception robbed all doctrines laid down in words of their effect, and who always threaten to turn the blessing into a curse."[8] Given his great admiration for Tolstoy, it would seem that Wittgenstein did, in fact, hold church theological doctrines in the same regard as Hegelian and related metaphysical doctrines. Tolstoy's critique (apparently on the basis of his own private *gnosis*)[9] of the catechismal doctrines of the Russian Orthodox Church—an institution that went well beyond

7. *The Invisible Writing, op. cit.*, p. 352.

8. *Memoir, op. cit.*, p. 136.

9. Tolstoy begins his translation of the Gospel of John on the gnostic note: "The comprehension of life became the beginning of all and the comprehension of life stood for God" (*The Four Gospels Harmonized and Translated*, vol. 1, Leo Wiener translation, Dana Estes and Co., Boston, 1904, pp. 24, 26). In the same volume, reminiscent to a considerable extent of Fox and Barclay, Tolstoy writes: "The kingdom of God is not in time and not in any place; it is like lightening—here and there and everywhere, and it has no time and no place because here it is within you . . . We must exalt the son of God in man . . . in order that men relying upon it, may not know death, but shall have non-temporal life in the kingdom of God . . . God and the kingdom of God are in men . . . The son of man is the comprehension. It has to be exalted and deified and by it we must live. He who lives in the comprehension lives non-temporally" (pp. 200-202). *cf* Wittgenstein's: "If one understands eternity to mean, not unending time (temporal duration), but timelessness, then the man who lives eternally is the one who lives in the present." (6.4311). "For life in the present there is no death." (*Notebooks*, 8.7.16.).

either the right Hegelians in Germany or the pro-Hapsburg Thomists in Austria in invoking theological-metaphysical symbols in deification of the existing order—foreshadows the *Tractatus*:

> I could not help noticing that the exposition of the theology [of the Russian Orthodox Church] was clearly directed, not to the explanation of the meaning of life . . . but only to the confirmation of the most incomprehensible and useless of propositions, and to the refutal of all those who did not recognize those propositions . . .[10]
>
> It was impossible to condemn or reject the ideas expressed, because it was impossible to catch a single clearly expressed idea. The moment I got ready to take hold of an idea, in order to pass judgement upon it, it slipped away from me, because it was purposely expressed obscurely.[11]
>
> God can do anything but this: he cannot talk nonsense.[12]

But like Wittgenstein, the motivating core of Tolstoy's opposition to church doctrine penetrated far deeper than an academic concern with clarity and precision of expression:

> I saw that the Orthodox people regarded all those who did not profess the same faith with them as heretics, precisely as the Catholics regarded Orthodoxy as a heresy; I saw that toward all who did not profess faith with external symbols and words, as Orthodoxy did, Orthodoxy, though trying to conceal it, assumed a hostile attitude . . . This hostility increases in proportion as the knowledge of the doctrine increases . . .
>
> The offence is so manifest to us educated people, who have lived in countries where several religions are professed, and who have seen that contemptuous, self-confident, imperturbable negative attitude which a Catholic assumes toward an Orthodox or a Protestant, and an Orthodox toward a Catholic or a Protestant, and a Protestant toward both the others . . .
>
> And I, who had assumed the truth to be in the union of love, was involuntarily startled to find that that religious teaching [which promised . . . that it would unite all in one faith and love] destroyed precisely that which it ought to build up.[13]

10. *The Four Gospels, Ibid.*, p. 6.
11. *Critique of Dogmatic Theology*, Leo Wiener translation (Dana Estes and Co., 1904), p. 94.
12. *The Four Gospels, op. cit.*, p. 11.
13. *My Confession*, Leo Wiener translation (Dana Estes and Co., 1904), pp. 82-83.

The revulsion that Wittgenstein felt with expressing and interpreting his private experience(s) through existing metaphysical and theological symbols and the systems built around them, issues forth in the very obliqueness with which they are woven into the *Tractatus*. In an effort to shield what is sacred (*Hoeheres, das Mystische*) from profanation by the vulgar (especially the educated vulgar), "out-of-the-world" is used deliberately to bring to mind something preposterous. And the same concern over profanation determines the form of the *Tractatus* as a *via negativa*. Although Wittgenstein never expected the misunderstanding of the work to be as total and widespread as it actually was, at the time he wrote the Preface, he clearly acknowledged that it was to be understood only by the few: "This book," the Preface begins, "will perhaps only be understood by someone who himself has already had the thoughts that are expressed in it—or at least similar thoughts."[14] But Wittgenstein never imagined—which may well be the key to understanding his radical shift in the 1930s away from the *Tractatus*—that his book would inspire a messianic materialistic movement that in its revolt against certain philosophical traditions, would throw the spiritual baby out with the metaphysical bath water.

It hardly needs to be remarked at this point that nothing is more alien to the *Tractatus* than the Promethean spirit of scientistic progressivism. Even Rudolf Carnap had found praiseworthy, upon his first, partial reading of the *Tractatus*—before he came to Vienna and read it together with members of the Vienna Circle—the humble rank which it had accorded to science in relation to an overall perspective on the human predicament. In the concluding paragraph of *Aufbau*, he wrote of the *Tractatus*:

> Wittgenstein has set forth clearly both the proud thesis concerning the all-powerfulness of rational science together with the humble insight concerning its importance for practical life . . . Unfortunately his treatise has remained practically unknown. It is, it is true, difficult to understand and insufficiently clarified, but very valuable both for its logical derivations and also for the ethical attitude with which it speaks.[15]

The *Tractatus* even attacks directly at one point the hubris of modern man, and finds more to praise in the superstitions of the ancients:

---

14. *Tractatus*, p. 2. "Thought"—*Gedanke*—is obviously used here in an everyday sense, not in the technical sense used throughout the *Tractatus*.

15. *Aufbau, op. cit.*, p. 261.

> The process of induction consists of accepting the *simplest* law that can be brought into agreement with our experience.
>
> (6.363)
>
> This process, however, has no logical, but only a psychological foundation.
>
> (6.3631)
>
> That the sun will rise tomorrow is a hypothesis; which means, we do not *know* if it will rise.
>
> (6.36311)
>
> The whole modern world-view is based on the illusionary deception that the so-called laws of nature (natural laws) offer explanations of natural phenomena.
>
> (6.371)
>
> Thus modern man sticks to natural laws as something inviolable, just as men of past ages stuck to God and Fate.
>
> (6.372)
>
> And they in fact are both right and both wrong. The ancients, however, are clearer in that they recognize a clear terminus, while, with the new system, it is supposed to appear as if *everything* is explained.
>
> (6.372)

This view is not at all, as Max Black characterizes it, "an excessively sceptical and deflationary view of the achievements and capacities of science",[16] and, in fact, is not inconsistent with the understanding of the nature of the scientific enterprise of a thinker such as Karl Popper.[17] Nevertheless, the example chosen of the sun not rising tomorrow may seem indicative of a whimsical flight of fancy, unless one considers it together with the statements about the psychological foundations of inductive certainty (6.3631) and the attack on the overweening pride and self-confidence of modern man (6.372). Just as an unexpected earthquake or tidal wave, the sun not rising would strike those who experienced such an event as frightening, horror-filled, and uncanny—in other words, as a *psychic* trauma. But for someone who knows the "absolute safety" of the ecstatic experience, there is no such trauma, for he knows that his

16. *A Companion to Wittgenstein's Tractatus, op. cit.*, p. 364.

17. "Science is not a system of certain, or well-established statements; nor is it a system which steadily advances towards a state of finality. Our science is not knowledge (*episteme*); it can never claim to have attained truth, or even a substitute for it, such as probability . . . *We do not know: we can only guess* . . . The old scientific ideal of *episteme*—of absolutely certain, demonstrable knowledge—has proved to be an idol. The demand for scientific objectivity makes it inevitable that every scientific statement must remain *tentative for ever*." (emphasis in original, *The Logic of Scientific Discovery*, Harper and Row, N.Y., p. 1959, pp. 278, 280).

psychic being (consciousness) has another resting place besides its attention to objects in the world—he knows that he is safe in the hands of God. *Dem Ich,* one might say in untranslatable German, *dass in Transzendenz beheimatet ist, kann nichts unheimlich sein.* The hubris of modern man is in holding what he can predict and control—i.e., the objects attended by consciousness—for ultimate reality in denial of the reality of Transcendence.[18] Through the occlusion of pride, he deifies the results of his own efforts. Wittgenstein's attack on the pride of inductive prediction should thus be seen, as Plato's parallel attack on the hubris of the enlightened sophists—i.e., on the shadow-callers, prideful of their ability to recall the sequence of shadows, believing themselves thereby to have explained *everything*[19]—as an affirmation of the ultimacy of Transcendence, of that which one can know only if one is willing to accept the penultimacy of the realm which science can control. Ultimate Reality is what one can come to know only if one is willing to look beyond the cave.

This point might also help to explain a deficiency in the *Tractatus* that served as the basis for considerable controversy within the Vienna Circle itself. Despite the fact that the whole logical and linguistic system which the *Tractatus* presents is founded upon the "elementary proposition" (*elementaerer Satz*) as its basic unit, not a single example is given of what these units correspond to in concrete reality. As more recent commentators have remarked,[20] there is nothing in the *Tractatus* which one could call an epistemology, and within the Vienna Circle itself, the debate soon arose as to whether these "elementary propositions"[21] were to refer to simple sensations in the Machian sense (the "sense data" of later British philosophy), sensations grouped in Gestalt wholes, or physical objects.[22] It must indeed have seemed strange that a work which attempted to construct a whole world out of atomic building blocks, should contain no discussion of what these blocks were made of. Critics of Wittgenstein have seen this as evidence of a rationalistic or formal-

18. Concerning the pride of scientific achievement, Wittgenstein says in the "Lecture on Ethics": "I believe to be one of the lowest desires of modern people . . . the superficial curiosity about the latest discoveries of science" (p. 4).

19. *Republic* 516d.

20. E.g., G.E.M. Anscombe, *An Introduction to Wittgenstein's Tractatus, op. cit.*, pp. 27-28; James Griffin, *Wittgenstein's Logical Atomism* (Clarendon Press, Oxford, 1964), p. 5.

21. In Carnap's terminology: "Erste Saetze", "Protokollsaetze", or "Beobachtungssaetze".

22. See Carnap's "Ueberwindung", *Erkenntnis*, Band 2, Heft 4, p. 222.

istic *apriorism*,[23] but it is nothing of the sort. It is merely a reflection on the fact that the primary concern of the *Tractatus* was *not* with building up a world from atomic units, but with distinguishing a profane, logical sphere, from a sacred, translogical one. Its purpose was to distinguish consciousness intensified and absorbed in the participatory experience of mystical union, from consciousness attending objects in the world, not to speculate on the relationship between consciousness and its attended objects or on the nature of objects in themselves. The non-multiplicitous, non-spatio-temporal, non-inner-worldly transcendence of the divine Encounter was to be radically separated from all else, and the nature of this "all else"—i.e., how it is known and of what it consists—was thus of secondary concern.

The depth and intensity of feeling accompanying Wittgenstein's opposition to all attempts to diminish or debase the *ganz andere* nature of the mystic experience, is brought out well in a passage from the "Lecture on Ethics". Speaking of the experiences which have constituted for him "absolute value", Wittgenstein first sets up a hypothetical argument against his own contention that such experiences cannot be talked about meaningfully in language:

> You will say: Well, if certain experiences constantly tempt us to attribute a quality to them which we call absolute or ethical value and importance, this simply shows that by these words we *don't* mean nonsense, that after all what we mean by saying that an experience has absolute value *is just a fact like other facts* and that all it comes to is that we have not yet succeeded in finding the correct logical analysis of what we mean by our ethical and religious expressions.[24]
>
> (emphasis in original)

Then, displaying the wounds and past anguish of a uniquely sensitive man desperately struggling against a vulgarian culture that threatens to engulf him, Wittgenstein replys, in the only emotional point in the "Lecture":

> Now when this is urged against me I at once see clearly, as it were in a flash of light, not only that no description that I can think of would do to describe what I mean by absolute value, but that I would reject every significant description that anybody

23. See, for instance, C.W.K. Mundle, *A Critique of Linguistic Philosophy* (Clarendon Press, Oxford, 1970) pp. 166-184; and Max Black, *op. cit.*, pp. 11-12.
24. P. 11.

could possibly suggest, *ab initio*, on the grounds of its significance.[25]

Here, in the flash of light,[26] lay the real driving force behind Wittgenstein's opposition to metaphysics, the force which sustained him throughout the 7-year period in which he composed the *Tractatus*, and which very likely moved him to take up the study of logic in the first place.

Some Problems with the Tractatus: *A Theocentric Ethic Without Fallen Man*

With its prime task to circumscribe a profane sphere, thus securing the sacrality of what lay beyond it, a number of difficulties emerged in working out the *Tractatus* system, some of which Wittgenstein seems to have been conscious of, others not. Of those which he was conscious of, ethics seems to have been one of the most troub-

---

25. *Ibid.* Immediately following this remark in the "Lecture", Wittgenstein suggests that to describe the experiences that constitute for him absolute value one would have to go beyond the world:

> I see now that these nonsensical expressions were not nonsensical because I had not yet found the correct expressions, but that their nonsensicality was their very essence. For all I wanted to do with them was just *to go beyond* the world and that is to say beyond significant language.
>
> (p. 11, emphasis in original)

One would have to go beyond the world to describe certain experiences in Wittgenstein's view because the experiences themselves go beyond the world, or at least give insight into what lies beyond the world. Elsewhere in the "Lecture" Wittgenstein speaks of ethics having a "supernatural" status:

> I can only describe my feelings by the metaphor, that, if a man could write a book on Ethics which really was a book on Ethics, this book would, with an explosion, destroy all the other books in the world. Our words used as we use them in science, are vessels capable only of containing and conveying meaning and sense, *natural* meaning and sense. Ethics, if it is anything, is supernatural and our words will only express facts . . .
>
> (p. 7, emphasis in original)

26. *Cf.* Pascal.

lesome. There can be no value in the world (6.41) because God, in matters of ethics and values the measure of all things, does not reveal himself in the world (6.432). Just as one cannot express the mystical union in language, so there can be no propositions of ethics: ethical propositions, like metaphysical propositions about God and the Absolute, "can express nothing which is higher" (6.42).

Beyond the inexpressibility and theocentric nature of ethics[1], however, Wittgenstein seems to have had little to say on the subject. In the *Notebooks*, for example, he comments briefly on ethical imperatives—why they are to be obeyed and the effects which obeying or disobeying such imperatives would have—but then enters the doubting comment: "All this is in some sense deeply mysterious!" Immediately following this doubt he states emphatically the one thing he *is* sure of: "*It is clear* that ethics does not *lend* itself to being expressed!" (30. 7. 16.)—a statement which, without the emphasis or exclamation point, is taken over directly into the *Tractatus* (6.421), where the elucidation is added, "Ethics is transcendental."

Having located ethics in the same outside-of-the-world realm as God, Wittgenstein ran into serious difficulties in trying to relate ethics to the human will, and the human will to the world. Although unsure as to what exactly the will was at the time of writing his *Notebook* entries, [2] and even less sure regarding the relationship between will and world,[3] a definite stance was taken in the *Tractatus*,

---

1. Besides the statements in the *Tractatus* and *Notebooks*, the theocentric nature of ethics is stressed in remarks Wittgenstein made to Friedrich Waismann. The remarks were made in conjunction with a discussion of Moritz Schlick's view of ethics:

> Schlick says there are two conceptions of the nature of the good in theological ethics: according to the shallower interpretation, that which is good is good because God so wills it; according to the more profound, God wills what is good because it is good. I say that the first conception is the more profound: good is that which God commands . . .
>
> The first conception states clearly that the nature of the good has nothing to do with the facts and thus cannot be explained through any proposition. If there is any proposition that explains just what I mean, it is this: Good is that which God commands.
>
> (from *Wittgenstein und der Wiener Kreis*, edited by Brian McGuinness. Blackwell, Oxford, 1967, p. 115)

2. "What my will is, I do not know yet." (8. 7. 16.).

3. "Good and evil enter first thru the *subject*. And the subject does not belong to the world, but is a border of the world.

"One could say (Schopenhauer-like): the world of representation is neither good nor evil, only the willing subject is. *I am aware of the complete unclarity of all these propositions.*

at least regarding what the will was not, and the relation of will to world:

> The will cannot be spoken of as the bearer of the ethical.
> And the will as phenomenon is of interest only to psychology. (6.423)
> If a good or evil exercise of the will alters the world, it can alter only the boundaries of the world, not the facts; not what can be expressed by language.
> In short, the world must thereby become a completely different world. It must, so to speak, increase or decrease as a whole.
> The world of the happy man is a different world from that of the unhappy man. (6.43)

Regarding the first proposition, it is obvious that Wittgenstein was primarily concerned with establishing the "otherness" of the transcendental experience, the experience which he says in the "Lecture on Ethics", is the source of "absolute good" and "absolute value"; it is an experience which can never be completely articulated since it would require going "beyond the world . . . beyond significant language".[4] Here, however, Wittgenstein was painting himself into a corner. The radical in/out schema of the *Tractatus*, designed to establish both the *ganz andere* nature of God together with the fact that man's ethical obligation is a divine obligation (i.e., an obligation to the God who is *ganz andere*) was to prove an insurmountable obstacle for developing a paradigm of ethical action. Specifically, it left no place for what in traditional Christian, Kantian, and Schopenhauerian ethics had played so central a role—namely, the human will. Since the world-transcendent God is the real source of "what is valuable", of "what is really important", of "what makes life worth living"[5], and since the "world" transcended by the world-transcendent God is the world of natural science, the relationship of the will to the world became extremely problematic. In saying that "the will cannot be spoken of as the bearer of the ethical", Wittgen-

---

"According to the earlier proposition, therefore, the willing subject would have to be happy or unhappy, and happiness and unhappiness cannot belong to the world. As the subject is not a part of the world, but a precondition of its existence, so good and evil are predicates of the subject, not properties of the world. *Completely veiled stands the nature of the subject here.*"

(2. 8. 16.)

(emphasis added except in first line)

4. "Lecture on Ethics", *op. cit.*, p. 11.
5. *Ibid.*, p. 5.

stein was, to be sure, not trying to depricate man's ethical strivings. But this is how it had to appear carrying the in/out schema to its logical conclusion. Given such a formulation, it is easy to understand how even so sympathetic a critic as G.E.M. Anscombe can find the treatment of ethics and will in the *Tractatus* to be "obviously wrong".[6]

Desiring to avoid the conclusion that the will was a pseudo-entity, or at best an inefficacious one, powerless to do anything that could be designated as good, Wittgenstein was forced to retreat back to Schopenhauer's contention that the will is that which can make the difference between the serene and happy man living in an expanded, fused world, and the unhappy man living in his own, anxiety-ridden private world. While Wittgenstein does not accept Schopenhauer's model of the good man as one who wills the end of his own ego-striving, or the equation of happiness with *apatheia*,[7] he does fall back on a Schopenhauer-like formulation when he speaks of the world "increasing or decreasing as a whole" as a result of a "good or evil exercise of the will" (6.43). Such a formulation, however, is in direct conflict with 6.373 where it is said that "the world is independent of my will." And the contention that a good or evil exercise of the will can alter the boundary (border) of the world obviously does not harmonize well with the representation of the human world border as an extensionless "I" point (5.632-5.64). Wittgenstein was aware of this clash in metaphors, which is why he qualifies what he says about the world increasing or decreasing with "so to speak" (*sozusagen*). But the need for a qualifier pointed to the real need to abandon the schema.

The world-increasing/world-decreasing distinction is, in fact, a new schema, bearing the stamp of last minute patchwork designed to shore up a critical inadequacy in the old. In its concern for placing the theophanic event beyond the pale of concretizing metaphysical and theological systems, the *Tractatus*, in fact, teeters on the very brink of a Gnostic-Manichean-like fracture between an alien, God-forsaken world, and a radically other, world-transcendent God. Such a fracture, historically speaking at least, tends to lead in the realm of ethics to two extremes: either an ascetic withdrawal from all "worldly" involvement, or at the opposite extreme, to a libertine-

---

6. *An Introduction to Wittgenstein's Tractatus, op. cit.*, pp. 171-172.

7. Traces of Schopenhauer's stoic-ascetic ideal can still be seen in the *Notebooks*, however, specifically when Wittgenstein writes: "I can only make myself independent from the world—and thus in a certain sense master it—by renouncing all influence upon what happens." (11. 6. 16.)

anarchistic contempt for all accepted standards of "worldly" morality.[8] Wittgenstein comes to within a hair's breadth of such a fracture when he says that the world, or at least *how* the world is, is a matter of complete indifference to what is higher (6.432), and he draws away from the brink only by adding:

> Not how the world is, but that it is, is the Mystical.
>
> (6.44)

This statement parallels a previous one holding that the pre-requisite for logic is the experience *that* something (i.e., the world) exists at all, and not the experience of *how* anything (i.e., any multiplicitous, in-the-world object) behaves (5.552).[9]

---

8. This was the situation at least, in some of the Gnostic sects which accompanied the growth of Christianity. On Gnostic rejection of moral obligation, see Hans Jonas, *The Gnostic Religion* (Beacon Press, Boston, 1963), pp. 266-289. The similarity between Wittgenstein's in/out schema and gnostic symbolization can be seen from Jonas's description of the latter:

> If the 'Life' [pneuma, spirit, God] is originally alien, then its home is 'outside' or 'beyond' this world. 'Beyond' here means beyond everything that is of the cosmos, heaven and its stars included. And 'included' literally: the idea of an absolute 'without' limits the world to a closed bounded system . . . the limitation by the idea of the 'beyond' deprives the 'world' of its claim to totality . . . if the cosmos ceases to be the All, if it is limited by something radically 'other' yet eminently real, then it must be designated as 'this' world. All relations of man's terrestrial existence are 'in this world', 'of this world' . . . (p. 51)

And such a symbolization Jonas explains, is not likely to accord much of a place to divine obligation in the world:

> Virtue in the Greek sense (*arete*) is the actualization in the mode of excellence of the several faculties of the soul for dealing with the world . . . The absence of a doctrine of virtue in gnostic teaching is connected with the . . . denial of any worth to the things of this world and consequently also to man's doing in the world. (p. 267)
>
> Generally speaking, the pneumatic [i.e., Gnostic] morality is determined by hostility toward the world and contempt for all mundane ties. From this principle, however, two contrary conclusions could be drawn, and both found their extreme representatives: the ascetic and the libertine. The former deduces from the possession of gnosis [i.e., the knowledge of the mystical experience] the obligation to avoid further contamination by the world and therefore to reduce contact with it to a minimum; . . . [For the Gnostic libertine, however] the law of 'Thou shalt' and 'Thou shalt not' . . . is just one more form of the 'cosmic tyranny'. . . . As the pneumatic is free from the heimarme [Fate], so he is free from the yoke of moral law. To him all things are permitted. (p. 46)

9. In the first part of the dichotomy "experience" (*Erfahrung*) is placed in quotation marks to distinguish it from the second, *Erfahrung* proper: "The 'experience' which

What Wittgenstein is referring to here, and its relation to ethics and the mystical experience of *ekstasis*, can be best discerned from statements in the "Lecture on Ethics". *Ekstasis* or the "absolute safety" experience was only one of three types Wittgenstein had mentioned in the "Lecture" as the basis of ethical obligation. The most important in this connection, in fact, was not the experience of absolute safety, but another experience which he describes as "seeing the world as a miracle":

> . . . what have all of us who, like myself, are still tempted to use such expressions as "absolute good," and "absolute value," etc., what have we in mind and what do we try to express? . . . if I want to fix my mind on what I mean by absolute or ethical value . . . in my case, it always happens that the idea of one particular experience presents itself to me which therefore is, in a sense, my experience *par excellence* and this is the reason why, in talking to you now, I will use this experience as my first and foremost example. . . . I will describe this experience in order, if possible, to make you recall the same or similar experiences, so that we may have a common ground for our investigation. I believe the best way of describing it is to say that when I have it *I wonder at the existence of the world.* And I am then inclined to use such phrases as "how extraordinary that anything should exist" or "how extraordinary that the world should exist".
>
> . . . the experience of wondering at the existence of the world . . . is the experience of seeing the world as a miracle.[10]
>
> (emphasis in original)

The experience alluded to here should not be confused with any kind of aesthetic experience—the sublimity one might feel, for instance, before the Himalayan mountains or some other overpowering beauty of nature. The world as a whole, without mention of anything specific, is the object of wonder. The wonder is the wonder of the world's "thatness" rather than the wonder of some particularly beautiful thing. "How extraordinary that something should exist", clearly refers to the same experience symbolized in the *Tractatus* as the mystical "that something exists", which is also identified as the pre-condition of logic (5.552, 6.44). The connection between logic, morality, and the Mystical, will come into clearer view if one can conceive the experience symbolized here as "seeing the world as a miracle", not as a different type of experience from the "absolute

we need to understand logic is not that something acts in such and such a way, but that something *is*: this, however, is not an experience."

10. "Lecture", *op. cit.*, pp. 7-8, 11.

safety" of *ekstasis*, but only a different moment and shifting perspective in the same experience-complex of mystic flight. While concretely, both moments and perspectives might not present themselves with equal clarity at any one time, they may be sufficiently distinguished on separate occasions to be joined together later for meditative renewal and more precise analysis of subsequent experiences.

"Seeing the world as a miracle" articulates the experience of mystic flight from the perspective of its immediate aftermath. The *world* is beheld as miraculous on such an occasion precisely because it serves as the adhering object for the re-attending consciousness, thus bringing to reflection both the dis-attending component of flight and the miraculous process of attention, disattention, and re-attention that comprises the entire experience. The fresh memory of *ekstasis* coalesces with a renewed concentration on the world thus constituting a border experience, which, in contrast to the ecstatic moment, takes on the softer hues of a twilight encounter.[11] Miraculous for Wittgenstein is not only the flight aspect of the mystical experience—i.e., the ecstatic ascent to, and absorption in God—but equally the descent or return to the world—in Christian mystic symbols, the moment of Creation. And here is where Wittgenstein parts company with Gnosticism. Implicit in the symbolization of the returned-to-world as a miracle, is its acceptance as the God ordained home of man—and this is precisely what gnostic systems reject. It is the world of God's creation, to be accepted by man in humility and thanksgiving. In contrast to Manichaean and other Gnostic systems of which the *Tractatus* bears a certain resemblance, Wittgenstein accepts the authenticity of the re-attending moment, and even recognizes it as the basis of allegorical representations of Creation:

> Now all religious terms seem . . . to be used as similes or allegorically. For when we speak of God and that he sees everything and when we kneel and pray to him all our terms and actions seem to be parts of a great and elaborate allegory . . . But this allegory also describes the experience whith I have just referred

11. Here, too, one can see the similarity between the re-attending moment in which the world is seen as miraculous, and an aesthetic experience. Both enter the same "border" region, but from different directions, the one from a lower level of the commonplace, everyday, the other from the higher level of the mystic peak. The one, one might say, is an intimation of immortality, the other, the wonder that ensues in the wake of immortality revealed. In actuality, however, the distinction does not always hold as experiences of external beauty can also be viewed in terms of an incarnational descent from the mystic peak.

> to. For the first of them [i.e., seeing the world as a miracle] is, I believe, exactly what people were referring to when they said that God created the world.[12]

The re-attending moment is both the miracle of world creation, and the source of man's moral obligation to the world in which he now finds himself. Re-attention, however, is also the pre-condition for logic, for it is only by virtue of this moment that consciousness assumes a multiplicitous form. From the peak of mystic ecstasy, it descends into a world, assuming in its attention to it, its logical structure. It is only in crossing from the "out" to the "in" that a logical structure comes into being, and hence, that the possibility emerges to represent such a structure. The foundations of both logic and morality thus have their origin in the same re-attending moment of the mystical experience.

Unlike Hindu mystical writers, Wittgenstein is fully willing to accept the reality of the world that comes into being at the moment of re-attention, but one of the consequences of re-attention which he does not accept is the reality of embodied (egoic) existence. No doubt wishing to place the theophanic experience beyond the reach of reductionistic psychology,[13] Wittgenstein came to deny that there was any such thing as an ego or embodied-self (5.631, 5.5421).[14] But

---

12. "Lecture", pp. 9-10. Despite his understanding of the experiential basis of creation-myths, the idea of creation apparently left Wittgenstein with a bad aftertaste. God as an artisan, the world as his artifact, must have appeared to him as grossly inadequate for expressing the *ganz andere* relationship, for in conversations with Norman Malcolm, he seems to have expressed contempt for the notion of creating the world (see Malcolm, *op. cit.*, p. 71). A comparison might be made here to Xenophanes' rejection of anthropomorphism.

13. The anti-psychologistic intent of the *Tractatus* is stressed by Engelmann, *op. cit.*, pp. 99-100.

14. Gnostic systems also denied the reality of embodied existence (along with creation myths), and the mystic experience upon which this denial was based apparently became the basis in many cases for an almost God-like pride (ego-inflation). Plotinus was apparently attacking this self-righteous pride when he attacked the Gnostics for inconsistency in their doctrine—for claiming simultaneously that actual divinity was encapsulated in the body (especially their own bodies), but denying that men (and especially themselves) were in any fallen state, i.e., that the divinity was really encapsulated:

> They first maintain that the Soul and a certain Wisdom declined and entered this lower sphere . . . then they tell us that the other souls came down in the descent and that these members of Wisdom took to themselves bodies, human bodies for example.
>
> Yet in the same breath, that very Soul which was the occasion of descent to the

in so doing, he sealed off the possibility of an ethic that could address itself to the moral strivings of everyday life, i.e., to man in his embodied existence.

In mythological representations, Shamanic tales,[15] and related mystic writings, the re-embodiment of the self that occurs in the descent from the mystic peak finds symbolic representation as a fall of man from a paradise or heaven, and the resulting embodied-man, with the passions and self-centeredness of his perspective, as the fallen or sinful nature of man. With the acceptance of this fallen state as the lot of man, a dynamic of fall and redemption (sin and grace) is then sketched where moral striving towards self-transcendence comes to play a significant role. Moral striving is seen as a striving to ascend beyond the perspective of the embodied-self to the self-transcending perspective of union with God. Wittgenstein, however, was unable to formulate even the most rudimentary dynamic, either in the *Tractatus* or the "Lecture on Ethics", because of his insistence that the spatio-temporarlly identified self was an illusion, and that the only reality which could be called a self or "I" was the extensionless border point revealed in the dis-embodying experience of mystic ecstasy.

The border-metaphor for man is not itself incompatible with a dynamic of fall and redemption, but when used in such a dynamic, embodied existence must be accepted as at least a shifting reality. St. Augustine offers a good example of just such a dynamic which uses a border-metaphor for man, yet accepts the full reality of embodied existence. In one of his *Homilies on the Gospel of John*, drawing heavily on neo-Platonic formulations, he exhorts all men to self-transcendence through moral striving:

> You are in the soul, are in the center; if you look below there is the body, if you look above, there is God. Withdraw from the body, rise above yourself.[16]

Body is here to be understood not only as the physical body and the consuming involvement (consciousness attention) in its passions

---

others is declared not to have descended. "It knew no decline, but merely illuminated the darkness . . ." (*Second Ennead*, II, 9, 10, translated by Stephen MacKenna, Pantheon Books, N.Y.)

15. Besides the myth of *Genesis*, see the shamanic tales discussed in Eliade, *Shamanism, op. cit.*, pp. 67, 68, 99, 130, 133, 250, 256, 484, 493.

16. Homilies, 20, 11. Quoted in "St. Augustine", *The New Catholic Encyclopedia*, volume 1, by O.J. DuRoy.

and desires, but anything with lastingness in time clung to, and identified with, as a transcendence denying "me" or "my"—e.g., clothes, possessions, social reputation, etc.

All the ingredients for such a dynamic are present in Wittgenstein's formulation, including the experience of estrangement from transcendence born of an evil exercise of the will (guilt). To the peak of mystical ascent (absolute safety in the hands of God), and the descending moment (the miraculousness of beholding the world), Wittgenstein adds a third experience as constitutive of ethics, the experience of "feeling guilty", of feeling that "God disapproves of our conduct" (p. 10). The mystic flight is thus linked with more everyday experience. Guilt is only possible, in contrast to the absolute safety of *ekstasis*—which is an ultimate assurance without guilt—when a finite, isolated piece of matter (a body), bounded in space and time, becomes the attended object of consciousness. Only in such a state can actions of a body be construed as "my" actions. Ethical action can than be seen, as in Augustine's exhortation, as the way of rising above oneself, as the way of moving closer to the ultimate Transcendence from which one has become estranged (fallen away from). Wittgenstein moves very near to an Augustinian-like understanding of God and man, but he is prevented from painting a more integrated picture because he is still, even in the "Lecture", committed too rigidly to the in/out framework of the *Tractatus*.

Problems II: "Legislative Linguistics"

The main target of Wittgenstein's critique of language in the *Tractatus* is metaphysical and theological propositions which talk about God and the Absolute as if they were describing a fact or event in the mundane world, displaying no recognition that there exists a problem in using sentences of the observational-descriptive form to express an experience which does not fit this form. But in his condemnation of the spiritual debasement of metaphysical and theological propositions, in his declaration that they are unsuitable for expressing what is higher, and in his entreaty to reverential silence as a functional substitute for them, Wittgenstein consigned all language—i.e., any communicative or symbolic form other than silence—to the same category as observational-descriptive propositions. He does this through the so-called picture theory of language, which, far from being a theory of any kind, is an *a priori* decree, similar to what would become known in later British philosophy as a "persuasive" definition.

The decree declaring that language (*die Sprache*) is a picture of the world, parallels in function and meaning the decree declaring that the world is the totality of facts—both were intended to circumscribe a profane sphere in order to stress the "otherness" of the divine. Viewed from the standpoint of actual languages, however—languages, that is, which are or have been spoken by actual peoples—such a decree is indeed, as a recent Wittgenstein critic charges, a kind of "legislative linguistics".[1] Much of the difficulty in interpreting the *Tractatus* derives from its attempt, through its oracle-like decrees, to transform what is essentially a "*may* not" prohibition against articulating an experience, into a "*can* not" fact of language structure—an attempt which, while projecting the assurance of incontestable facticity, directs the reader away from the experiential source of both the "may not" prohibition, and the oracle-like assurance with which it is put forth as a fact. Wittgenstein himself openly reflects on the decree-nature of the *Tractatus*'s statements about language when he declares at the end of the work that his own statements are nonsensical, unable to live up to the criteria of meaningful language set down in the *Tractatus* itself. Reflections of this kind notwithstanding, however, he does seem to have lost sight in his own mind of the decree nature of what was recorded in the *Tractatus.*—a fact which well indicates the spiritual anguish in which it was conceived.

When in the "Lecture", after describing the mystic experiences that form the basis of absolute value, Wittgenstein says:

> No description that I can think of would do to describe what I mean by absolute value . . . for all I wanted to do with them was just *to go beyond* the world and that is to say beyond significant language. My whole tendency and I believe the tendency of all men who ever tried to write or talk Ethics or Religion was to run against the boundaries of language.[2]

he is talking about the boundaries he himself has erected in support of reverential silence, against the profanation of metaphysical and

1. C.W.K. Mundle, *A Critique of Linguistic Philosophy* (Clarendon Press, Oxford, 1970), p. 16. The authority of the lawgiver, it should be kept in mind, however, does not proceed from whim or arbitrariness.

2. pp. 11-12.

theological systems. If one understands the *Tractatus*'s critique of language, not as an *a priori*, but as an *a posteriori* account (and Wittgenstein certainly thought of the picture theory in this way), then it is indeed, as Max Black suggests, a critique of a never-never language.[3]

In the fusion (and confusion) in his own mind of the "*may* not" and "*can* not"—i.e., of decree and fact—Wittgenstein has created a "theory" of language in the *Tractatus*, which, taken at face value, is naive in the extreme. Permitting only the simplest referent-symbol relationships, it leaves out the whole network of associations that words actually can and do evoke—i.e., the whole criss-crossing amalgam of images, experiences, impulses, feeling tones, memories, expectations, subconscious dispositions, etc. Certainly this "multivalence" of reference[4] is more characteristic of most of the words and phrases we use than the unilinear "picturing" of which the *Tractatus* speaks. And this is even more so in the case of metaphysical and theological language symbols. As Karl Popper has remarked in his autobiography, "Wittgenstein exaggerated the gulf between the world of describable ('sayable') facts and the world of that which is deep and cannot be said. There are gradations; moreover, the world of the sayable does not always lack depth."[5]

In his concern with metaphysical propositions, Wittgenstein takes no account at all of other communicative mediums, actual or potential, that lie between discursive propositions and silence. Thus, by inference, lyric poetry, allegory, parable, myth, dialogue,

---

3. *A Companion to Wittgenstein's Tractatus, op. cit.*, p. 11.

4. The term is from Mircea Eliade. Eliade's theoretical reflections on religious language-symbols can be found in *The Two and the One* (Harper and Row, N.Y., 1965), pp. 189-211.

5. *The Philosophy of Karl Popper*, edited by Paul Arthur Schilpp, (Open Court, La Salle, Illinois, 1974), p. 180. Popper continues on this topic:

> It is his facile solution of the problem of depth—the thesis 'the deep is the unsayable'—which unites Wittgenstein the positivist with Wittgenstein the mystic. Incidentally, this thesis had long been traditional, especially in Vienna, and not merely among philosophers. (p. 180).

Popper then directs the reader to a quotation from Robert Reininger reproduced in his *Logic of Scientific Discovery* (Harper and Row Publishers, N.Y., 1968). The quotation reads..

> Metaphysics *as science* is impossible because although the absolute is indeed experienced and for that reason can be intuitively felt, it yet refuses to be expressed in words. 'If the soul *speaks* then alas it is no longer the *soul* that speaks'. (p. 111)

protreptic, sacrament, rite, homily, and so on, are all condemned to the same fate as discursive propositions in their collective inability to express anything higher.[6] When one has ascended the ladder and seen the world aright, says Wittgenstein, one must keep silent.

---

6. Symbolic forms which have a richer capacity than discursive propositions are the subject of Susanne Langer's, *Philosophy in a New Key: A Study in the Symbolism of Reason, Rite, and Art* (Harvard University Press, 1973, first published 1942). Writing at the beginning of the Second World War, Dr. Langer was concerned in this book with breaking out of the intellectual straitjacket and moral nihilism represented by the Carnap-Ayer variety of positivism. Her plea on behalf of a "balanced active intelligence [for whom] reality is . . . the all inclusive realm of science, myth, art, and comfortable common sense" (p. 289) was made against a philosophy, which, it is charged, "knows only deductive or inductive logic as reason, and classes all other human functions as 'emotive', irrational and animalian" (p. 292). Seeking an ally to join in her defense of non-discursive modes of communication, Dr. Langer turned, of all people, to Wittgenstein, claiming to have found in the *Tractatus* support for her philosophical views. She begins the most important chapter in the book, which deals with the difference between discursive and non-discursive forms of communication, with the incredible statement: "The logical theory on which this whole study of symbols is based is essentially that which was set forth by Wittgenstein some twenty years ago, in his *Tractatus Logico-Philosophicus*." (p. 79).

Although sometimes linking Wittgenstein together with Carnap and the logical positivism she is trying to break free from, she tries to invoke the picture theory of the *Tractatus* (4.0311, 4.015, 4.0141) as support for her own philosophy of myth, rite, sacrament, and art symbolism. To achieve this, the opening lines of the *Tractatus*, where the world is represented as the "totality of facts", are re-interpreted as a dutiful recording (for reasons not explained) of the dominant views of modern man, rather than a true account of Wittgenstein's own beliefs. (pp. 272-273). And the in/out schema of the *Tractatus* is construed so that the "in" is expanded to include exactly what Wittgenstein says is "out". Thus, in reply to Bertrand Russell's restatement of the Wittgensteinian view that language shares the structure of the physical world and cannot express anything that may lie outside such a world, she says: "Now I do not believe that 'there is a world which is not physical, or not in space-time'; but I do believe that in this physical, space-time world of our experience, there are things which do not fit the grammatical [i.e., discursive-propositional] scheme of expression. But they are not necessarily blind, inconceivable, mystical affairs; they are simply matters which require to be conceived through some other symbolistic schema other than discursive language." (p. 88).

But Wittgenstein's picture theory of language, which Dr. Langer wants to call to her defense, describes the very physical world (the world of linearly time-structured sense-perception) *in* which all that Dr. Langer is concerned about in her book—i.e., art, music, ethics, religion—is absent. Regarding a theory of aesthetics, to the extent that the *Tractatus* can be spoken of as having any such theory at all, aesthetics is seen as belonging, in some unexplained manner, to the very same out-of-the-world mystic realm as God and ethics: "Ethics is transcendental. Ethics and aesthetics are one." (6.421). Wittgenstein's picture theory could be invoked in support of a theory of non-discursive symbolisms only by an enormous alteration of the flatness of the world pictured in the *Tractatus*, and a complete misunderstanding of the import of the book.

While no doubt true, one soon finds, after reaching such a height, that there is no longer anything to hold on to, and that, before long, one inevitably begins to fall back to lower rungs.[7] If the man on the top has thrown the ladder away, however, not only he himself, but all those clinging to the various rungs, are likely to find themselves in a terrifying fall into an unending abyss. And in such situations, it is not silence which men tend to listen to, but political demagogues and the new ideological ladders that they are only too eager to extend.

Problems III: The Rejection of History

The philosophy offered by Wittgenstein in both the *Notebooks* and the *Tractatus* is not only a-historical, but decidedly anti-historical. In the Preface to the *Tractatus*, for instance, Wittgenstein writes:

> Indeed, what I have written here makes no claim at all to novelty; and therefore, I offer no sources because it is a matter of indifference to me, if, what I have thought, someone else before me has already thought.[1]

7. *Cf.* the previously quoted account of Augustine:

> Thus by states I passed from bodies to the soul which uses the body for its perceiving, and from this to the soul's inner power to which the bodies senses present external things . . . and from there . . . to the reasoning power . . . [But I] withdrew my thought from its habitual way . . . [Then] in the thrust of a trembling glance my mind arrived at That Which Is . . . But I lacked the strength to hold my gaze fixed, and my weakness was [forced] back again so that I returned to my old habits, bearing nothing with me but a memory.
>
> (*Confessions,* VIII, 17, Sheed translation)

1. The last part of the German sentence rendered here in English served as the occasion for an eyebrow-raising mistranslation in Pears-McGuinness. The German is very simple: "*weil es mir gleichgueltig ist, ob das, was ich gedacht habe, vor mir schon ein anderer gedacht hat,*" where the "*was ich gedacht habe*" and the "*ein anderer gedacht hat*" are in symmetrical balance. This is translated in Pears-McGuinnes: "it is a matter of indifference to me whether the thoughts that I have had *have been anticipated* by someone else" (emphasis added). Here, the thoughts of the *Tractatus* are seen as the height of a never-before-reached pinnacle. No doubt the translators were thinking of the *Tractatus*, as Carnap and other members of the Vienna Circle did, pri-

And in the *Notebooks* he says more contemptuously: "Of what concern is history to me? Mine is the first and only world!" (2. 9. 16)

To understand this attitude towards history, one must take account of two factors: first, the centrality which the mystical experience has for Wittgenstein, and second, the climate of historicism in which he wrote, i.e., of Marxist and Hegelian ideological constructions of history in which history was portrayed as a determinate stream, surrounding and engulfing a helpless individual. The mystical experience, the meaning-revealing, out-of-the-world flight of an alone (to an Alone), stands as the very refutation of the historicist's claim. In opposition to historicism, Wittgenstein adopts what might be called a mystical existentialism, where the history of the historicists is replaced with the eternal Present revealed in the mystic flight:

> But can one so live that life ceases to be problematic? That one *lives* in eternity and not in time?
>
> *Notebooks* 6. 7. 16.
>
> Only one who lives, not in time, but in the present is happy.
>
> *Notebooks* 8. 7. 16.
>
> For life in the present there is no death.
>
> *Notebooks* 8. 7. 16.
>
> He who lives in the present, lives without fear or hope.
>
> *Notebooks* 14. 7. 16.
>
> The solution to the riddle of life in space and time lies *outside* of space and time.
>
> *Tractatus* 6.4312
>
> If one understands by eternity not unending time (temporal duration) but timelessness, then the one who lives eternally is the one who lives in the present.
>
> *Tractatus* 6.4311

The eternal Present, the Present in which life knows no death, i.e., knows no past/present/future flow of time, transcends history. Life in this Present knows no hope or fear because "hope" (*Hoff-*

---

marily as a development in the modern logic founded by Russell and Frege, and since both of these men were acknowledged by Wittgenstein in the lines immediately following ("I'll only mention that I am indebted to the magnificent works of Frege and the writings of my friend, Mr. Bertrand Russell, for a great deal of the stimulation to my thought"), the "newness" of modern logic seemed to be called in question taking the German lines as they stood. Thus, someone previously having thought what I have thought, became someone anticipating what I have thought. No such difficulty would have arisen had the logic in the *Tractatus* been understood in its instrumental role in the *via negativa*.

nung), though usually understood as something positive, refers here to a life that must always look forward to something. To live one's life in a perpetual looking-forward-to, in the continued expectations of an advancing career, for instance, or of a rising socio-economic status, or to identify oneself with science and technology "looking forward to" its perpetual progress, is a horror of horrors for anyone who can look far enough forward to see that nothing awaits them there but death.[2] The happy man lives without such hope, for he lives in the eternal Present, without looking foward or back.

Wittgenstein's eternal Present, transcending time and history, is virtually identical with the eternal Now symbol of Meister Eckhart:

> The person who lives in the light of God is conscious neither of time past nor of time to come but only of the one eternity . . . he gets nothing new out of future events, nor from chance, for he lives in the Now-moment . . . God himself is in that agent of the soul in that eternal Now-moment . . . for the Now-moment in which the last man will disappear, and the Now-moment in which I am speaking are all one in God, in whom there is only one Now.[3]

The closer one lives to God, the higher one ascends in his daily life to the Now-moment revealed in the mystic peak, the more one is liberated from enslavement to a purposeless, anxiety-ridden death sentence, which is the fate of all condemned to life in a linear time continuum. The man who lives in the eternal Present is the happy man who knows no death.[4]

---

2. It was an enchainment of such a kind to a past/present/future time dimension which nearly drove Tolstoy to suicide, as he relates it with such matchless passion in his *Confessions*. Men can break free from such a horror, Tolstoy proclaimed in later works, if they seek the Kingdom of God which is within them, if they break into the eternal life which God has placed at their disposal.

3. *Meister Eckhart*, (Raymond Blakney translation, Harper and Row, N.Y. 1941), pp. 209-210. Actually, the eternal Now symbol did not originate with Eckhart but has a long neo-Platonic history.

4. Wittgenstein here has obviously drawn heavily from Tolstoy's formulations in *The Gospel in Brief* where time is declared to be an illusion in life and the true life said to exist outside time in a meaning-conferring present. In the Preface to *The Gospel in Brief*, Tolstoy summons up the meaning of each of its 12 chapters in a brief sentence or two. Chapters 1, 2, 3, 7, 8, 9, and 10 are summed up as follows:

> Man is the son of the Infinite Source of Being; he is the son of this Father, not by the flesh but by the spirit.
>
> And therefore, man must serve the Source of his being, in the spirit.
>
> The life of all men has a divine Origin. This Origin only is sacred.

But in rejecting historicism, Wittgenstein rejected the study of history as well, and in so doing he was rejecting one of the few possibilities open to a philosopher to develop a genuine critique of the language into which he has been born. The debasement of Western culture with which Wittgenstein was preoccupied[5] could only have been fully comprehended and criticized through an empathizing study of the writers and thinkers in whose works that debasement was most clearly revealed. Without such an understanding, Wittgenstein could do little more than call attention to the degenerate state into which religio-philosophical language symbols had fallen, and recommend that they be replaced by silence. But culture is neither formed nor re-formed through silence, and in the face of corruption in man and society, silence, as Camus tells us,[6] is often the very language of acquiescence and despair. Wittgenstein did, it is true, read and admire the works of men who struggled with many of the same problems of de-culturation as he himself—e.g., Plato, Augustine, George Fox, Kierkegaard, Dostoyevsky, and Tolstoy.[7] But he seems never to have arrived at even the faintest understanding of the process of cultural degeneration itself. Had he, he might have gone on in the inter-war period to serve the therapeutic role of a desperately needed Jeremiah (or second Karl Kraus), instead of going on to become a recluse,[8] whom many people would take to be a kook.

This present life in time is the food of the true life.

And therefore, the true life is outside time; it is in the present.

Time is an illusion in life; the life of the past and the future clouds men from the true life of the present.

And therefore, one must aim to destroy the deception arising from the past and future, the life in time.

(*The Gospel in Brief*, Thomas Y. Crowell and Company, N.Y., 1896, pp. 2-3)

5. Allan Janik and Stephen Toulmin's designation of the *Tractatus* as the compliment to the critique of language and art debasement offered by Karl Kraus has much to commend itself (*Wittgenstein's Vienna*, Simon and Schuster, 1973, p. 196). The present writer is greatly indebted to Janik and Toulmin for their suggestion that the *Tractatus* has been generally misinterpreted in the more than fifty years since its publication. A debt of gratitude is also owed to their suggestion that the last ten pages of the *Tractatus* constitute its climax, though if the analysis offered here of the "world" symbol and the say/show-itself distinction is correct, it would have to be seen as the kind of climax which reveals that the butler did it—a fact which, when you view the movie the second time through, you can see was indicated all along from the very beginning, only you were too busy in following the plot to pick up the clues.

6. *The Rebel*, (Vintage Books, N.Y., 1956), p. 14.

7. See Georg von Wright, "Ludwig Wittgenstein, a Biographical Sketch", *The Philosophical Review*, October 1955, pp. 543-544.

8. Wittgenstein's inability to relate to his culture, either in conforming acceptance, or admonishing rejection, can be seen in the seriousness with which, on a number of occasions, he considered entering a monastery. (See von Wright, *Ibid.*, p. 534).

Problems IV: The Rejection of a Hierarchical Ontology

In an article on mysticism of surprising insight, Bertrand Russell describes how many mystical and metaphysical systems, in the interests of the higher reality of the mystical experience itself, are often more concerned with convicting natural science and everyday life of irreality than of offering an adequate account of them.[1] Wittgenstein, of course, had no desire to prove that the world of science was a world of illusion. On the contrary, as we have seen, he relied on the very non-illusionary reality of this sphere to provide the relational "than" in establishing the wholly other status of mystic theophany. But of everyday life, notwithstanding Bertrand Russell's own inability to distinguish such from the world of natural science, the *Tractatus* offers not even a minimally satisfying account.

In both the *Tractatus* and the "Lecture", Wittgenstein tries to picture the world of everyday life on the same ontological plane as that of physics. Consistent with the affirmation of the radical God/world contrast, and the rejection of an identifying self (i.e., an in-the-world self), he rejects any notion of an in-the-world hierarchy of being. All reality less than God is to be construed using the same framework as that of physical mechanics. Against both Aristotle and *Genesis*, no ontological distinctions are permitted between inanimate matter, plants, fish, animals, and human beings. This, of course, taken as a picture of the world of everyday life, cannot begin to do justice to its richness, a richness that derives from the identification each one of us makes with the creatures and things about us. Life as an extensionless border point, absorbed in the unspeakable wonder of mystic ecstasy, is only attained in the rarest of moments, even by shamans and saints, and does not describe the world of everyday life. Whether one views consciousness from its emergence in childhood, or in the re-attending moment of the mystic flight, sooner or later a definite piece of matter—a human body—is singled out from among the animals, plants, trees, and rocks as a "me". And as consciousness explores the nature of this "me" and the world in which it lives, it discovers empathetically both that there are other beings of the same nature as this "me" comprising the species

1. "Mysticism and Logic", *The Hibbert Journal*, volume xii, October 1913-1914, p. 793.

"man", as well as a variety of other beings, sharing only part of this nature, in descending rank-order depending on the degree to which they share in the multi-dimensionality of human nature. But Wittgenstein's rejection of self-identification is total, and, as a consequence, he is unable to make even the simplest ontological distinctions, as for instance, between sentient animals and insentient plants. He is not even able to proceed beyond a disembodied, solipsistic "I", to an embodied "I" and a nature of man.

Some of the inextricable philosophical difficulties that emerge when identification is disallowed can be seen in the following quotation from the "Lecture on Ethics", where the attempt is still made to defend the basic *Tractatus* position on the out-of-the-world status of ethics and religion, and the unidimensional plane to which, it is alleged, all in-the-world reality must conform:

> Suppose one of you were an omniscient person and therefore knew all the movements of all the bodies in the world dead or alive and that he also knew all the states of mind of all human beings that ever lived, and suppose this man wrote all he knew in a big book, then this book would contain the whole description of the world . . . If for instance in our world-book, we read the description of a murder with all its details physical and psychological, the mere description of these facts will contain nothing which we could call an *ethical* proposition. *The murder will be on exactly the same level as any other event, for instance, the falling of a stone.* (emphasis added in last sentence, p. 6)

Well suppose one were to read in the newspaper headlines: "Piano Wire Strangler Brutally Murders Fourth Victim." If murdering were really on the same ontological level as the falling of a stone, what justification could the editors possibly give for singling out the Strangler as perpetrator of the crime and not the piano wire? Or in a similar headline, "Gunman Murders Innocent Passerby"—why not, physics-like, speak of the bullet murdering the passerby, or the expanding gases in the gun barrel, or the electrochemical changes in the contracting muscles of the trigger-finger? Why might one not designate the heart which failed to supply the victim's brain with blood as the murderer, or the legs which brought the victim to the place and time where a bullet was passing? Why is the passerby here designated "innocent"?

To answer these questions obviously requires some understanding of identification and empathy, and the hierarchical ontology presupposed in our common-sense understanding of things. Without empathy and a hierarchical *Lebenswelt*, an event such as one man *murdering* (i.e., conscious, intentional, purposive killing) another man is unthinkable, just as the very notion of a "man" itself. In the same "Lecture" Wittgenstein himself implicitly accepts such a hierarchy in a quaint discussion of miracles:

> We all know what in ordinary life would be called a miracle. It obviously is simply an event the like of which we have never yet seen. Now suppose such an event happened. Take the case that one of you suddenly grew a lion's head and began to roar. Certainly that would be as extraordinary a thing as I can imagine. Now whenever we should have recovered from our surprise, what I would suggest would be to fetch a doctor and have the case scientifically investigated and if it were not for hurting him I would have him vivisected. And where would the miracle have gone? (p. 10)

But if identification and empathy are rejected, if all being is on the ontological level of a falling stone, what reasons could there be for *not* vivisecting the lion? Why should the lion receive any different treatment than an unusual mold that has grown on a piece of bread, or the chemical corrosion on a piece of copper? Ethical considerations of the type involved in opposition to animal vivisection can only proceed from a hierarchical ontology—which is just what the *Tractatus* and "Lecture" specifically reject.

The idea of a world-encompassing, monistic science, such as that presented in the *Tractatus*, certainly did not originate with Wittgenstein. It was, in fact, a common idea in certain intellectual circles in the latter half of the 19th century, being associated with such names as Helmholtz, Haeckel, and Mach. Wittgenstein accepted the monistic view of science (the later *Einheitswissenschaft*) quite uncritically, and even sharpened its claims because it proved congenial to the main purpose of the *Tractatus* in establishing the *ganz andere* character of theophany. But in bringing the nature of the mystic-ecstatic experience to great clarity—a clarity perhaps in its own way the equal to that of Pseudo-Dionysius—the *Tractatus* was to put forth an ideological construction of reality with consequences far removed from what Wittgenstein intended.

The Tractatus: *Final Characterization*

The *Tractatus* was Wittgenstein's *De Civitate Dei*, written in opposition to the profanation of the *majestas* of God, as paradigmatically represented in the great metaphysical and theological disputes of modern European history. It is an indictment of a corrupt, debased, idolatrous civilization. In contrast to Russell's, a proper Introduction might begin something like the following:

> The glorious city of God is the theme of this work, which it undertakes in defense against those who prefer their own gods to the Founder of this city—a city surpassingly glorious, even as it sojourns as a stranger in the midst of the ungodly.[1]

---

1. From *The City of God*, Book I, Preface (translated by Marcus Dodds, The Modern Library, N.Y., 1950), edited and adapted.

III

From Prophecy to Scripture: The Canonization of Ordinary Language

For this commandment which I command you this day is not too hard for you, neither is it far off. It is not in heaven, that you should say, "Who will go up for us to heaven, and bring it to us, that we may hear it and do it?" . . . But the Word is very near you; it is in your mouth and in your heart, so that you can do it.

Deuteronomy 30:11-14

The Holy Spirit departed from Israel.

(decree of the rabbis at the Council of Jamnia explaining the passing of prophecy with Malachi)

The salvation of Russia comes from the people. And the Russian monk has always been on the side of the people. . . . Of course I don't deny that there is sin in the peasants too. The fire of corruption is spreading visibly, hourly, working from above downwards. . . . But God will save Russia, for though the peasants are corrupt and cannot renounce their filthy sin, yet they know it is cursed by God and that they do wrong in sinning. Our people still believe in righteousness, have faith in God and weep tears of devotion. It is different with the upper classes. They, following science, want to base justice on reason alone . . . They have already proclaimed that there is no crime, that there is no sin. And that's consistent, for if you have no God what is the meaning of crime? . . . But God will save Russia as He has saved her many times. Salvation will come from the people, from their faith and their meekness.

Father Zossima, in Dostoyevsky's *The Brothers Karamazov*
(Constance Garnett translation)

Showing the Truth of the Tractatus: *A Choice of Vocations*

With the completion of the *Tractatus* in the summer of 1918 and the end of the First World War shortly thereafter, Wittgenstein was ready to move on to a new occupation. He had entered the field of philosophy and logic with a specific purpose in mind, namely, to clarify the distinction between what can be said in language, and what cannot be said in language but only shown or manifested in a non-verbal way; and believing that he had solved this "cardinal problem of philosophy" in a final and definitive manner,[1] it was only natural with the completion of the *Tractatus* that Wittgenstein should give up his philosophical concerns and seek other endeavors. The idea of being an academic philosopher had never appealed to him, and even in the 30s, after he had returned to academic life and actually become a philosophy professor, he seems to have had an attitude towards academic philosophy bordering almost on contempt.[2]

There were two vocations in particular which Wittgenstein gave serious attention to after the war, both of which can be viewed as another way of "showing" the moral and spiritual message of the *Tractatus*. The first, and the one he was actually to pursue, was that of a rural school teacher. The Wittgenstein family, which was one of the wealthiest in Austria, had a long tradition of social service,[3] and

1. *Tractatus*, Preface, p.5.

2. Norman Malcolm, for instance, relates how Wittgenstein actively tried to discourage him from becoming a professor of philosophy: "Wittgenstein wished to persuade me to give up my plan to become a teacher of philosophy. He wondered whether I could not do some manual job instead, such as working on a ranch or farm. He had an abhorrence of academic life in general and of the life of a professional philosopher in particular. He believed that a normal human being could not be a university teacher and also an honest and serious person" (*Ludwig Wittgenstein: A Memoir*, Oxford University Press, London, 1962, p. 30). Elsewhere in Malcolm's *Memoir* Wittgenstein refers to the "absurd job of a professor of philosophy" (p. 43), and at another point says that it is a wonder to him how anyone can read the British philosophical journal *Mind* "with all its impotency and bankruptcy" in preference to a certain American detective magazine (pp. 35-36).

3. William Bartley III, *Wittgenstein* (J.P. Lippincott Company, Philadelphia, 1973). p. 87. This book offers the most detailed account of Wittgenstein's years as an elemen-

as in most urban, industrialized nations, one may assume it was the poor of the Austrian countryside, even more than the poor of the cities, who had the least opportunity for educational advancement. The decision to become a rural school teacher in this context might be seen as something akin to the actions of the American VISTA volunteer of the 1960s who saw it as his duty to help the underprivileged of Appalachia. Wittgenstein's specific choice of a teaching vocation may well have been influenced by the example of Tolstoy, who even before his great religious crisis and his subsequent praise of peasant life, had taken an active interest in peasant education, helping to set up a number of rural schools near his home at Yasnaya Polyana.[4] It would not, in fact, be going too far here, in view of the impact which Tolstoy and his writings had on Wittgenstein, to see in his involvement with the rural poor a conscious *imitatio Tolstoyi.*

---

tary school teacher. It is, however, while valuable, unfortunately diminished in stature by what might be described as the author's penchant for the sensational—more specifically, by the author's claim, which he apparently bases on the flimsiest of hearsay evidence, that Wittgenstein was a promiscuous and uncontrollable homosexual who went on periodic binges in the parks of Vienna and the pubs of London. No references or substantiation of any kind are given for these assertions, and the reader is left wondering just where or from whom they came. In a subsequent letter to the *Times Literary Suppliment* (January 11, 1974), Bartley says that the reason he did not give the names of his sources was to protect their confidentiality, but the reader is still left wondering why the sources were not given at least pseudonyms, and their relationship to Wittgenstein explained in a general kind of way. Wittgenstein may well have been homosexual in his erotic orientation—many people, after all, are—but given his reclusiveness, his desire to live in remote regions, as well as his known affinity for the thought of Otto Weininger, Augustine, and the later Tolstoy, it would seem that in both theory and practice he approached much closer to the ideal of chastity in sexual matters than to either an active homosexual or heterosexual life-style. Bartley, of course, recognizes much of this, but with a speculative license and imagination worthy of the worst tabloid press writers, chooses to see in Wittgenstein's "monklike retreats" to remote areas of Europe part of a "strategy Wittgenstein used to protect himself from himself" (p. 50). No doubt Maurice Drury was nearer the mark when he says that "sensuality in any form was entirely foreign to his [Wittgenstein's] ascetic personality" (*Times Literary Suppliment*, February 22, 1974). Similarly, Fania Pascal, Wittgenstein's Russian teacher, writes: "I can only say that to my husband and myself, and as far as I know to all others who knew him, Wittgenstein always appeared a person of unforced chastity. There was in fact something of *noli me tangere* about him, so that one cannot imagine anyone who would ever dare as much as to pat him on the back, nor can one imagine him in need of the normal physical expressions of affection. In him everything was sublimated to an extraordinary degree." (*Ludwig Wittgenstein: Personal Recollections*, edited by Rush Rhees, Rowman and Littlefield, Totowa, N.J., 1981, p. 60).

4. Tolstoy's educational activities are explained in Ernest J. Simmons' *Tolstoy* (Routledge and Kegan Paul, London, 1973), Chap. 6.

The other vocation to which Wittgenstein gave serious attention after the war was that of a religious contemplative. His ideas about entering a monastery at this time were conveyed to Bertrand Russell when the two of them met at the Hague in December of 1919 to discuss the *Tractatus*. Russell describes the meeting in a letter to Lady Ottoline Morrell, which fortunately has been preserved. The letter is an invaluable document not only for grasping Wittgenstein's thoughts immediately after the war, but for understanding the fundamentally religious nature of Wittgenstein's motivation and personality. The letter, in part, reads as follows:[5]

> I have much to tell you that is of interest. I leave here today [December 20, 1919, the Hague] after a fortnight's stay, during a week of which Wittgenstein was here, and we discussed his book every day. I came to think even better of it than I had done; I feel sure it is really a great book, though I do not feel sure it is right. . . .
>
> I had felt in his book a flavour of mysticism, but was astonished when I found that he has become a complete mystic. He reads people like Kierkegaard and Angelus Silesius, and he seriously contemplates becoming a monk. It all started from William James's Varieties of Religious Experience,[6] and grew (not unnaturally) during the winter he spent alone in Norway before the war, when he was nearly mad. Then during the war a curious thing happened. He went on duty to the town of Tarnov in Galicia, and happened to come upon a bookshop, which, however, seemed to contain nothing but picture postcards. However, he went inside and found that it contained just one book: Tolstoy on The Gospels. He bought it merely because there was no other. He read it and re-read it, and thenceforth had it always with him, under fire and at all times. But on the whole he likes Tolstoy less than Dostoyevsky (especially Karamazov). He has penetrated deep into mystical ways of thought and feeling, but I think (though he wouldn't agree) that what he likes best in mysticism is its power to make him stop thinking. I don't much

5. In *Letters to Russell, Keynes, and Moore*, edited by G.H. von Wright (Cornell University Press, Ithaca, 1974), p. 82.

6. Wittgenstein read James's *Varieties* in June of 1912 and mentions it in one of his earliest letters to Russell (*Ibid.*, p. 10). Russell's account here might be somewhat misleading (e.g., "he has *become* a complete mystic"), to the extent, at least, that it suggests a major change in Wittgenstein from the writing of the *Tractatus* to the time Russell and he met at the Hague. Wittgenstein's interest in mysticism, as Russell remarks, pre-dates the war and the writing of the *Tractatus*, any major change having taken place from this time being one in Russell's understanding of Wittgenstein rather than one in Wittgenstein.

> think he will really become a monk—it is an idea, not an intention. His intention is to be a teacher. He gave all his money to his brothers and sisters, because he found earthly possessions a burden. I wish you had seen him.

Though Wittgenstein did become a school teacher, and not a monk, the thought of entering a monastery was more than just a wild idea or flight of fancy. In the summar of 1920 Wittgenstein spent his vacation working as a gardener's assistant at a monastery outside of Vienna, and several years later, after he had left rural school teaching, he was actually to inquire at a monastery about the possibility of becoming a monk, though according to Norman Malcolm, he was discouraged in his pursuit by the father superior.[7] In the summer of 1926, he again worked as a gardener's assistant at a monastery.[8] Wittgenstein was thus quite serious in his thoughts about becoming a monk, though Russell seems reluctant to concede this point. In his reference to the power of mysticism to make Wittgenstein stop thinking, Russell alludes to a definite tendency in Wittgenstein to become so engrossed in his thoughts that he would be unable to turn them off—a tendency, of course, which if properly directed, can be the mark of true genius. Malcolm, referring to this same tendency, explains how Wittgenstein, in order to get his mind off the problems he had been thinking about in his lectures, would resort to the expedient of taking a seat in the very first row of a movie theater, thereby becoming totally absorbed in the film.[9] But this was certainly *not* Wittgenstein's interest in religious mysticism, or at least not his primary interest. The simple fact of the matter is that Wittgenstein, in considering the idea of becoming a contemplative monk, was consciously trying to pursue what he saw as a religious calling. This simple and obvious explanation, which Russell does not consider, goes hand in hand with the fact that Wittgenstein gave away all his wealth after the war, and for the rest of his life chose to live in the humblest of surroundings, often under conditions of the severest austerity.[10]

Tolstoy's *The Gospel in Brief*, which Russell refers to in the letter, no doubt had a catalytic effect on Wittgenstein's pursuit of a

---

7. See Malcolm's article on Wittgenstein in *The Encyclopedia of Philosophy*, volume 8, p. 328; and Wittgenstein's letter to Engelmann, 19. 7. 20., in *Paul Engelmann: Letters from Ludwig Wittgenstein* (Horizon Press, N.Y., 1968), p. 35.

8. Malcolm, *Ibid.*

9. Malcolm, *Ludwig Wittgenstein—A Memoir, op. cit.*, pp. 27-8.

10. *Ibid.*, p. 10. See also Bartley, *op. cit.*, pp. 106-108, and Engelmann, *op. cit.*, p. 60.

new vocation. His sister Hermine describes how the soldiers around Wittgenstein used to call him "the one with the Gospel", so often was he seen carrying Tolstoy's work.[11] In this work, Tolstoy seeks to present in a compact form[12] his interpretation of the meaning of Jesus's message to mankind. The Gospels are divided into 12 chapters, since such a division, Tolstoy claims, flows naturally from the actual nature of Jesus's teaching.[13] Within the present context, the first six chapters are the most significant. These are summarized by Tolstoy in the Preface to his work as follows;

> 1. Man is the son of the Infinite Source of Being; he is the son of this Father, not by the flesh but by the spirit.
> 2. And therefore, man must serve the Source of his being in the spirit.
> 3. The life of all men has a divine Origin. This Origin only is sacred.
> 4. And therefore man must serve this Source of all human life. This is the will of the Father.
> 5. Service of the Will of the Father of Life is life-giving.
> 6. And therefore, it is not necessary to life that each man should satisfy his own will.[14]

Here, in doctrinal-didactic form, one can see most clearly the struggle of the religious personality as it strives to bring its life into conformity, not with its own will, but with the will of that which it experiences as greater than itself: the *amor sui* struggles to give way to the true life in the *amor Dei*. In eager acceptance of the sovereignty of God and the servanthood of man, the self has found its true calling—"Not as I will, but as thou wilt" (*Matt.* 26:39). Wittgenstein's actions after the war—his renunciation of his inheritance, his decision to become an elementary school teacher, the humble conditions under which he chose to live, and the seriousness with which, on a number of occasions, he considered becoming a monk—must all be seen in the light of this simple Christian-Tolstoyan imperative, which Wittgenstein was henceforth to adopt as his own.

---

11. Bernhard Leitner, *The Architecture of Ludwig Wittgenstein*, (New York University Press, N.Y., 1976). p. 27.
12. Tolstoy's more elaborate treatment of the Gospels is contained in his *The Four Gospels Harmonized and Translated, op. cit.*
13. *The Gospel in Brief* (Thomas Y. Crowell and Co., N.Y., 1896), p. 2.
14. *Ibid.*

Breaking Silence—Wittgenstein's Encounter with Paul Engelmann

In his memoir, Paul Engelmann describes how Wittgenstein, when he first came to visit him during the War, suffered from a kind of speech defect. He had difficulty articulating what he wanted to say, and Engelmann would often have to come to his assistance to provide the words he was looking for. Engelmann describes this situation as follows:

> At the time of his first stay in Olmuetz Wittgenstein suffered from a minor defect of speech which, however, disappeared later on. He used to struggle for words, especially when he was trying hard to formulate a proposition. Often enough I was able to help him to find the right words by stating myself the proposition he had in mind. I could do it because I really had a sensitive understanding for what he wanted to say. More than once on such occasions he exclaimed with relief, "If I can't manage to bring forth a proposition, along comes Engelmann with his forcepts and pulls it out of me!"[1]

It is difficult from this passage alone to discern the exact nature of Wittgenstein's malady. Symptomatically it might simply be described as a kind of mutism. But given what is known about Wittgenstein's thoughts and sensitivities during this period, it would not be too speculative to see in what Engelmann describes here the travail of a man whose experienced alienation from society is so extreme that he has lost all confidence in his ability to communicate with others. Wittgenstein—"lonely, forlorn, marooned in the desert", as Engelmann describes him[2]—had, in fact, first sought out Engelmann hoping to find someone with whom he might discuss some of his more intimate thoughts and feelings. And in this regard, at least, he was not disappointed.

Wittgenstein had gone to Olmuetz in 1916 as part of his military training, and had been given Engelmann's name by Adolf Loos, the prominent Viennese architect, who was Engelmann's teacher at the time.[3] Wittgenstein was to encounter in Engelmann a sympathetic listener, who was able to understand his ideas on moral and spiritual matters because he himself had thought deeply about

1. Engelmann, *op. cit.*, p. 94.
2. *Ibid.*, p. 62.
3. *Ibid.*, p. 63.

these things, and like Wittgenstein, suffered intensely from a sense of personal moral inadequacy.[4] "In me," Engelmann explains, "Wittgenstein unexpectedly met a person who, like many members of the younger generation, suffered acutely under the discrepancy between the world as it is and as it ought to be according to his lights, but who tended also to seek the source of that discrepancy within, rather than outside, himself. This was an attitude which Wittgenstein had not encountered elsewhere and which, at the same time, was vital for any true understanding or meaningful discussion of his own spiritual condition."[5] Explaining further, he says: "It was my own spiritual predicament that enabled me to understand, from within as it were, his utterances that mystified everyone else. And it was this understanding on my part that made me indispensable to him at that time."[6]

As Engelmann describes in his memoir, he and Wittgenstein had discussions ranging over a number of topics, which included poetry, art, music, philosophy, the justice of the world war, morality, religion, suicide, human sinfulness, and many more. Engelmann says that the subject matter of discussion usually focused on two broad areas, one being the philosophical conceptions of the *Tractatus*, the other, religion and morality.[7] Perhaps what is most striking to the reader of Engelmann's memoirs who comes to them with a knowledge of the *Tractatus*, is the fact that the great preponderance of topics which Wittgenstein seems to have taken up with Engelmann are precisely those which he declares in the *Tractatus* one must be silent about. Wittgenstein's vow of silence, one might say, was broken almost at the same time it was taken. The desire for communication with other human beings is certainly a very strong impulse in man, as Wittgenstein, in his isolation, had probably come to know better than anyone. What his talks with Engelmann show is a movement away from strict adherence to the *Tractatus* doctrines and a clearer understanding of the fact that at least under certain circumstances, with the right people, and at the right time, verbalization concerning moral and spiritual matters is appropriate and legitimate. Silence, while it may sometimes be the best mode of communication for one's deepest thoughts and feelings, is not necessarily so. This realization on Wittgenstein's part was destined to play a major role in his later rejection of the *Tractatus* and his subsequent acceptance of all common ways of speaking.

4. *Ibid.*, p. 73.
5. *Ibid.*, pp. 74-5.
6. *Ibid.*, p. 73.
7. *Ibid.*, pp. 74-76.

Creating a Monster

"This book," Wittgenstein had declared in the opening line of the Preface to the *Tractatus*, "will perhaps only be understood by someone who himself has already had the thoughts expressed therein—or at least similar thoughts." "Its purpose would be achieved if it gave pleasure to just one person who read it and understood it." From these words it can be seen that Wittgenstein from the start had no illusions about the *Tractatus* being understood by very many. Not only did it demand of the reader at least a rudimentary knowledge of modern logic, but it required in addition, a high degree of empathetic understanding for certain states of mystic-religious illumination which radically transcend the normal modes of consciousness and experience. As it turned out, the *Tractatus* proved even more incomprehensible than Wittgenstein had originally thought. Other than Engelmann, not a single person, in fact, really understood it—not Bertrand Russell, nor Moritz Schlick, nor Rudolf Carnap, nor A.J. Ayer, nor Friedrich Waismann, nor any other member of the Vienna Circle really grasped its import. Moreover, not only did those who read it fail to understand it, but many were to derive from it attitudes and conclusions the exact opposite from those which Wittgenstein had intended.

Carnap, as has already been explained in the previous section, was radicalized by the *Tractatus* into rejecting, not merely as unscientific (as he had previously, in his more tolerant days done), but as absolute and useless nonsense any proposition outside the domain of the natural sciences. His opposition to metaphysical and theological systems was in one regard the same as that of the *Tractatus* author; both men saw metaphysics, at least metaphysics of the Hegelian type, as pompous, muddled, and needlessly obscure. But beyond their agreement on this superficial level, Carnap and Wittgenstein were of two entirely different minds. Whereas Wittgenstein was primarily concerned with maintaining the wonder and majesty of "the Inexpressible", and in cultivating a silent piety, Carnap, in common with Neurath and certain other members of the Vienna Circle, wished to banish all but natural science from man's field of awareness. In Carnap's *Logische Syntax der Sprache* (1934) the difference between the two men is brought to a head when Carnap applies his criterion of meaningfullness to certain bothersome propositions of the *Tractatus* itself. Speaking of what he calls the "mythology of the inexpressible", Carnap lists nine propositions taken from within the

Vienna Circle camp, each of which, he explains, is totally without meaning.[1] Three of these nine propositions are taken over directly from the *Tractatus*:[2] "There is indeed the inexpressible" [6.522]; "What can be shown cannot be said" [4.122]., "Philosophy will signify what cannot be said by presenting clearly what can be said" [4.115].[3] And in another section, which he designates the "mythology of higher things", four nonsense propositions are listed, all of which are taken over directly from the *Tractatus*: "The sense of the world must lie outside of the world" [6.41]; "How the world is, is completely indifferent to what is higher" [6.432]; "If a good or bad willing changes the world, it can only change the limits of the world, not the facts" [6.43]; "Propositions cannot express anything higher" [6.42].[4] What was for Wittgenstein the most important distinction of the *Tractatus*—i.e., that between what can be said and what must be shown, between the world and what lies beyond the world, between the lower and the higher, the logical and the translogical—is thus in Carnap completely lost. A propositional logic which is taken over from the *Tractatus* has come to be used in such a way as to push out of man's awareness the very mode of experience and Reality the majesty of which Wittgenstein was most concerned with defending in his original development of logical theory.

The same rejection of a "higher", "inexpressible", "transcendent" realm is to be found in the pamphlet prepared by Neurath, Carnap, and Hahn in 1929 in honor of Schlick, bearing the title "Die Wissenschaftliche Weltauffassung: Der Wiener Kreis" ("The Scientific Conception of the World: The Vienna Circle").[5] From its content, which reflects a certain knowledge of Marxism and the history of philosophy, it is clear that Neurath was its chief architect. It will be recalled from the previous section Neurath's rebuke to the Wittgensteinian notion of "higher things"—that in questions of metaphysics, "one must indeed be silent, but not *about* anything." This same attitude dominates the pamphlet. "Everything is accessible to man," it boldly proclaims, "and man is the measure of all things." "Here is an affinity with the Sophists, not with the Platonists; with the Epicureans, not with the Pythagoreans; with all those who stand for earthly being and the here and now. The scientific world-

1. *The Logical Syntax of Language* (Routledge and Kegan Paul, 1964), p. 313.
2. *Ibid.*, p. 314.
3. Pears-McGuinness translation.
4. Carnap, *op. cit.*
5. An English translation has been published in Otto Neurath, *Empiricism and Sociology,* edited by Marie Neurath and Robert S. Cohen (D. Reidel Publishing Co., Boston), pp. 299–318.

conception knows no *unsolvable riddle*."[6] Elsewhere in the pamphlet it is explained how "neatness and clarity are striven for, and dark distances and unfathomable depths rejected. In science there are no 'depths'; there is surface everywhere."[7]

Wittgenstein is favorably mentioned several times in the pamphlet, and is listed in the appendix as one of the "leading representatives of the scientific world-conception".[8] It is easy, however, to see the difference between the spirit motivating the above declarations and that behind the *Tractatus*. "*The riddle* does not exist," Wittgenstein had said in the *Tractatus*, because "if a question can be framed at all, it is also *possible* to answer it" (6.5). The riddle, in the sense of an unanswerable question, does not exist, because "when the answer cannot be put into words (*aussprechen*), neither can the question be put into words" (6.5). But an "answer", Wittgenstein believed, clearly exists, even if it cannot be put into words. "The solution of the riddle of life in space and time," he says, "lies *outside* of space and time" (6.4312)—though this "outside-of", transcendental realm, which provides the answer to the riddle, cannot be fathomed by language or human conceptual structures. It cannot be so fathomed *not* because it does not exist, but because of the expressive limitations of language. Moreover, aside from any technical impossibilities, even to attempt to do so would represent a profaning. Wittgenstein would certainly agree with the view that *in science* their are no depths, but that, he would say, only shows the limitations of science; it certainly does not, in his view, diminish the importance to life (indeed for Wittgenstein the centrality to life) of the unfathomable, unspeakable depths of human experience in man's communion with what, vis-a-vis science and the world, is wholly other.

Nothing could be more out of tune with the philosophy of the *Tractatus* than the Protagorean notion of "man the measure". The

6. *Ibid.*, p. 306.

7. *Ibid.* Neurath's attitude here (he is the obvious author of these passages) is perhaps better described as a theophobia (or logophobia) rather than a simple skepticism or atheism. It is an echo of the words of Prometheus quoted by his mentor Karl Marx at the beginning of his doctoral dissertation: "In a word, I hate all the gods." Such an attitude, one must realize, has little in common with the theoretical skepticism of the kind one finds, for instance, in a Bertrand Russell. At some level of his being, at least, Neurath *knows* that there is a Depth dimension of reality beyond the level of the phenomena accessible to the natural sciences. He protests so strenuously against the Depth for the very reason that he knows that it is there, and suspects that it threatens the position of man as the measure of all things. For a similar attitude in 20th century European thought, one would have to turn to Sartre.

8. *Ibid.*, p. 318.

very purpose of the work as a *via negativa* is that man may leave himself behind, i.e., ascend the ladder, abandon self and world, and in pious silence behold the mystery of the divine Beyond (5.632, 5.641, 6.54, 7). It is interesting to see that one of the few classic philosophers whom Wittgenstein seems to have read and enjoyed was Plato.[9] One can hardly imagine a lesser affinity with Epicurean or Sophistic philosophy.

By the late 1920s, after Wittgenstein had returned to Vienna from rural school teaching and met privately with several members of Schlick's Circle, it must have become quite apparent to him, not only that no one understood the *Tractatus*, but that in its influence on the emerging positivist movement in Vienna, it was having the complete opposite effect from the one he had intended. Instead of producing a heightened moral and spiritual awareness in men, it had become the theoretical basis for an aggressively anti-spiritual movement of a truely extremist variety. With a sense of frustration and despair, Wittgenstein must have come to the painful realization in the late 1920s that, like Dr. Frankenstein, he had, despite the best of intentions, unwittingly created a monster. When "Die Wissenschaftliche Weltauffassung" was being written (1929), Schlick was away on sabbatical leave in America. Wittgenstein was told by Friedrich Waismann of what was being planned in the pamphlet and how it was to be presented to Schlick upon his return to Vienna. In a letter to Waismann, Wittgenstein set forth his opposition to the Circle's anti-metaphysical bravado, and warned against doing anything that would embarass Schlick, a man for whom Wittgenstein had the greatest respect. One can discern from the letter something of the frustration Wittgenstein felt from his inability to influence others along the lines of the say/show message of the *Tractatus*. Part of the letter is reproduced below and needs no further comment.

> Just because Schlick is no ordinary man, people owe it to him to take care not to let their "good intentions" make him and the Vienna school which he leads ridiculous by boastfulness. When I say "boastfulness" I mean any kind of self-satisfied posturing. "Renunciation of metaphysics!" As if *that* were something new! What the Vienna school has achieved, it ought to *show* not *say*. . . . the master [i.e., master craftsman] should be known by his *work*.[10]

9. Malcolm, *Memoir, op. cit.*, p. 20.

10. *Wittgenstein and the Vienna Circle*, edited by Brian McGuinnes, (Harper and Row Publishers, 1979), p. 18, emphasis in original.

Remarks on Frazer

Wittgenstein's attitude toward the Carnap-Neurath-Ayer style of positivism—the monster which he himself had helped to create—is perhaps best reflected in a series of remarks he wrote in the early 1930s on Sir James Frazer's *The Golden Bough.* In Frazer one finds the same basic attitude as in Central European positivism: a progressivist belief in the superiority of Western modernity over all previous cultures together with a ridiculing, debunking attitude towards the customs and beliefs of pre-modern people. It would seem from what Wittgenstein says about Frazer that it was this kind of debunking attitude, and the conceit that goes along with it, that more than anything else stirred Wittgenstein to anger.

Frazer, Wittgenstein explains, interprets the magical and religious practices of primitive peoples as errors or superstitions—as forms, that is, of human stupidity. But in this regard he is simply wrong. "Frazer's account of the magical and religious notions of men is unsatisfactory," Wittgenstein declares; "it makes these notions appear as *mistakes*." "Was Augustine mistaken," Wittgenstein asks rhetorically, "when he called on God on every page of the *Confessions*?"[1] "Well, one could say, if he was not mistaken, then the Buddhist holy man, or some other, whose religion expresses quite different notions, surely was."[2] "But *none* of them was making a mistake," Wittgenstein says, "except where he was putting forward a theory."[3] Frazer, according to Wittgenstein, wrongly interprets the beliefs and practices of pre-modern men as false sciences. There is much more to it than that, he holds, and moreover, there are many ways modern people act very similar to the primitives whom Frazer ridicules.[4]

The primitive practice of burning someone in effigy, for instance, is not so very different, according to Wittgenstein, from the practice of a modern person kissing a picture of a loved one.[5] In both

---

1. "Remarks of Frazer's *Golden Bough*", edited by Rush Rhees, translated by A.C. Miles (Humanities Press, Inc., Atlantic Highlands, N.J. 1979), p. 1. Most of the translations used here are taken over from Miles, though I have altered some of them where it seemed appropriate.

2. *Ibid.*

3. *Ibid.*

4. *Ibid.*, p. 4.

5. *Ibid.*

cases the actions give expression to a wish and make the person performing the action feel satisfied.[6] Primitives on the whole, Wittgenstein believes, are much smarter than Frazer thinks: "The same savage who, apparently, in order to kill his enemy, sticks his knife through a picture of him, really does build his hut of wood and cuts his arrow with skill and not in effigy."[7]

Primitive religious practices, Wittgenstein stresses, may express a genuine spirituality which moderns should not belittle. In matters of the Spirit, in fact, it is Frazer and his kind, says Wittgenstein, who are the real primitives: "What narrowness of spiritual life [*seelischen Lebens*] we find in Frazer!," Wittgenstein declares. "And as a result: how impossible for him to understand a different way of life from the English one of his time!" "Frazer cannot imagine a priest who is not basically an English parson of our time with all his stupidity and feebleness."[8] In an even more direct attack Wittgenstein writes: "Frazer is much more savage than most of his savages, for they are not as far removed from an understanding of spiritual matters [*geistigen Angelegenheit*] as an Englishman of the twentieth century. His explanations of primitive observances are much cruder than the meaning of the observances themselves."[9]

Frazer and the nominal Christians of modern times are thus seen by Wittgenstein as the crudest of Philistines, whose understanding of spiritual things is greatly inferior to that of even the most uneducated of men. Moreover, to their ignorance is added the worst kind of arrogance and conceit which parades ignorance as enlightened wisdom. The statement "Frazer is much more savage than most of his savages," where the text switches to Frazer's original English term "savage" rather than the German *Wilde*, suggests something of the passion evoked in Wittgenstein by an attack of the educated upon the religiosity of less sophisticated people. In explaining Wittgenstein's personal disdain for him, Carnap said that he had the distinct feeling in personal discussions that any ideas which smacked of Enlightenment were repugnant to Wittgenstein.[10] In this regard, Carnap was no doubt wholly correct.

---

6. *Ibid.*
7. *Ibid.*
8. *Ibid.*, p. 5.
9. *Ibid.*, p. 8.
10. See Section II, p. 66.

The Shift to Ordinary Language: A Celebration of the Common Man

With his return to academic life in 1929, Wittgenstein began a process of reassessing his earlier views—a process spurred on, no doubt, by his ongoing meetings with members of the Vienna Circle[1] and the increasing influence in European thought of the Viennese-style of logical positivism. His views at the beginning of 1929 were still substantially those of the *Tractatus*, as can be seen in his brief article "Some Remarks on Logical Form"[2]; but by 1930 Wittgenstein's ideas were definitely in a state of transition, which can be seen in his *Philosophical Remarks*,[3] and by the mid-30s, with the dictation of the *Blue Book* and the *Brown Book*[4] and the completion of the *Philosophical Grammar*,[5] all the main ideas that comprise Wittgenstein's later philosophy were substantially complete. One can speak of nothing less than a revolution in his thought between 1929-1935, and while continuity certainly exists, Wittgenstein's later philosophy must be seen as a radical break with the *Tractatus* in both substance and method.

The most significant aspect of this break was the shift in focus from the formal, *a priori* systems of symbolic logic, which had previously been seen as the way to revealing the basic structure of language and the world, to a new preoccupation with the various ways in which ordinary men use ordinary words. The very terms "ordinary-" and "everyday-language" (*alltaegliche Sprache*, *Umgangs-*

1. Although Wittgenstein remained in residence at Cambridge during most of the school terms from 1929 to the outbreak of the Second World War, the long summer vacations found him back in Vienna, where he carried on his discussions with Schlick and Waismann. On just how thoroughly Viennese the influences on Wittgenstein were, see the remarks in Bartley, *op. cit.*, pp. 24-5.

2. *Aristotelian Society Proceedings*, Supplementary Volume IX, 1929, pp. 162-171. Ordinary language, for instance, was seen as disguising true logical structure and leading to misunderstandings which could only be cleared up by the substitution of a logical-notational symbolism. Wittgenstein, however, begins to move away from the simple picture theory of the *Tractatus*, in that elementary propositions are no longer seen as necessarily independent of one another. On this, see Anthony Kenney, *Wittgenstein* (Harvard University Press, Cambridge, 1973), pp. 103-106.

3. English translation by Raymond Hargreaves and Roger White (Harper and Row Publishers, N.Y., 1975).

4. Harper and Row Publishers, N.Y. 1965.

5. Translated by Anthony Kenney (University of California Press, Berkeley, 1974).

sprache, gewoehnliche Sprache), so prominent in Wittgenstein's later thought, are, in fact, essentially contrast terms. They derive their meaning from their contrast with the highly "extraordinary" and unusual languages of mathematical logicians and natural scientists—i.e., from just those kinds of languages represented by Russell and Whitehead's *Principia Mathematica* and Wittgenstein's own *Tractatus*. "The task of philosophy," Wittgenstein declares in the *Philosophical Grammar*, "is not to create a new, ideal language, but to clarify the use of our language, the existing language" (par. 72). Earlier he had explained to Friedrich Waismann the shift in his thinking on this matter: "I used to believe that there was the everyday language that we all usually spoke and a primary language that expressed what we really knew, namely phenomena. I also spoke of a first system and a second system. Now I wish to explain why I do not adhere to that conception any more. I think that we have only one language and that is our everyday language. We need not invent a new language or construct a new symbolism, but our everyday language already is *the* language, provided we rid it of obscurities."[6]

Ordinary language is thus pushed to the center of the stage and is accorded a new respect totally absent from the *Tractatus*. It is true that Wittgenstein says in *Tractatus* 5.5563 that "all the propositions of our everyday language (*Umgangssprache*) are, just as they stand, logically in perfect order," but this is a rather obscure passage, and runs counter to the whole reformative thrust of the book. Wittgenstein was apparently thinking here only of simple discursive statements of everyday language (e.g., "Your tea is ready"; "The mailman is at the door"; "It's very cold outside"), which were seen to share a common logical form with the world, and to depict accurately the logical multiplicity of various states of affairs in the world. He was probably not thinking here of such non-discursive statements of everyday language as expressions of wishes, questions, interjections, commands, and the like, all of which would come to play an important part in the discussion of langauge in his later works, and he was most certainly not thinking of everyday moral, aesthetic, and religious judgments (e.g., "Murder is wrong"; "My, what a nice day!"; "God loves us as his children"), all of which were confined in the *Tractatus* to the realm of silence. It was, in fact, these alternate, non-discursive modes of everyday language and the desire to accord them a new status of respect that led Wittgenstein

6. *Wittgenstein and the Vienna Circle, op. cit.*, p. 45.

to abandon the simple picture theory of language found in the *Tractatus* and work out an entirely different theory.[7]

Hand in hand with the new respect that was accorded to ordinary language went the subordination of logic and logical analysis. From now on, logic was not to be used to construct a language more ideal than the ordinary; the ordinary, with all its complexity and subtlety, was now seen as ideal enough just as it stood. Logical analysis, it was held, can serve to clarify ordinary language, but not to alter or replace it in any fundamental way. This major change of heart on Wittgenstein's part can be seen as early as 1930, in the *Philosophical Remarks*:

> How strange if logic were concerned with an 'ideal' language and not with *ours*. For what could this ideal language express? Presumably, what we now express in our ordinary language; in that case, this is the language logic must investigate. . . . Logical analysis is the analysis of something we have, not of something we don't have. Therefore it is the analysis of propositions *as they stand*. (It would be odd if the human race had been speaking all this time without ever putting together a genuine proposition). (par. 3, emphasis in original)

---

7. David Pears' remarks on this point are well worth quoting:

". . . when he said that beyond the line of demarcation which he drew in the *Tractatus* there must be silence, he did not merely mean that there must be scientific silence. He meant that any attempt to put nonscientific truths into words would necessarily distort them by forcing them into the mold of scientific discourse. So religion, ethics, and aesthetics . . . all slide into the limbo reserved for transcendental subjects, because factual discourse really does occupy the dominant position—indeed the only position. . . . But . . . the pressure exerted by those other kinds of discourse was going to change the map of logical space. In the *Tractatus* he had pushed them off the map not, of course, in any intolerant positivistic way, but in a subtle, sympathetic, transcendental way, and at least two of them, ethics and aesthetics, seem not to be amenable to this treatment.

"There were also much stronger disruptive pressures within the logical space of factual discourse. For his early theory of factual propositions was a theory about their essence, and so he did not pay much attention to the specific differences between the various forms of factual proposition."

Ludwig Wittgenstein (The Viking Press, N.Y., 1969), pp. 97-8.

Pears' statement rightly emphasizes the narrow vision of the *Tractatus*, and would well be kept in mind by those who, like Susanne Langer and Janik and Toulmin, want to read into the *Tractatus* what is clearly not there. The *Tractatus* is not a plea for poetry, myth, fable, or other forms of non-discursive language—it is a plea for the natural-scientific mode of discourse, and beyond that, for silence.

Ordinary language is thus seen as possessing a certain wisdom which isn't to be improved upon through an ideal or logically perfect language such as those sought after by positivist logicians. Ordinary language, in other words, is not in need of any radical transformations. "It is wrong," says Wittgenstein in the *Blue Book*, "to say that in philosophy we consider an ideal language as opposed to our ordinary one. For this makes it appear as though we thought we could improve on ordinary language." "But ordinary language is all right" (p. 28). In the *Philosophical Investigations*,[8] Wittgenstein explains how the idea of an ideal language had distorted his earlier perceptions. The idea of an ideal, he says, "is like a pair of glasses on our nose through which we see whatever we looked at. It never occurs to us to take them off" (par. 103).[9] In the early thirties, Wittgenstein was to take these glasses off and cast them aside for good.

Coupled with the new respect for ordinary language went a new appreciation for its richness and diversity. In the *Tractatus*, the only linguistic forms which were considered were descriptive propositions and the tautologies of mathematics and logic. In Wittgenstein's later philosophy there emerged a new appreciation for the many different linguistic uses one finds in everyday life, and a new tolerance concerning their appropriateness and legitimacy. Giving orders, speculating about an event, play-acting, making up a story, singing, telling a joke, thanking, greeting, praying—all these and more, Wittgenstein came to realize, go to make up the totality of actual language (PI 23). "It is interesting," he writes, casting an aspersion upon his own previous work, "to compare the multiplicity of the tools in language and of the ways they are used, the multiplicity of

8. Translated by G.E.M. Anscombe (Basil Blackwell, Oxford, 1968). I have altered some of these translations slightly.

9. See also par. 81. This metaphor brings out perhaps better than any other just how much the persuasiveness of Wittgenstein's attack on his earlier philosophy is a matter of whether or not one already accepts the basic premises of the later philosophy, and especially, the new status of respect accorded to ordinary language. For the logical positivists and the early Wittgenstein, these glasses were *corrective* lenses (not shaded or distorting ones), which brought clarity and precision to what would otherwise be muddle, confusion, and metaphysical nonsense. To Russell and Carnap they would always remain so. Only if ordinary language is affirmed as an invaluable means of communication, and accorded a certain degree of respect, does an appeal to it begin to carry any weight against the claims made on behalf of various formal-constructional systems and the *a priori* principles which underlie them. It was in their unwillingness to accord any special status to ordinary language that separated Russell, Carnap, and their followers from the later Wittgensteinians. On this point, see J.O. Urmson, *Philosophical Analysis: Its Development Between the Wars* (Oxford University Press, 1956), pp. 160-161.

kinds of words and sentences, with what logicians have said about the structure of language (including the author of the *Tractatus-Logico-Philosophicus*)" (PI 23). Words, he stresses, do many jobs, and do not simply refer to objects as he had earlier believed. One must, Wittgenstein came to believe, look to the actual use of a word in our everyday language, not postulate *a priori* what the functions of words must be. And having done this, one will see that the use of words is quite various. Just as money, Wittgenstein suggests in the *Philosophical Grammar*, can purchase many things besides a material object—e.g., permission to sit in a theater, a title of nobility, fast travel, etc.—so words have many different uses besides referring to things (par. 27). "Think of the tools in a tool-box," Wittgenstein says in an often quoted passage in the *Philosophical Investigations*; "there is a hammer, pliers, a saw, a screw-driver, a rule, a glue-pot, glue, nails and screws. The function of words are as diverse as the function of these objects" (par. 11). The *Tractatus*, he came to believe, had not sufficiently taken account of this fact.

Bertrand Russell, in one of his autobiographical works, offers an assessment of this new respect Wittgenstein showed towards ordinary language which is well worth considering, even if, in its characterization of Wittgenstein's motives, it is not wholly correct. Suggesting that few of Wittgenstein's desciples really knew what manner of man he was, Russell makes the following comment:

> There are two great men in history whom he somewhat resembles. One was Pascal, the other was Tolstoy. Pascal was a mathematician of genius, but abandoned mathematics for piety. Tolstoy sacrificed his genius as a writer to a kind of bogus humility which made him prefer peasants to educated men and *Uncle Tom's Cabin* to all other works of fiction. Wittgenstein, who could play with metaphysical intricacies as cleverly as Pascal with hexagons or Tolstoy with emperors, threw away this talent and debased himself before common sense as Tolstoy debased himself before the peasants—in each case from an impulse of pride. I admired Wittgenstein's *Tractatus* but not his later work, which seemed to me to involve an abnegation of his own best talent very similar to those of Pascal and Tolstoy.[10]

10. *My Philosophical Development* (Simon and Schuster, N.Y., 1959), p. 214. In a conversation with Ved Metha, Russell had similar remarks: "When his *Tractatus* came out I was wildly excited. I think less of it now. At that time, his theory that a proposition was a picture of the world was so engaging and original. Wittgenstein was really a Tolstoy and a Pascal rolled into one. You know how fierce Tolstoy was; he hated competitors.... And you know how Pascal became discontented with mathematics and science and became a mystic; it was the same with Wittgenstein. He was a

As in his remarks on Wittgenstein's mysticism, and Wittgenstein's intention to become a monk, these comments reflect Russell's general inability to ascribe to Wittgenstein any genuine moral or religious motive. Pride and vanity are vices to which few men are immune, least of all those who, like Wittgenstein, are endowed with powerfully magnetic personalities. But even those displaying enormous pride and vanity are sometimes moved by higher motives, and Tolstoy and Wittgenstein would certainly seem to be good examples. Just how debasing oneself before common sense and the peasantry constitutes an act of pride is not something Russell explains very well in these remarks. Nevertheless, Russell's comparison of Wittgenstein with Tolstoy and Pascal is a good one. Like Pascal, Wittgenstein was a man called to a life of piety and public mission by an intense personal religious experience.[11] And like Tolstoy, he came to see the university educated intellegentsia of the West as the carrier of a moral and spiritual corruption that had thrust human civilization into a new Dark Age. And also like Tolstoy, he looked towards the uneducated masses of mankind as the source, if not of moral renewal, at least of resistance to still further corruption and disintegration.

This, it would seem, is the real key to understanding Wittgenstein's later turn to the uncritical acceptance of ordinary language. His earlier philosophy, instead of having the regenerative influence he had no doubt hoped for it, had given birth to a radically anti-spiritual movement which was only exacerbating the existing cultural situation. But in the ordinary language of the ordinary man, Wittgenstein was to see a way out of the general corruption and moral nihilism which threatened to engulf Western society. Common people, he thought, know the difference between right and wrong, between justice and injustice, even if, in actual decisions, they don't always make the right choices. They are genuinely aware of beauty, of truthfulness, of love, and can be heard all the time talking about these things. Moreover, they are not at all concerned about metaphysical speculation or the arguments of theologians, for their concern with life and the health of the soul is something daily and something real. Wittgenstein was certainly disillusioned to some extent with many of the people he encountered during his

---

mathematical mystic. But after [the] *Tractatus* he became more remote from me, just like the Oxford philosophers."

(*Fly and the Fly Bottle: Encounters with British Intellectuals*, Little Brown and Company, Boston, 1963, pp. 42-3).

11. See the remarks on Pascal in the previous Section.

teaching days in the Austrian countryside, as one can gather, for instance, from a letter he wrote to Russell.[12] From Tolstoy he had taken over what proved to be a highly romanticized view of the European peasants. Nevertheless, however much the peasants and common people may have deviated from his original romanticized image, they always seem to have represented for Wittgenstein a vast improvement over the urban intelligentsia. The *anomie* and moral nihilism, no less than the metaphysical disputes which one found among the latter, were not to be found in their world.

With the new respect now accorded to the common man and his language, it was not surprising that under the influence of Wittgenstein's later philosophy many areas previously tabu to positivist-oriented intellectuals would once again come to be the focus of philosophical reflection. Although Wittgenstein only laid the groundwork, and did little of the actual concrete analysis, under his influence there would appear in Britain and America after his death a whole host of books and articles on such topics as the language of morals, of religion, of political philosophy, of art, of literary criticism, of prayer, etc. Discussion of "higher" things—or at least discussion of what other people had to say about such things—would become legitimate once again, and henceforth no one would be accused of talking nonsense when this was done. A new respect for the richness of life as reflected in the richness of the common man's language would come to replace in Anglo-American philosophical circles the flatness of the world of the *Tractatus*.

From Prophetism to the Spirit of Jamnia: A New Conservatism and a New Epoch

Wittgenstein's new attitude towards ordinary language is part of what might be described as a new conservatism. The *Tractatus*, in its relationship to existing culture, had all the hallmarks of a revolutionary manifesto. It recognized only discursive propositions and tautologies as legitimate speech, and attempted to confine all of what traditionally fell under the headings of ethics, aesthetics, and

12. *Letters to Russell, Keynes, and Moore*, *op. cit.*, p. 94; see also the letter of 28. 11. 21., p. 97.

religion to a realm of devotional silence. In the later philosophy, however, the spirit of the revolutionary gives way to that of the conservative—to one, that is, who accepts cultural norms as given, refusing on principle to criticize or attack them. "What belongs to a language game," Wittgenstein explains, "is a whole culture."[1] "To imagine a language is to imagine a form of life (*Lebensform*)" (PI 19). And this culture or form of life, he says, must be accepted by the philosopher as it is: "What has to be accepted, the given, so one could say, are the forms of life" (PI II, p. 226). "Philosophy may in no way interfere with the actual use of language; it can in the end only describe it . . . It leaves everything as it is" (PI 124).

There is something of a Burkean quality in all this, though Burke certainly allowed himself more license in criticizing existing social custom than Wittgenstein. Existing language is seen as adequately fulfilling all the functions for which it is used, and while certain improvements are allowed for, in general, ordinary language is taken by Wittgenstein to be normative. The philosopher's role, therefore, becomes one of scribe and exegete, who is expected to clear up misunderstandings which may arise when linguistic custom is not properly grasped, though he is never to alter or criticize that custom itself. In the new Wittgensteinian world-view, ordinary language, in effect, comes to serve the same regulative function which the word of scripture serves in the world-view of religious fundamentalists.

In keeping with the religious analogy, one might characterize the transition in Wittgenstein's thought as that from a basically mystic or prophetic mode of existence, to that of a rabbinic or priestly one. In the *Tractatus* and "Lecture on Ethics", Wittgenstein had looked towards the Beyond, towards the world- and language-transcending vision of *das Mystische*, as the source of orientation in life. In his later philosophy, however, the Ineffable is no longer directly present, for the center of man's existential orientation has shifted to the world-immanence of linguistic custom, which is now seen to possess an almost scripture-like authority. The prophet one might say, has descended the mountain to join the priests and rabbis below, as the immediate pastoral needs of society have come to overshadow the former concern with maintaining the truth and purity of mystic theophany. Men must now seek their transcendence within the immanent order itself, though they will not have much trouble

1. *Lectures and Conversations on Aesthetics, Psychology and Religious Belief* (University of California Press, Berkeley, 1967), p. 26.

finding it there, for in the form of ordinary language, including all moral, religious, and aesthetic discourse, it is already contained in the specific life-form of the culture.

One might draw a comparison here between the development of Wittgenstein's later philosophy and the actions of the council of Jamnia in 90 A.D.[2] In the face of the extreme anxiety and cultural disorientation aroused by the Roman destruction of Jerusalem and its temple, the rabbis who met at Jamnia in that year gathered together many of the religious and spiritual writings that had come down from Israel's past and stamped upon them a new status of unchanging cannonical authority. At the same time, they declared that the age of prophecy, the age when men had direct converse with Yahweh, was now past; that after Malachi the Spirit had departed Israel; and that now men were to order their lives not by the aid of prophetic inspiration, but by conforming to the word of scripture. Similarly Wittgenstein, in the face of the most devastating war mankind had ever known—a war whose devastation was as much moral and spiritual as physical[3]—turned to what he saw as the basic sanity and decency still alive in the traditions of the common man, and elevated these, in so far as they manifested themselves in language, to a new status as scripture. And with the proclamation of ordinary language as scripture, Wittgenstein—again like the rabbis—was simultaneously announcing the end to the age of prophecy, including, in this case, his own prophetic mission.

One might also compare the transition from Wittgenstein's early to his later philosophy to the shift in Plato's thought from the *Republic* to the *Laws*. The former, with its center of meaning in the Allegory of the Cave, was a mystic-prophetic work that found the solution to the problem of justice and the Good in a world transcending vision. In the latter work, Plato has lowered his sights and resigned himself to the fact that for the vast majority of mankind, orientation in life cannot procede from the depths of the soul in its direct attunement to the Divine, but requires the existence of an elaborate system of external laws, which the citizens of the polis are forbidden to break.[4] In a similar manner, Wittgenstein in his later

2. On Jamnia and the development of a Jewish cannon, see Bernhard Anderson, *Understanding the Old Testament* (Prentice Hall, Inc., Engelwood Cliffs, N.J., 1966), pp. 554-559.

3. In a letter to Russell, Wittgenstein observes how the Austrians since the war had sunk to the very lowest level (*bodenlos tief*), which is even too sad to talk about. (*Letters, op. cit.*, p. 97).

4. The interpretation of Plato suggested here follows that of Eric Voegelin in his *Plato and Aristotle* (Louisiana State University Press, Baton Rouge, 1957).

philosophy has resigned himself to the fact that few, if any, can live at the spiritual heights of the *Tractatus*, with its center of meaning in the ladder metaphor and its invocation of silence, but must rest content with the common sense wisdom and common decency of the ordinary man. Linguistic custom in Wittgenstein's later philosophy thus comes to parallel in function the laws of Plato's Cretan city state.

Here too, one might also see a further influence of Tolstoy. Paul Engelmann has described how Wittgenstein read and apparently admired Tolstoy's *What is Art?*, in which Tolstoy criticizes much of European art for not being accessible to the common man.[5] True art, for Tolstoy, is comprehensible to intellectual and peasant alike; it edifies both as a Biblical story does. The *Tractatus*, one might say applying Tolstoy's criterion, was seriously flawed because its content was accessible only to those trained in the highly esoteric discipline of symbolic logic, and even among those so trained, few if any seemed capable of grasping its meaning. The medium of ordinary language, on the other hand, was something everyone could grasp quite readily, and while perhaps not as edifying as a Biblical story (or one of Tolstoy's *Twenty-Three Tales*, which Wittgenstein also read with great admiration)[6], at least helped to re-inforce the basic value-system of a society. It had a universal appeal absent from the philosophy of the *Tractatus*.

Accompanying Wittgenstein's switch to ordinary language in the 30s was a powerful self-consciousness that saw in this switch the beginning of a whole new philosophical epoch. The most important statements in this regard come from certain lectures Wittgenstein delivered in 1933—lectures which were attended and later summarized in written form by G.E. Moore. The relevant passages from Moore's summary are as follows:

> I was a good deal surprised by some of the things he [Wittgenstein] said about the difference between "philosophy" in the sense in which what he was doing might be called "philosophy" . . . and what has traditionally been called "philosophy". He said that what he was doing was a "new subject", and not merely a stage in a "continuous development"; that there was now, in philosophy, a "kink" in the "development of human thought," comparable to that which occurred when Galileo and his contemporaries invented dynamics; that a "new method" had been discovered, as had happened when "chemistry was developed

5. Engelmann, *op. cit.*, p. 91.
6. Engelmann, *op. cit.*, p. 80.

> out of alchemy"; and that it was now possible for the first time that there should be "skillful" philosophers, though of course there had in the past been "great" philosophers. . . . As regards his own work, he said it did not matter whether his results were true or not: what mattered was that "a new method had been found."[7]

Someone who sees in his own turn of mind an historical-philosophical event of epoch-making proportions, one comparable to the development of chemistry out of alchemy, might reasonably be thought of as a megalomaniac, but it must be kept in mind that Wittgenstein had already witnessed when he made these remarks the enormous impact his *Tractatus* had had on influential thinkers, and he also must certainly have been aware of the near hypnotic power he continued to exert throughout his life on students and friends. Under such circumstances, a shift in his own thinking, it might reasonably be concluded, would portend a parallel shift in the thinking of large segments of the philosophical public. And here, of course, Wittgenstein proved to be correct.

The "new subject" Wittgenstein talks of in the lecture, is that of ordinary language, the "new method", its analysis within actual linguistic contexts (language games)—i.e., the subject matter and method which actually did come to dominate Anglo-British philosophy. On the succeeding page of Moore's notes, Wittgenstein gives examples of what he means by the traditional philosophers—the "greats" who are now to be replaced by the men of "skill"— specifically naming Plato and Berkeley. From this it would seem that what he is intending in the quoted passage, in this most poignant moment of his lectures (Moore's account, one assumes, has accurately captured the pathos of the occasion), is something akin to a proclamation that the age of prophecy is now past. From now on, men are seen to live in an entirely new epoch, the epoch of ordinary language and the common man. The prophets and visionaries of old —the Platos and the Berkeleys, the Hegels and the Schopenhauers, the Heideggers and the Bergsons—these "greats" are now to be superceded by that whole mass of unrecognized ordinary people who lead a quiet and pious life. With the prophets and visionaries go too their destructivist counterparts, i.e., the skeptics and "critical philosophers"—the Epicuruses and the Protagorases, the Humes and the Comtes, the Carnaps and the Ayers. Philosophy henceforth will be neither edifier nor corrupter, for after clearing up misunder-

7. "Wittgenstein's Lectures in 1930-1933", in *The Classics of Analytic Philosophy*, edited by Robert R. Ammerman (McGraw Hill, N.Y., 1965), p. 283.

standings, it will leave everything as it is. It will no longer seek to transform lesser metals into gold—nor to debase them into dirt—but will accept them for what they are, seeking only to determine their nature.

Off to Russia

As previously explained, the main features of Wittgenstein's post-*Tractatus* philosophy were already complete by the mid-30s. Although he planned to publish the results of his later reflections in the form of a comprehensive work, subsequent hesitation, and a desire to expand and revise what he had already done, resulted in the fact that a synoptic formulation of his new ideas wasn't completed until 1945, when he finished Part I of the *Philosophical Investigations*. By 1935, however, the major contours of his new philosophy were completely worked out, and so it is perhaps not too surprising to find him at this time once again wanting to leave academic life and pursue a new vocation. In the autumn of 1935, he took a trip to the Soviet Union in the hope that he might be able to settle there permanently and perhaps take up the study of medicine. His plans for this extraordinary move are discussed in two letters he wrote to his friend John Maynard Keynes the summer before his actual Russian visit.[1] Knowing that it would be difficult to get permission to stay in Russia, he prevailed upon Keynes to use his influence to help set up a meeting with the then Russian Ambassador to England, Ivan Maisky. Maisky, it was hoped, might have the right contacts in Russia to help Wittgenstein get the permission he sought. Keynes was to oblige Wittgenstein's request by giving him a letter of introduction to Maisky, which reads, in part, as follows:

> Dear Monsieur Maisky:
>
> May I venture to introduce to you Dr. Ludwig Wittgenstein, a fellow of Trinity College, Cambridge, who is anxious to find means of obtaining permission to live more or less permanently in Russia.
>
> Dr. Wittgenstein, who is a distinguished philosopher, is a very old and intimate friend of mine, and I should be extremely grateful for anything you could do for him. I must leave it to him

1. *Letters to Russell, Keynes and Moore*, *op. cit.*, pp. 132, 134.

> to tell you his reasons for wanting to go to Russia. He is not a member of the Communist Party, but has strong sympathies with the way of life which he believes the new regime in Russia stands for.[2]

Wittgenstein seems to have been moderately left-socialist in his political views, though he definitely was not a Marxist or revolutionary. Paul Engelmann, in fact, says that Wittgenstein tended to show great respect towards all legitimately constituted political authority (he had, it will be recalled, dutifully served in the armies of Franz Josef) and throughout his life, tended to look upon revolutionary convictions as immoral.[3] It was certainly not the ideology of Marx and Lenin that attracted him towards Russia at this time; he had, in fact, little knowledge of political philosophy, and was not what one would call a "political person". But if it was not a faith in Communist ideology that attracted him to Russia, what then was it? The answer to this question can be discerned from one of his letters to Keynes, where he describes the people he hoped to see in Russia:

> Now what I wanted with Maisky was this: I wanted to see him and have a conversation with him. I know that there is VERY little chance that I or my case could make a good impression on him. But I think there is an off chance of this happening. There is further a small chance of knowing some official at Leningrad or Moscow to whom he might introduce me. I want to speak to officials at two institutions; one is the "Institute of the north" in Leningrad, the other the "Institute of national Minorities" in Moscow. These Institutes, as I am told, deal with people who want to go to the "colonies", the newly colonized parts at the periphery of the USSR. I want to get information and possibly help from people in these Institutes.[4]

Here one can see clearly that it is contact with the rural populace that Wittgenstein is most interested in—those in the "colonies", at the periphery of the USSR. It is not the party officials, nor the Communist intellectuals, nor even the urban factory workers with whom he is interested in living, but the Russian peasants. And of course, what he knew of the Russian peasants, was what he had gathered from the writings of Tolstoy and Dostoyevsky.[5] Once

2. *Ibid.*, pp. 135-136.
3. Engelmann, *op. cit.*, p. 121.
4. *Letters to Russell, Keynes, and Moore, op. cit.*, p. 134.
5. This may be why in the same letter to Keynes he describes his reasons for wanting to go to Russia as "partly childish." On this, Fania Pascal, Wittgenstein's Russian

again Wittgenstein yearned to work among the common people, though this time in a nation that was officially dedicated to the ideals of brotherhood and co-operation—ideals which Wittgenstein affirmed from his own Christian-Tolstoyan religious perspective. Wittgenstein had, in fact, thought of going to Russia as early as 1922, only a few years after the revolution, though his brief remarks in this regard contained in a letter to Engelmann, seem to have been more of a passing fancy than anything serious.[6]

From our present perspective, one can look back upon Wittgenstein's intention to settle in Russia as incredibly naive. But it must be kept in mind that few outside of Russia at this time had any firm knowledge of the horrors of the Gulags, the forced collectivizations, or the purge trials. Bertrand Russell, Wittgenstein's former mentor, had, it is true, seen the potential tyranny of the Bolshevik regime even in Lenin's time, but it is doubtful if Wittgenstein ever read Russell's work on the subject (*The Practice and Theory of Bolshevism*), and even if he had, he probably would have mistrusted Russell's assessment, not thinking him particularly astute in matters of morals and politics. The fact is that for many non-communist intellectuals in the thirties, the Soviet Union represented a great experiment in human community—a truely grass roots society built on the foundation of factory workers and farmers, which was dedicated to a true communal socialism where envy and greed would come to be replaced by a spirit of solidarity and mutual care. Most Westerners at this time knew little of the ruthlessness of Stalin and his henchmen; "Uncle Joe" was even conceived by some as something of a Russian folk hero. One might recall in this regard the statement of one of Roosevelt's ambassadors to Russia, to the effect that even to question the good faith of Stalin was "bad Christianity, bad sportsmanship, bad sense".[7]

Wittgenstein, of course, never did settle in Russia, though whether it was because of an inability to obtain official permission,

---

teacher, writes: "To my mind, his feeling for Russia would have had at all times more to do with Tolstoy's moral teachings, with Dostoevsky's spiritual insights, than with any political or social matters. He would view the latter, which certainly were not indifferent to him, in terms of the former. His rarely expressed political opinions might be naive" (*Ludwig Wittgenstein: Personal Recollections*, edited by Rush Rhees, *op. cit.*, p. 57). Similarly, R.L. Goodstein, a friend of Wittgenstein, writes: "What attracted him was the Russia of Dostoievski and Tolstoy, not the Russia of Stalin" (Quoted in "Wittgenstein and Russia", by John Moran, *New Left Review*, May-June 1972, p. 89).

6. Engelmann, *op. cit.*, p. 52.

7. The ambassador was Joseph Davies. Quoted in Samuel Eliot Morison, *The Oxford History of the American People* (Oxford University Press, N.Y., 1965), p. 1046.

or the increasing realization of the tyranny of the regime, is not clear.[8] In 1937, a year after he returned from Russia, he went back to Norway to live in the hut he had built before the World War. One could say that here at least he was among rural folk, though he seems to have stayed pretty much to himself, working on what would become the *Philosophical Investigations*. With the outbreak of the Second World War, however, Wittgenstein volunteered to become an orderly in a hospital in London, and was later transfered to another hospital where he worked as an X-Ray technician. Hence, his desire to "practice medicine" and serve his fellowmen was at least partially and temporarily fulfilled.

The Triumph of Ordinary Language Philosophy in Britain

During the 30s, Wittgenstein began to attract around him at Cambridge a number of very gifted students, who would later continue on in the master's style of philosophical analysis. In addition to students, there were some who held fellowships and professional chairs during the time of his Cambridge tenure who would also be greatly influenced by him. Among these Cambridge people who came under Wittgenstein's direct influence were G.E.M. Anscombe, Friedrich Waismann (who had moved to Cambridge from the University of Vienna), Norman Malcolm, John Wisdom, Alice Ambrose, and Morris Lazerowitz. Of greater impact, however, was the influence exerted by Wittgensteinian ideas on Oxford thinkers, an influence so great that the term "Oxford philosophy" would later come to designate a whole school of applied Wittgensteinians. Among the people in this latter group were Gilbert Ryle, Stuart Hampshire, H.L.A. Hart, R.M. Hare, J.O. Urmson, Geoffrey Warnock, and perhaps most important of all, J.L. Austin.[1] The sweeping impact of later Wittgensteinian philosophy in Britain, its virtual triumph in the major British universities, was a development in modern intel-

8. Georg von Wright suggests (Malcolm, *Memoir*, *op. cit.*, p. 16) that the latter was at least in part responsible—"the harshening of conditions in Russia", as he calls it.

1. This important episode in British intellectual history is taken up briefly in V.C. Chappell's introduction to his edited work, *Ordinary Language* (Prentice-Hall, Inc., Englewood Cliffs, N.J., 1964), pp. 1-4; and in John Passmore's *A Hundred Years of Philosophy* (Basic Books, Inc., N.Y., 1966), pp. 448-449.

lectual history that is truly astounding. It is true that some of the groundwork had already been laid by G.E. Moore in the early decades of the century, but the influence of Moore's common sense ideas in the 20s and 30s was nothing like that exerted by Wittgenstein's ideas in the 40s and 50s. The near total domination of British philosophy in the late 1940s by Wittgensteinian modes of thought no doubt had much to do with Wittgenstein's powerful personality, but this does not explain the eager acceptance of his ideas outside of Cambridge by people who had little personal contact with him.

For an explanation of the tremendous success of Wittgenstein's ideas in Britain, one must turn to the great historical events of the period 1930-1945, and in particular, to the rise of Nazism in Germany, and the collective effort of resistance to Nazism that culminated in the Allied victory in the Second World War. As mentioned in the previous Section, it was a popular belief among natural science oriented thinkers before World War II, that public pontification on the "great issues" of good and evil, justice and injustice, God and the world, etc., in addition to being unconfirmable through the methods of natural science, was disruptive of the public peace. But as a result of the war and the full disclosure of the enormity of the Nazi crimes, a moral consensus emerged in the Western nations—a moral lowest common denominator, one might say—which, while decrying various absolutisms (political, philosophical, and religious) came to believe that at least a minimal agreement on certain basic issues of right and wrong was necessary for civilized society to exist. No longer did thinkers believe—as Moritz Schlick and Hans Kelsen once believed—that pluralism, tolerance, and harmony would follow once people abandoned their moral and ethical convictions as unsupported and unsupportable. Moral vacuums, it was discovered, are as abhorred by nature as physical ones, and tend to be filled with a maniacal vengeance. Moreover, it was just those without a sense of right and wrong, those for whom one value was as good (or bad) as another, who seemed least capable of summoning forth from their inner depths the will and courage that was needed to resist the various criminals and madmen who would inevitably try to fill such vacuums.[2]

The impact of the war in this regard cannot be easily exaggerated—the sense of moral and spiritual solidarity in an actual life and death struggle against a demonic foe was even too much for

2. The effect of positivism and value-neutralism as a force contributing to the success of National Socialism in Germany is stressed by John Hallowell in his *The Decline of Liberalism as an Ideology* (University of California Press, 1943).

many a confirmed logical positivist. Through the medium of Wittgenstein's later philosophy, moral values would once again enter the universe of British philosophers with a respect they had not previously received. Even when it was believed that no cognitive or scientific basis existed for making choices in moral and spiritual matters, the importance of such choices was almost universally recognized as the iconoclastic-debunking spirit which had characterized such earlier works as Ayer's *Language, Truth and Logic* almost completely faded from the scene.[3] Bertrand Russell, it is true, never abandoned his basically emotivist view of ethics, nor his wish to see philosophy conform more closely to the natural sciences, but his influence in British academic circles was on the wane. The "silly things" that "silly people" say, as Russell was to characterize the language of the common man,[4] had by the end of the Second World War in Britain become the basis for a new moral and ideological consensus.

It would be a mistake, of course, to think of linguistic philosophers as particularly interested in issues of a moral, political, or religious kind. Some certainly were. Most, however, were more interested in other kinds of issues, such as the nature of human action, the philosophy of mind, linguistic performatives, psychoanalysis, the language of social science, the concept of law, and many others. But whatever their individual concerns, in contrast to positivists and logical atomists, none of the later linguistic philosophers were interested in doing away with moral-evaluative discourse or in making philosophy more like mathematics and physics.

In reflecting on this chapter in British intellectual history, there certainly seems something ironic—if not pathetic—in self-styled "philosophers", men on the very highest rung of the intellectual ladder, deferring to the linguistic conventions of the common man for their orientation and guidance in life. But this goes to show that all men, intellectuals as well as others, crave such orientation, and when it is not present in one place, it will be sought in another. Logical positivism, many British thinkers came to realize, was at best a philosophy of the natural sciences, and the real world is certainly much richer than that of the natural sciences. Natural science, many came to believe, while it plays an indespensable role in

3. Ayer himself seems to have been somewhat chastened after the war. In the 1946 introduction to the second edition of *Language, Truth and Logic*, he speaks of his former pride as "being in every sense a young man's book", and says that "much of its argument would have been more persuasive if it had not been presented in so harsh a form." (Dover Publications, Inc., N.Y., p. 5).

4. *My Philosophical Development, op. cit.*, p. 230.

our daily lives, is not much of a guide outside of its limited domain. Ordinary language philosophy, whatever one may say in criticism of it, appealed to many British thinkers after the war as a vast improvement over the single-vision and moral nihilism of its logical positivist predecessor.

IV

Linguistic Tribalism and the Revolt Against *Innerlichkeit*[1]

1. *Innerlichkeit*—inwardness, spiritual depth.

And the Lord said to Moses, Go down and warn the people, lest they break through to the Lord to gaze and many of them perish.

Exodus 19:29

There were four men who entered Paradise. Ben Azzai (the first) beheld it and died. Ben Zoma (the second) beheld it and went insane. Aher (the third) beheld it (and became a sorcerer). Only Rabbi Akiba (the fourth) entered in peace and returned in peace.

The Babylonian Talmud (*Hagigah* 14b)

Ich fuerchte mich oft vor dem Wahnsinn.

Ludwig Wittgenstein,
Culture and Value

This Being-with-one-another dissolves one's own Dasein into the kind of being of "the Others", in such a way, indeed, that the Others, as distinguishable and explicit, vanish more and more. In this inconspicuousness and unascertainability, the real dictatorship of the "they" is unfolded. We take pleasure and enjoy ourselves as *they* take pleasure; we read, see, and judge about literature and art as *they* see and judge; likewise we shrink back from the "great mass" as *they* shrink back; we find "shocking" what *they* find shocking. The "they" . . . prescribes the kind of Being of everydayness.

Martin Heidegger, *Being and Time*

Saving Society / Saving Oneself

In the previous section, Wittgenstein's late philosophy was looked at from the standpoint of the morally and culturally destructive effect of logical positivism and Wittgenstein's desire to provide some kind of counterbalance to it. This perspective is important and illuminating, yet taken by itself, it gives only a partial picture of the motivation and goals of Wittgenstein's later thought.[1] Wittgenstein

---

1. In interpreting Wittgenstein's later thought, the following works were found to be helpful: K.T. Fann, *Wittgenstein's Conception of Philosophy* (University of California Press, Berkeley, 1971) [concise account of both early and late philosophy; extensive bibliography]; Anthony Kenny, *Wittgenstein* (Harvard University Press, Cambridge, 1973) [particularly good for the works between the *Tractatus* and the *Philosophical Investigations*]; David Pears, *Ludwig Wittgenstein* (The Viking Press, New York, 1969) [valuable introductory essay]; George Pitcher, *The Philosophy of Wittgenstein* (Prentice-Hall, Englewood Cliffs, N.J., 1964) [contains one of the clearest and best accounts of Wittgenstein's philosophy, both early and late]; David Pole, *The Later Philosophy of Wittgenstein* (The Atholone Press, London, 1958) [good criticism of the "conservatism" of Wittgenstein's late philosophy, though perhaps overly timid]; Ernst Sprecht, *The Foundations of Wittgenstein's Late Philosophy* (Manchester University Press, Manchester, 1969) [clear presentation of the salient features of Wittgenstein's later thought; good bibliography]; Wolfgang Stegmueller, *Main Currents in Contemporary German, British, and American Philosophy* (Indiana University Press, Bloomington, Indiana, 1969) [extensive summary material on Wittgenstein's thought, though without the critical perspective found in the rest of the work]; Geoffrey Warnock, *English Philosophy since 1900* (Oxford University Press, London, 1958) [contains a short, concise chapter on the *Philosophical Investigations*; also an extremely valuable introductory chapter on idealism in Britain]. Of articles on Wittgenstein, the most valuable proved to be Peter Strawson's "Critical Notice" on the *Philosophical Investigations* (*Mind*, vol. 63, 1954, pp. 70-99) [a first rate review in all respects: informed, well-written, well-organized]; Paul Feyerabend's "Wittgenstein's *Philosophical Investigations*" (*Philosophical Review*, vol. 64, 1955, pp. 449-483) [stresses Wittgenstein's criticism of linguistic essentialism]; and Norman Malcolm's article on Wittgenstein in the *Encyclopedia of Philosophy* [this superb overview of Wittgenstein's life and thought is much better in its treatment of the late philosophy than the same author's widely read review of the *Philosophical Investigations* (*Philosophical Review*, vol. 63, 1954, pp. 530-559), which stands so close to the original in thought and vocabulary that it resembles more of a reduced photocopy than an independent explanation or interpretation]. And finally, of the critical works on Wittgenstein, both C.W.K. Mundle's *A Critique of Linguistic Philosophy* (Clarendon Press, Oxford, 1970), and Ernest Gellner's *Words and Things* (Routledge

was concerned, to be sure, with developing a philosophical position that would not shake the basic ethical and religious foundations of society. In this sense, it can be said, his philosophy of ordinary language was worked out with the welfare of the social order in mind. But Wittgenstein was also concerned in his later thought with his own personal predicament—or at least the predicament of others who might find themselves in a similar situation—and in particular, with the problem of overcoming the deeply rooted sense of isolation and social estrangement that had haunted him for most of his adult life. Viewed from this perspective, his philosophy can be seen as as much an exercise in self-rescue as an attempt to save society. Both of these perspectives, the personal and the social, must be taken together as divergent aspects of a more complex whole. The self-rescue aspect of his thought, moreover, can be divided into two separate but closely related themes. One might characterize these as (1) the re-integration of the self into society; and (2) the rescue of the self from the potential chaos of its own psychic depths. The first of these themes will be taken up in the material which immediately follows, while the second will be addressed, directly or indirectly, throughout most of the remainder of the section.

"Our *Language*"

The misunderstanding of the *Tractatus* was not something Wittgenstein could bear with personal equanimity. He had invested the energies of seven years of some of the most intensive thought and study imaginable, and his frustration and sense of hopelessness at the inability of even such men as Russell and Frege to grasp what he was saying proved to be acute. This can be clearly discerned in a letter he wrote to Russell (quoted in part previously) where he explains how Russell had not really understood the main contention of the book:

---

and Kegan Paul, London, 1979) proved not only helpful, but enormously refreshing [the latter, it is true, as Professor Ayer once said in a review, contains a few "cheap shots", but it also contains much trenchant polemic, and after more than 25 years still remains something of a minor classic; the 1979 edition contains a new introduction which stresses the role of Wittgenstein's late philosophy in providing a valid re-enchantment to a world threatened by the disenchanting influences of the natural sciences].

Cassino
19. 8. 19

Dear Russell,

Thanks so much for your letter dated 13 August [1919]. . . . Now I'm afraid you haven't really got hold of my main contention, to which the whole business of logical prop [ositions] is only a corollary. The main point is the theory of what can be expressed (gesagt) by prop [osition]s—i.e. by language—(and, which comes to the same, what can be *thought*) and what can not be expressed by prop [osition]s, but only shown (gezeigt); which I believe, is the cardinal problem of philosophy.

I also sent my M.S. to Frege. He wrote to me a week ago and I gather that he doesn't understand a word of it all. So my only hope is to see *you* soon and explain all to you, for it is VERY hard not to be understood by a single soul![1]

(emphasis in original)

A month and a half later, not long before their meeting at the Hague, Wittgenstein again mentions Frege in a letter to Russell:

> I've had a correspondence with Frege. He doesn't understand a word of my work and I'm totally exhausted from explaining it.[2]

The frustration of not being understood "by a single soul" would eventually become even more intense for Wittgenstein after his futile attempt to explain the *Tractatus* to Russell during their meeting at the Hague (December, 1919). Some months after this meeting he received a copy of Russell's Introduction, which indicated clearly that Russell had not understood what he was trying to say. "I'm in pretty poor shape and urgently need a talk with you," Wittgenstein wrote to his friend Paul Engelmann, after explaining how "impossible" Russell's Introduction was—especially in translation—and how he could not bring himself to have it appear in print alongside the *Tractatus*, even if this meant that the book would never be published.[3] Commenting on Wittgenstein's sense of failure and frustration in the matter, Engelmann writes

> . . . Russell's introduction may be considered one of the main reasons why the book, though recognized to this day as an event of decisive importance in the field of logic, has failed to make

1. *Letters to Russell, Keynes and Moore, op. cit.*, p. 71.
2. *Ibid.*, p. 76.
3. Engelmann, *op. cit.*, p. 31.

> itself understood as a philosophical work in the wider sense. Wittgenstein must have been deeply hurt to see that even such outstanding men, who were also helpful friends of his, were incapable of understanding his purpose in writing the *Tractatus*. And the deep depression manifest in these letters of the next few months . . . sprang from his doubt as to whether he would ever succeed in making himself understood as a philosopher.[4]

Wittgenstein's return to Cambridge in 1929 must have been the occasion for deep reflection concerning both his previous philosophy and his own relationship to the world about him. In particular, it must have been the occasion for him to reflect on the kind of mystic-prophetic philosophy which he had developed in the *Tractatus*, on where it had brought him, and on what it had done for others. And one can well imagine the results of such reflections: What good is a mystic-prophetic message, Wittgenstein must have said to himself, if it is universally misunderstood, if, in its misunderstood form, it has an actual corrupting effect on people, and if it seems to succeed only in isolating the philosopher-prophet still further from society —indeed, isolating him so completely that he has almost lost the capacity to speak? Prophetic existence, to be sure, is always a lonely, tempestuous affair, but what good is it, what beneficial purpose does it possibly serve, if no one understands what the prophet is talking about? These and similar considerations must have been in Wittgenstein's mind in 1929 and 1930 when he made the switch to ordinary language. In the uncritical acceptance of the language and culture of the ordinary man, Wittgenstein was to discover not only a measure of morality and decency for society, but a home for a tormented soul, a place of refuge from its inner isolation and estrangement. The philosopher and the common man would form a single community if only the philosopher lowered his sights and accepted the existing culture (the culture of the *Volk*) for what it was. Moreover, such a community could serve as a body to which other philosophers and intellectuals might be invited to join, provided of course, that they were willing to give up their role as critic and debunker, as well as the sense of intellectual superiority which they normally felt towards those less educated than themselves.

The key document for grasping what the acceptance of ordinary language meant for Wittgenstein personally is the *Philosophical Remarks*, his first book-length endeavor after his return to philosophy in 1929, and the first work in which he clearly begins to move

4. *Ibid.*, p. 117.

away from the *Tractatus*. On the very first page he makes the following statement:

> I do not now have phenomenological language, or 'primary language' as I used to call it, in mind as my goal. I no longer hold it to be necessary. All that is possible and necessary is to separate what is essential from what is inessential in *our* language.
> (emphasis in original)

Similarly, on the next page, Wittgenstein writes (in a remark previously quoted):

> How strange if logic were concerned with an 'ideal' language and not with *ours*. For what would this ideal language express? Presumably, what we now express in our ordinary language; in that case, this is the language logic must investigate.
> (emphasis in original)

The single italicized word "our" tells the whole story in these passages, and one can assume that it must have come to Wittgenstein as something of a catharsis. In the proclamation of ordinary language as "our" language, Wittgenstein, the alienated outsider, has decided to join the world of the common man. The philosopher is no longer to stand apart from society, either as positivist critic or prophetic reformer, and there will be little chance of what he says being seriously misunderstood, for philosophy will now seek no more than to elucidate how "we"—that is, everyday people and the philosophers who join them—ordinarily speak. In the acceptance of ordinary language as "our" language, Wittgenstein has found for the philosopher both a new home and a new task.

Closely associated with this acceptance of the community-constituting role of the public language is the emphasis which Wittgenstein places on participation in linguistic activity as a source of life and vitality. As mere sounds or marks on paper, words, Wittgenstein explains, are lifeless and dead. But when words are written or spoken as part of the ongoing activity of an actual linguistic community, they take on, he explains, a new character pregnant with vitality and meaning. "Every sign *by itself*," he says in the *Philosophical Investigations*, "seems dead." "What gives it life? In use it is alive" (PI 432). In their use as part of a language-game within an existing linguistic community, words, Wittgenstein stresses, take on a new character which they don't have in isolation. "Only in the stream of thought and life do words have meaning," he says in *Zettel* (par. 173).[5] And elsewhere: "The stream of life, or the stream of the world flows on and our propositions are so to speak verified only at instants" (*Philosophical Remarks* par. 48).

Participation in the actual linguistic life of society has thus opened up for Wittgenstein a whole new *Lebenswelt.* No longer must the philosopher be an outsider to life, shut up within his own private world, unable to communicate with those outside. With the acceptance of ordinary language as "our" language the rigid boundary between self and other has begun to disappear. Participation in the linguistic life of society, one might say, has come to replace in Wittgenstein's later thought the private meditative experience of the mystic as Wittgenstein's preferred mode of self-transcendence.

Coming in Out of the Storm: Metaphysics, Mysticism, and the Significance of the Mental Health Metaphors

One of the chief tenets of Wittgenstein's later thought is that it is a prime task of philosophy to clear up the "metaphysical" perplexities and confusions which emerge from the misuse and misunderstanding of ordinary language. Frequently the process of eliminating these perplexities and confusions is referred to by Wittgenstein in terms of metaphors drawn from the areas of psychology and mental health. In the *Blue Book*, for instance, Wittgenstein speaks of the "mental cramps" and "mental discomforts" which emerge when we become dissatisfied with ordinary language (p. 59), while in lectures given around the same time (1934), besides "mental cramps", he speaks of philosophical problems arising from "certain obsessions".[1] In the *Philosophical Investigations*, the mental health metaphors are even more pronounced:

> The philosopher's treatment of a question is like the treatment of an illness. (255)

5. *Zettel,* translated by G.E.M. Anscombe (University of California Press, Berkeley, 1967).

1. *Wittgenstein's Lectures, Cambridge 1932-1935*, edited by Alice Ambrose (Rowman and Littlefield, Totowa, N.J., 1979), pp. 90, 97-99.

> What is your aim in Philosophy? To show the fly the way out of the fly-bottle. (308)
>
> The real discovery is the one that makes me capable of stopping doing philosophy when I want to.—The one that gives philosophy peace, so that it is no longer tormented by questions which bring *itself* in question . . . There is not *a* philosophical method, though there are indeed methods, like different therapies. (133)
>
> Philosophy is a battle against the bewitchment of our intelligence by means of language. (109)

Although he doesn't offer many examples from the history of philosophy, one type of such obsession and mental cramp which Wittgenstein spends a good deal of time on (and which will be taken up in more detail later) is the search for the universal essence of a term. The assumption that each general term in a language—the word "good", for instance,—must correspond to one and only one type of object, is an assumption, according to Wittgenstein, that has led to all kinds of needless metaphysical wranglings and confusions. What must be done to clean up such needless difficulties, he says, is simply to look at the multifarious meanings which words have in actual usage. "What we do is bring words back from their metaphysical to their everyday use" (PI 116). "[Philosophical problems] are . . . not empirical problems; they are solved, rather, by looking into the workings of our language, and that in such a way as to make us recognize those workings" (PI 109). When actual usage is taken into account, we will see, according to Wittgenstein, that most universal terms have no single "essence", and that all the efforts philosophers have made in the past to determine such an essence were based upon a simple misunderstanding of the actual function of words in a language. "A philosophical trouble," he says, "is an obsession, which once removed, it seems impossible that it should ever have had power over us. It seems trivial."[2]

Thus the "torments", the "troubles", the "mental cramps", together with the "metaphysical" confusions that give rise to them—these, according to Wittgenstein, are to be eliminated from philosophy through a better understanding of the workings of ordinary language. The reader who reflects on this important theme in Wittgenstein's later thought will perhaps find himself a bit perplexed. To be sure, there have been, and no doubt will continue to be, problems in philosophy which have arisen out of a misunderstanding of language, whether it is the case of a misunderstanding of an ordi-

2. *Ibid.*, p. 98.

nary term, or a technical-philosophical one. Here few people could disagree with what Wittgenstein has to say. Moreover, it would not seem entirely inappropriate to refer to the elimination of such problems in terms of therapy or the elimination of mental cramps, even if one may not agree with the contention that the workings of ordinary language always contain the key to the solution of various difficulties. Nevertheless, though the mental health metaphors may not be entirely inappropriate, they do seem to be somewhat exaggerated. "Cramp" and "trouble" would seem to be all right, as would "therapy", but "obsession" seems to be somewhat overdrawn, and "torment" and "sickness" would seem to be definitely out of place. One has the suspicion here that there is more involved than meets the eye, and this suspicion is greatly increased when one reads what Wittgenstein has to say about the task of the philosopher in his *Remarks on the Foundation of Mathematics*:

> The philosopher is a man who has to cure himself of many sicknesses of the understanding before he can arrive at the notion of the sound human understanding. If in the midst of life we are in death, so in sanity we are surrounded by madness (*Wahnsinn*).[3]

Here the mental health metaphor is so overdrawn—with talk of "life" and "death", "sanity" and "madness"—that it would seem as if something extraneous, some personal element, for instance, has crept into the discussion. It has already been remarked how Wittgenstein could become so engrossed in a philosophical problem that it would take on the quality of an obsession, and how he would try to overcome one obsession by the superimposition of another (such as viewing a motion picture from the very first row of a theatre). And Wittgenstein, no doubt, thought of certain kinds of philosophical puzzles and perplexities in terms of such obsessive behavior. But as he says in the above quotation, the philosopher must cure himself of *many* sicknesses before he can arrive at health, and the fact of the matter is that obsessive thinking, at least of the kind involved in his academic work, was hardly the most serious of Wittgenstein's mental problems, or the one that was most likely uppermost in his mind in his use of the more radical type of mental health metaphor. A fear of madness and insanity were, in fact, not something Wittgenstein spoke of second-hand, nor, it would seem in the quotation from the *Remarks on the Foundation of Mathematics*, metaphorically. As can be discerned from the testimony of those who

3. (MIT Press, Cambridge, 1967), sec IV, par. 53, p. 157e.

knew him best and from what he himself says in several letters to friends, an actual fear of psychic disintegration and mental chaos was one which haunted Wittgenstein throughout much of his adult life. George von Wright, for instance, in his "Biographical Sketch", describes the situation in its simplest terms:

> It is probably true that he [Wittgenstein] lived on the border of mental illness. A fear of being driven across it followed him throughout his life.[4]

The only thing one might quarrel with in this statement is the use of the term "mental illness". What von Wright clearly means here is "insanity". Wittgenstein's own description of his psychic states at various times of his life renders any lesser term clearly inappropriate. In one of his letters to Engelmann, for instance, which was written not long after the rejection of the *Tractatus* by a large publishing house, Wittgenstein describes the following about himself:

> . . . as far as the merits of my case are concerned I am beyond any outside help.—In fact I am in a state of mind that is terrible to me. I have been through it several times before: it is the state of *not being able to get over a particular fact*. It is a pitiable state, I know. . . . But this is just like what happens when a man who can't swim has fallen into the water and flails about with his hands and feet and feels that he is simply incapable of staying above water. That is the position I am in now. I know that killing oneself is always a rotten thing to do. Surely one cannot will one's own destruction, and anybody who has considered what is involved in the act of suicide knows that suicide is always an attempt to take oneself by surprise. And nothing is worse than to have to take oneself by surprise.[5]

Thoughts of suicide were nothing new to Wittgenstein at this time. Not only does he mention them in two other letters to Engelmann, but he once told his friend David Pinsent that before coming to Cambridge in 1912, hardly a day went by without him thinking of suicide as at least a possibility.[6] And though for a time such thoughts apparently subsided, his torments certainly did not end with his study in Cambridge. For instance, writing to Russell in January of 1914 from his hut in Norway, he vividly describes the

4. Malcolm, *Memoir, op. cit.*, p. 3.
5. Engelmann, *op. cit.*, pp. 33-34.
6. See Malcolm's article on Wittgenstein in *The Encyclopedia of Philosophy*, volume 8, p. 327.

psychic horrors he had recently had to endure, and his inability as a result to do any substantial thinking in logic:

> . . . It's VERY sad but I've once again no logical news for you. The reason is that things have gone terribly bad for me in the last few weeks. (A result of my "holidays" in Vienna.) Everyday I was tormented alternately by a horrible sense of dread and by a depression, and even after these had subsided I was so exhausted I couldn't even think of doing work. It's terrifying beyond all description the kinds of mental torment there can be! It wasn't until two days ago that I could hear the voice of reason over the howls of the demons (*Laerm der Gespenster*) and could begin to do work again. And *perhaps* I'll get better now and be able to produce something decent. But *never* did I imagine what it's like to feel just *one* step away from insanity (*Wahnsinn*).—Let's hope for the best![7]

In another letter to Russell written in the summer of the same year, Wittgenstein again speaks of the volatility of his psychic condition and his temporary inability to do work in logic:

> . . . Here I feel different every day. Sometimes things inside me are in such a ferment that I think I'm going mad: then the next day I am totally apathetic again. But deep inside me there's a perpetual seething, like the bottom of a geyser, and I keep on hoping that things will come to an eruption once and for all, so that I can turn into a different person. I can't write you anything about logic today.[8]

During the time of his employment as a rural school teacher, Wittgenstein wrote a letter to his sister Hermine in which he describes what a great struggle it had been for him in just maintaining his mental equilibrium. His sister, who had found it strange that he had not sought to put his higher education to a more appropriate use, simply could not understand, Wittgenstein says in the letter, the struggle that was going on within him:

> You are like someone who, looking through a closed window, can't explain the strange movements of a passerby. He doesn't know what kind of a storm is raging outside and that this person is perhaps only with great effort keeping himself on his feet.[9]

7. *Letters to Russell, Keynes and Moore, op. cit.*, p. 47.
8. *Ibid.*, pp. 57-58.
9. Bernhard Leitner, *The Architecture of Ludwig Wittgenstein, op. cit.*, p. 19.

Wittgenstein may have been better at keeping himself on his feet after his return to academic life, though his psychic instability had by no means passed. In a letter to Malcolm as late as February, 1948, for instance, he could write:

> I am now in very good bodily health and my work isn't going bad either. I have occasionally queer states of nervous instability about which I'll only say that they're rotten while they last, and teach one to pray.[10]

Malcolm himself, whose acquaintance with Wittgenstein dates from the late 30s, speaks in his *Memoir* of Wittgenstein's great depression, and of the "intensity of his mental and moral suffering."[11]

Thus when Wittgenstein talked of sanity and madness, of mental sickness and mental health, he did so from the standpoint of a life situation in which problems of this nature were real and of overriding importance. Still, the initial perplexity which proceeds from a reflection on the mental health metaphors is hardly eliminated by the knowledge that some personal element may be involved here. One still is left with the question of why the elimination of "metaphysical" and other confusions of language should be referred to by what would seem to be highly exaggerated metaphors which are apparently pregnant with meaning for their author. Could Wittgenstein really have wanted to suggest some kind of relationship between insanity, in the literal and full meaning of the term, and his later philosophy of ordinary language? As it turns out, this is just what Wittgenstein did want to suggest, and the connection between the two is to be discerned from a conversation he had with Maurice Drury. Drury, who was a medical doctor, had discussed with Wittgenstein certain psychiatric symptoms which he had encountered that puzzled him greatly. Wittgenstein, in reply, made the following remark:

> You should never cease to be amazed at symptoms mental patients show. If I became mad the thing I would fear most would be your common-sense attitude. That you would take it all as a matter of course that I should be suffering from delusions.[12]

Wittgenstein here is, of course, trying to provide Drury with information that would be of some comfort to his patients. The world

10. Malcolm, *op. cit.*, p. 74.
11. *Ibid.*, p. 99.
12. Quoted in K.T. Fann, editor, *Ludwig Wittgenstein: The Man and His Philosophy* (Humanities Press, N.Y.), p. 67.

of ordinary language and common sense Wittgenstein knew from first-hand experience, cannot begin to fathom the nature of those radically altered states of consciousness—whether beatific or horrific—which often lead to the severe psychic imbalances that wind people up in mental hospitals.[13] Knowledge of this would certainly be reassuring to those who have experienced such states of consciousness and met only with the uncomprehending inhabitants of the ordinary, common-sense universe.[14] But what is most important here for present purposes is the corollary warning which can be derived from what Wittgenstein has told Drury.[15] This corollary warning, which again was something the truth of which Wittgenstein knew first-hand, might be phrased something like the following: "While you may have great insights, once you leave the world of common sense and ordinary language, you run the risk of social isolation and outright madness." From the standpoint of such a warning, of course, it can easily be seen how acceptance of the world of ordinary language and common-sense could come to be

---

13. The relation between altered states of consciousness and mental imbalance cannot be taken up here. The present writer, however, is in agreement with Anton Boisen (*The Exploration of the Inner World, Out of the Depths*) that the difference between, on the one hand, the Beatific and Dark Night experiences associated with prophets and saints, and on the other, the manic flights and psychotic crashes associated with people who wind up in mental institutions is to be sought not on the phenomenological plane (where the experiences are often quite similar), but on the plane of personality transformation. The value and importance of an experience is always to be seen in terms of how a person has responded to it—how, that is, the experience has been integrated into the person's life, and what changes have followed from it.

14. Again the issue raised here cannot be taken up within the present context, though the present writer, it should be mentioned, believes there is much truth in R.D. Laing's contention that many psychiatrists have more to learn from their patients than the patients from the psychiatrists.

15. Wittgenstein, it should be mentioned, seriously thought in the mid-30s of becoming a psychiatrist, no doubt believing that he had a better understanding of the experiences and inner torments of mental patients than most other people. On this, Drury writes: "[I received] another letter from Wittgenstein, in which he suggested that if he did qualify as a doctor he and I might practise together as psychiatrists. He felt that he might have a special talent for this branch of medicine." Drury also explains how Wittgenstein, during a visit to Dublin, sought access to some of the mental patients at a local hospital: "During his visit to Dublin Wittgenstein asked me if I could arrange for him to have discussions with patients who were seriously mentally ill. He said this would be a matter of great interest to him. . . . Wittgenstein then went two or three days a week and visited some of the long stay patients who had few to visit them. He became particularly interested in one elderly man, of whom he said: 'This man is much more intelligent than his doctors.' . . . I was fascinated to see how gently and helpfully Wittgenstein was able to discuss with him." (*Ludwig Wittgenstein: Personal Recollections*, edited by Rush Rhees, *op. cit.*, pp. 151, 154, 155)

closely associated in Wittgenstein's mind with sanity and mental health.

And metaphysics could become the great temptation to be overcome in Wittgenstein's later philosophy precisely because, next to logical positivism, it was metaphysics which offered the greatest challenge to the sovereignty of ordinary language and the common-sense way of viewing things. This point, however, is in need of further elaboration. In his account of Wittgenstein's lectures, G.E. Moore records the following remarks Wittgenstein made about the new method he was introducing into philosophy:

> He said also that we were "in a muddle about things," which we had to try to clear up; that we had to follow a certain instinct which leads us to ask certain questions, though we don't even understand what these questions mean; that our asking them results from "a vague mental uneasiness," like that which leads children to ask "Why?"; and that this uneasiness can only be cured "either by showing that a particular question is not permitted, or by answering it."[16]

Wittgenstein seems to be reflecting here on what might be called man's primordial sense of wonder—i.e. on that certain instinct in man which leads him as a child to ask Why?, and as an adult to pursue metaphysical—philosophical forms of questioning. "Why is there something, and not nothing?," "Why are things the way they are and not different?," Heidegger and Leibnitz ask; "Why am I, and why is the whole world?" is Tolstoy's question. In each case, the primordial sense of wonder has given rise to a metaphysical form of inquiry. Elsewhere Wittgenstein identifies this kind of inquiry, in so far as it deals with the character of existing language and culture, with the dimension of depth in man. "The problems arising through a misinterpretation of our forms of language," he says in the *Philosophical Investigations*, "have the character of *depth*. They are deep disquietudes" (PI 111).

Metaphysical constructions, and the linguistic confusions often contained therein, Wittgenstein realized, proceed from deep existential yearnings—what he previously had called the "urge to the mystical." Stirred by wonder, desiring to know "Why?", men often undertake the philosophical quest to discover the ultimate origin of their own being and the being of the universe. "For it is owing to their wonder," as Aristotle says in his *Metaphysics* (982B), "that men both now begin and at first began to philosophize." In the

16. "Moore Lecture," *op. cit.*, p. 284.

Tractatus Wittgenstein had sought to dispel metaphysical constructions so as to *heighten* the "urge to the mystical" and the language-transcending experience towards which it leads. This, as was explained in Section II, was in the long tradition of the *via negativa*. But now, in his late philosophy, Wittgenstein seeks to dispel metaphysical constructions—i.e. "bring words back from their metaphysical to their everyday use"—not merely because of the linguistic confusions such constructions often involve (this was, of course, also a motive in the *Tractatus*), but for the very reason that they proceed from the mystical urge. It is the mystical, i.e., the depth region of the soul where the divine seeks out the human, and where the "deep disquietudes" and "vague mental uneasiness" have their origin, that Wittgenstein wishes to dispel from man's consciousness, at least in so far as the truth of this dimension is not already externally represented in existing public language games (in the language of aesthetics and religion, for instance). In this incredible about-face from the *Tractatus*, Wittgenstein has chosen to stress the fact that the wonder and disquietudes which often give birth to metaphysics, while they can lead to private insights and ultimate assurances of being "absolutely safe", can also open up regions of the mind and modes of experience that lead to social estrangement, psychic imbalance, or outright insanity. The depressions and dark nights, Wittgenstein knew, are as much a part of the depth dimension as the ecstasies and illuminations, and the new focus of his philosophy has come to be the avoidance of the former rather than the experiencing of the latter. We must be "cured" of the desire to enter the depth—to go beyond the ordinary—as from an "illness".

Metaphysics and the urge to go beyond ordinary language are thus intimately tied up with Wittgenstein's idea of philosophy as a mental health therapeutic—and this idea, once again, is to be taken quite literally. It is not just the linguistic muddles and confusions involved in running up against ordinary language which concerned Wittgenstein. While he certainly was concerned with these, at a profounder level, his concern with the inviolability of ordinary language and the common-sense way of viewing things was a concern with sanity itself and the mental stability of the philosopher.[17] To

17. Of the more widely read commentators on Wittgenstein, Peter Strawson seems to have been the only one to have detected at least an inkling of this element. In his review of the *Philosophical Investigations* (*Mind*, vol. 63, 1954, pp. 70-99), he rightly attributes to Wittgenstein a "fear of legitimizing certain metaphysical doubtings and wonderings" (p. 99). Strawson himself is in favor of what he calls a "purged kind of metaphysics". The idea, he suggests, "that the *sole* purpose of the distinctions we draw attention to, the descriptions we give of the different ways in which words func-

go beyond ordinary language and the world of common sense, as mystics and metaphysicians try to do, was to court psychic chaos. In rejecting metaphysics and the depth dimension of the soul, Wittgenstein, one might say, voted to come in out of the storm. His tormented soul was to seek its peace in the security of the ordinary.

Towards a Behaviorist View of Mind: The Revolt Against Inwardness

If the mental health metaphors and the remarks made to Drury, together with known facts from Wittgenstein's personal history, lead one to the conclusion that at least part of the motivation for Wittgenstein's later philosophy was the fear of unleashing potentially imbalancing forces in the depths of the human psyche, the most important theoretical manifestation of this state of affairs is to be found in the quasi-behaviorist account of mental terms which Wittgenstein develops. Wittgenstein's philosophy of mind is one of the most important aspects of his later thought, and owing in part to its systematic elaboration and further development by Gilbert Ryle in his *The Concept of Mind*,[1] one which has been much discussed by commentators. Yet there has been virtually no effort, at least as far as the present writer is aware, to relate the philosophy of mind to Wittgenstein's personal psychic and social situation.

The salient features of Wittgenstein's philosophy of mind can be summed up in the following statement: The so called "inner" or mental aspects of human experience are significant to human life only as part of an external, publicly observable process of actions

---

tion, is to dispel particular metaphysical confusions," is "unduly restrictive." "Even if we *begin* with a therapeutic purpose," he says, "our interest might not exhaust itself when that purpose is achieved." "It is surely over-puritanical to hold that, just because the claims made [on behalf of metaphysical doctrines] for such new ways [of looking at things] were too large, we should be concerned solely with preventing ourselves from seeing the world afresh. We might make room for a purged kind of metaphysics, with more modest and less disputable claims than the old. . . . Could not the activities we call 'doing philosophy' also form a family?" (p. 78). If the interpretation offered in this section is correct, it would have to be realized that Wittgenstein didn't *want* to see the world afresh. It was the very security offered by established linguistic custom and common ways of viewing things that, in part at least, attracted him to ordinary language.

---

1. Barnes and Noble, Inc., N.Y., 1949.

and events. As Wittgenstein says in the *Philosophical Investigations*, "an 'inner process' stands in need of outward criteria" (PI 580). This may sound a good deal like psychological behaviorism, and indeed it is. Wittgenstein, it is true, does acknowledge in certain places inner activities and events which he does not try to translate into, or reduce to, the external manifestations of those activities and events.[2] Nevertheless, the thrust of his entire analysis is so much towards the external, publicly observable aspects of mental activities, that in practical terms his position is hardly distinguishable from that of conventional behaviorism. Perhaps the major difference between Wittgenstein's philosophy of mind and that held by most behaviorists is Wittgenstein's greater stress on the situational context, and in particular, on the rules and customs of the society in which linguistic behavior is observed.

The flavor and content of this view of mind might be gathered from what Wittgenstein says about the activity of thinking:

> It is misleading then to talk of thinking as of a "mental activity". We may say that thinking is essentially the activity of operating with signs. This activity is performed by the hand, when we think by writing; by the mouth and larynx, when we think by speaking; and if we think by imagining signs or pictures, I can give you no agent that thinks. If then you say that in such cases the mind thinks, I would only draw your attention to the fact that you are using a metaphor . . .
>
> If again we talk about the locality where thinking takes place we have a right to say that this locality is the paper on which we write, or the mouth which speaks.
>
> (BB pp. 6-7)

One might normally conceive of thinking as an activity which goes on in the mind, but here and elsewhere Wittgenstein is willing to concede the mind as a possible site of thought only with great hesitation, for he clearly prefers to conceive of thinking as the publicly observable use of language. As such, its organ is not in the mind, but in the hand of the writer or the mouth of the speaker. Thinking is not something internal, but external; not private, but public. "Thinking is not something that accompanies talking," Wittgen-

2. E.g. "'I noticed that he was out of humor.' Is this a report about his behavior or his state of mind? . . . Both, not side-by-side, however, but about the one *via* the other." (PI II, p. 179). "My attitude towards him is an attitude towards a soul. I am not of the *opinion* that he has a soul." (PI II, p. 178). In general, one might say that there are more concessions to the introspectivist (non-behaviorist) view of mind in the *Blue Book* than in the *Philosophical Investigations*.

stein says in one of his lectures; "it may just be the talking."[3] "Don't look to the inner, look to the outer," might be Wittgenstein's slogan here. In the *Philosophical Grammar*, thinking is compared to the activity of a sewing machine, with the understanding that what really counts is the outer stitch, rather than the internal workings of the machine:

> We ask: "What is a thought? What kind of thing must something be to perform the function of thought?" This question is like: "What is a sewing machine, how does it work?"—And the answer which would be like ours would be, "Look at the stich it is meant to sew; you can see from that what is essential in the machine; everything else is optional." (PG, par. 63)

The case is similar with understanding. Understanding, for Wittgenstein, is not to be equated with an inner insight, with a flash in the mind for instance, that assures a person that he has understood something, say, the formula for a mathematical series. Understanding rather, is to be seen as just those outward acts—e.g. the writing of a correct mathematical formula—which show that understanding has taken place. Wittgenstein, however, doesn't want the reader to think of understanding as taking place in one realm—an inner, mental realm—only then to be communicated through, or expressed in, another. Rather, as in the case of thinking, he wants the reader to shift his notion of the site where understanding takes place to the outer, public realm itself. "In the sense in which there are processes (including mental processes), which are characteristic of understanding, understanding," says Wittgenstein, "is not a mental process" (PI 154). "Try not to think of understanding as a 'mental process' at all—For that is the expression which confuses you. But ask yourself: in what sort of case, in what kind of circumstances [i.e. in what sort of external situations and contexts] do we say, 'Now I know how to go on' [i.e. with a mathematical series] . . . " (PI 154).

The activities of wishing, remembering, and meaning a thing by a word are similarly for Wittgenstein not to be seen as primarily inner or mental activities. When one utters a word and means something by it, Wittgenstein holds, the meaning of the word is not a mental accompaniment of the word, but just the utterance itself within its linguistic and non-linguistic context. "The question, 'What do I mean by that?'," says Wittgenstein, "is one of the most misleading of expressions. In most cases one might answer: Nothing

3. *Wittgenstein's Lectures, Cambridge, 1932-1935, op. cit.*, p. 52.

at all—I *say* . . . "[4] "And nothing is more wrong-headed than calling meaning a mental activity! Unless, that is, one is setting out to produce confusion" (PI 693). "The meaning of a phrase for us is characterized by the use we make of it. The meaning is not a mental accompaniment to the expression" (BB p. 65).

When Wittgenstein speaks of the use of a term, he is particularly interested in stressing the external context, including all rules and social customs, in which the term appears. He frequently compares the use of a word to making a move in a game of chess: "Words and chess pieces are analogous; knowing how to use a word is like knowing how to move a chess piece . . . knowing how a piece is to be used is not a particular state of mind which goes on while the game goes on. The meaning of a word is to be defined by the rules for its use, not by the feeling that attaches to the words."[5]

With the activities of wishing and remembering, Wittgenstein is equally concerned with de-emphasizing the significance of inner processes of any kind. While he does not deny that processes of this kind may go on in cases where one can speak of wishing, remembering, thinking, etc., the tendency in his writings is to view such processes as epiphenomenon, whereas the core of the phenomenon is to be sought on the plane of observable behavior. Wittgenstein in fact comes very close in certain places to actually identifying mental states and mental activities with the outer linguistic expression of those states and activities. "Remember," he says, "that the expression of a wish can be the wish, and that the expression doesn't derive its sense from the presence of some extraordinary spirit" (PG par. 103). And with remembering: "Remembering . . . isn't at all the mental process that one imagines at first sight. If I say, rightly, 'I remember it' the most *varied* things may happen; perhaps even just that I say it" (PG par. 42). Summing up a good deal of discussion on this general topic, Wittgenstein writes in the *Blue Book*: "I have been trying in all this to remove the temptation to think that there '*must* be' what is called a mental process of thinking, hoping, wishing, believing, etc., independent of the process of expressing a thought, a hope, a wish, etc. . . . If you are puzzled about the nature of thought, belief, knowledge, and the like, substitute for the thought the expression of the thought, etc." (BB pp. 41, 42).

Some mental activities, one might think, such as imagining or thinking to oneself, have no external mode of expression. While Wittgenstein does not deny this, he suggests that in principle at

4. *Zettel, op. cit.*, par. 4.
5. *Wittgenstein's Lectures, Cambridge,* 1932-1935, *op. cit.*, p. 3.

least, all that goes on in the mind in most instances might just as well transpire on the external, physical plane. "There is one way," says Wittgenstein, "of avoiding at least partly the occult appearance of the process of thinking, and it is, to replace in these processes any working of the imagination by acts of looking at real objects." ". . . why should I not substitute seeing a red bit of paper," he says, "for imagining a red patch? The visual image will only be the more vivid. Imagine a man always carrying a sheet of paper in his pocket on which the names of colours are co-ordinated with coloured patches" (BB p. 4). "We could perfectly well, for our purposes," says Wittgenstein, "replace every process of imagining by a process of looking at an object or by painting, drawing or modelling; and every process of speaking to oneself by speaking aloud or by writing" (BB p. 4). In this manner, according to Wittgenstein, the "occult appearance" of the process of imagining and thinking would disappear.

In assessing Wittgenstein's philosophy of mind (or anti-philosophy of mind, as it is perhaps better described) the interpreter must at first confront what is surely a glaring contradiction. On the one hand, Wittgenstein's later philosophy offers a manner of looking at language and the world which has the effect of exalting the common-sense and linguistic conventions of the ordinary man. On the other hand, in his quasi-behaviorist account of mental activities and mental terms, Wittgenstein suggests a way of looking at mental processes which differs radically from the usual common-sense view, and is actually much closer to that of the logical positivists and linguistic constructivists whom he opposes.[6] Surely no descriptive account of how ordinary people use ordinary mental terms would suggest a view of mind anything like that suggested by Wittgenstein. Consider, for instance, the following: "*Now* I understand why she was so rude to me last summer at the party"; "Despair was certainly a constant temptation, but we never gave up hope"; "When I was a little boy I used to dream that I was falling through a well"; "There's nothing wrong with his body, it's his mind that's sick"—In each of these very ordinary statements there is pre-supposed an introspectivist understanding of mind that is clearly at odds with the philosophy of mind outlined by Wittgenstein. The simple fact of the matter is that for most people the activities designated by such terms as "thinking", "understanding", "meaning", "wishing", "remembering", "imagining", etc., are understood primarily as inner, mental operations, though ones, of course, not necessarily uncon-

6. This, no doubt, accounted for much of its appeal to a one-time positivist such as Ryle.

nected with an external, physical world. This, it would seem, is implicitly recognized by Wittgenstein in the great deal of effort he invests in countering the common-sense protests of his hypothetical interlocutors. Similarly, the activities designated by such terms as "running", "jumping", "swimming", "driving a car", "cleaning house", "shining shoes", etc., are seen primarily as external, physical activities—though again, in like manner, not necessarily unconnected with an inner realm of mind. The great lot of mankind it would seem, believes that it is important, at least for certain purposes, to distinguish a mental from a physical aspect of human experience without trying to reduce the one to the other. Most people, in other words, are implicitly dualists.

This striking contradiction between the common sense/ordinary language aspect of Wittgenstein's later philosophy, and its quasi-behaviorist elements has not gone unnoticed by commentators. William Barrett, for instance, in his *The Illusion of Technique*, asks rhetorically just how far one can go in Wittgenstein's behaviorist-like direction without abandoning the normativeness of ordinary language:

> The force thus of Wittgenstein's emphasis upon the intrinsic connection of meaning and use is to turn us away from the fictitious inner cabinet of the mind into the open and public world, where people talk and behave toward each other in the ordinary situations of life. The emphasis is thus plainly behaviorist throughout. The question remains: How far does this behaviorist tendency in Wittgenstein go? Indeed, how far can it rightly go if ordinary language is taken as an arbiter?[7]

In a similar spirit Grover Maxwell and Herbert Feigl, in their article "Why Ordinary Language Needs Reforming", attack both Gilbert Ryle and Norman Malcolm for accepting uncritically this basic contradiction in Wittgenstein's thought:

> . . . Professor Gilbert Ryle adduces a kind of ontological proof or transcendental deduction of the nonexistence of private mental states or events such as pain, anger, elation, etc. He purports to do this by exhibiting our actual use of such terms and comes to the remarkable conclusion that they *mean* or refer to nothing but actual and/or possible behavior. . . . it would be hard to imagine a more radical departure from common sense and ordinary usage than that which Professor Ryle proposes. We are more sure of the fact that when we token 'Jones is in pain', we do

7. Doubleday and Company, Garden City, N.Y., 1979, p. 76.

not *mean* or intend to refer to his actual or possible behavior than we are of any philosophical thesis.

. . . Professor Norman Malcolm goes even further and suggests that sentences such as 'I am in pain' are perhaps not reports at all but are to be classified with such acts as limping, crying, holding one's leg, etc. It is one of those delightful ironies of philosophy that Professor Malcolm, for whom *any* departure from ordinary language was, at least at one time, anathema and who emphatically maintained that ordinary use is *correct use* should propose the most radical departure from ordinary language of which we have ever heard. Professor Malcolm arrives at his position, of course, by following the footsteps of the master [i.e. Wittgenstein].[8]

C.W.K. Mundle has similar comments to make about Ryle's unwillingness to accord to mind any independent existence as either substance or cause. Speaking of "Ryle's claim that all sentences which conjoin or disjoin terms like 'body' and 'mind', or 'mental . . .' and 'physical . . .' are category-mistakes, are not 'proper', are 'absurd' and 'make no sense'," Mundle writes:

As examples of such absurd conjunctions he [Ryle] gives: "there exist both minds and bodies", "there occur physical processes and mental processes," "there are mechanical causes . . . and mental causes of corporeal movements." Ryle certainly appears here to be correcting, and not describing English usage; for his dicta involve treating as senseless sentences which are commonly used and understood, like "He is strong (healthy or resilient) in mind and body" or "His behavior had both mental and physical causes."[9]

The source of Ryle's piece of *a priori* and/or legislative linguistics is the fact that he seeks support from ordinary language for rejecting a theory which is, and for affirming theories which are not, built into the grammar of English.[10]

Stuart Hampshire finally, in his review of *The Concept of Mind*, suggests criticisms of the Ryle-Wittgenstein view of mind almost identical to those of Mundle:

. . . common-sense language is in fact, for better or for worse, firmly dualistic, in the sense that we do operate—and have op-

8. In *The Linguistic Turn*, edited by Richard Rorty (University of Chicago Press, 1967), p. 199.

9. *A Critique of Linguistic Philosophy*, *op. cit.*, p. 42.

10. *Ibid.*, p. 45.

> erated since the earliest known literature—a distinction, or rather a whole st of distinctions, involving various and shifting criteria, between mental and physical states and events: we constantly ask, and are beginning to answer, various more or less general questions about the relation between a person's body and his mind, questions which cannot therefore be dismissed as "improper" if ordinary usage is to be authoritative; it is Professor Ryle, and not only Descartes, who displays an *a priori* theory of language involving a conflict with established usage, when he rejects the dogma that "there occur physical processes and mental processes, that there are mechanical causes of corporeal movements, and mental causes of corporeal movements," and argues that "these and other analogous conjunctions are absurd" . . .[11]

The Wittgensteinian account of mental activities and mental terms as presented in all his later works, must be seen, in fact, as one continuous series of persuasive definitions rather than a simple description. So understood the question naturally arises as to what exactly Wittgenstein is trying to persuade us of, and what he hopes to gain by so doing. A first approach to an answer should be clear as to what exactly Wittgenstein is *not* trying to do through his quasi-behavioral account of mental activities, for there are many reasons which can move people in the direction of a behaviorist outlook. For some, the simplicity and seeming scientific precision offered by behaviorist method is the chief allurement, and as a philosophical position, behaviorism is frequently arrived at by research scientists—or at least by those who identify closely with the task of research scientists—who, recognizing the positive value of behavioral methodology, tend to expand that methodology into a reality encompassing world-view. For others, however, the allurement of behaviorism is not merely in its greater theoretical precision and simplicity, but in the feeling of superiority over people which it conveys by virtue of the inevitable selective application of the behaviorist viewpoint to the thoughts and actions of those other than the behaviorist himself. Behavioral psychologists in particular—and here Skinner and Watson are prototypical cases—inevitably envision themselves in the role of conditioners rather than conditioned, and interpret their own beliefs as the result of scientific inquiry and rational reflection, rather than a mere manifestation of verbal behavior. There are still others, finally—though these cases are quite rare and hardly exist in a pure form at all—for whom the allurement of be-

11. *Mind,* April 1950, pp. 237-255.

haviorism must be sought in the one-sidedness of their own personal and psychological development such that a behaviorist view of mind can appear as a fully satisfying account of the dynamics of the human psyche.

With Wittgenstein, however, none of these reasons apply. His rejection (or near-rejection) of an inner or mental realm independent of an external world had nothing to do with the requirements of a research methodology. He had no special interest in advancing behavioral research, and no desire whatever to condition people according to his will. Moreover, his inner mental life was hardly so stunted in its development, so one-sidedly warped in its growth, that the depth and richness of the human psyche could appear to him as fully accounted for by a behaviorist view of mind. (On the contrary, his remarks to Drury about mental patients, together with his continued interest in spiritual and introspectivist authors, would show that he clearly held an opposite view). But if Wittgenstein didn't adopt a behaviorist outlook for the usual sorts of reasons that people do, the question still remains as to what his reasons were. And the answer here must be sought in that same fear of the potentially imbalancing effect of a plunge into the soul's depths that has given rise to the mental health metaphors.

Wittgenstein's fear of insanity, as we have seen, was quite real, and his account of mental activities begins to make much more sense once it is viewed within the context of this fear. As previously explained, his defense of common-sense and ordinary language was at least partially motivated by a desire to direct the mind away from its own depth and inwardness, which was sensed as potentially dangerous. By directing the mind's attention to the outer realm of public discourse and public activities, it would be effectively saved from those radically altered states of consciousness which could prove so devastating to the introspectivist thinker. Like the man who has been nearly drowned and is determined never again to go near the water, Wittgenstein has decided never again to let his attention stray from the land. But there was a major difficulty with this kind of position. The ordinary language of public discourse, as it turns out, is shot through and through with mind-predicates which are usually interpreted in a clearly introspectivist manner. So unless the mind were to be permitted to reflect upon itself once again, these mind-predicates would have to be re-interpreted persuasively to refer to external activities and events. Hence, we have the curious combination of a defense of ordinary language and common-sense, coupled with a behaviorist-like view of mental activities and mental terms. It was the fear of the psyche and its depth which was responsible (in part) for Wittgenstein's acceptance of the world of common-sense and ordinary language, and it was this same fear which was again responsible for his rejection of common-sense and ordinary language at that one point where common-sense and ordinary language threatened to reopen what he had hoped to close.

Every effort is taken in his account of mental activities to direct the reader's attention to the external, sense-perceivable world so that, through a pre-occupation of the mind with the outer, all first-hand contact with the inner would be banished. The inner is permitted to live on only as it is expressed outwardly, either through linguistic or non-linguistic behavior. This obsessive pre-occupation with the external, one might say, is the price of psychic stability; a neurotic form of existence is set forth as a defense against the greater threat of psychotic disintegration and chaos. And thus all sorts of deprecating pejoratives are used in referring to the mind as an inner realm—"occult character", "extraordinary spirit", "a shadowy being"—so as to discredit the common-sense viewpoint. One casts aspersions upon the ghost in the machine (to use the metaphor of a later Wittgensteinian) so as not to conjure up the demon that lurks there.

Towards a Behaviorist View of Mind: The Revolt Against Privacy

The direction of attention away from the inner realm of consciousness and mind to the outer world of objects and things is closely tied to another aspect of Wittgenstein's later philosophy; namely, its rejection, at least for purposes of a philosophy of language, of the notion of a private or personal sphere inaccessible to public view. His remarks in this regard are part of an extended discussion in the *Philosophical Investigations* on the use of sensation words, and particularly of the word "pain". One of his main contentions is that words for sensations, as part of a public language, not only have a public meaning, but public referents as well. It is impossible, Wittgenstein holds, for words to refer to private objects—i.e., objects inaccessible to public view—and still remain part of a public language. This is stated perhaps most clearly in his famous allegory of the beetle in the box, where he tries to demonstrate the impossibility of interpersonal communication if the sensation words in a public language really referred to objects which each person knew only privately from his own personal case. The beetle can be taken as a metaphor not only for pain, but for any sensation or alleged inner, private event; the box for the human body, or at least that aspect of the human body which can normally be observed by others:

> Now someone tells me that *he* knows what pain is only from his own case!—Suppose everyone had a box with something in it: we call it a "beetle". No one can look into anyone else's box, and everyone says he knows what a beetle is only by looking at *his* beetle.—Here it would be quite possible for everyone to have something different in his box. One might even imagine such a thing constantly changing.—But suppose the word "beetle" had a use in these people's language?—If so it would not be used as the name of a thing. The thing in the box has no place in the language-game at all; not even as a *something*: for the box might even be empty.—No, one can 'divide through' by the thing in the box; it cancels out, whatever it is.
>
> That is to say: if we construe the grammar of the expression of sensation on the model of 'object and designation' the object [i.e. the private, inner object] drops out of consideration as irrelevant.
>
> (PI 293)

Wittgenstein seems to be saying two things here about the relationship between a private object and a public language, one of which is very radical—and very wrong—the other of which is less radical and much less disputable. The less disputable thesis holds that it would be very difficult, if not impossible, to communicate one's private sensations (one's beetle) to others if those sensations were not linked in some way to some kind of external, publicly observable criteria for their occurrence—if the only way open, in other words, for one mind to know the contents of another mind were through a kind of telepathy. But this relatively non-controversial thesis is interwoven in the bettle analogy with a much more radical one; namely, that in talk about sensations such as pain we can dispense with concern over the inner or private object altogether and concentrate instead exclusively on what is publicly observable. It is this latter idea, so obviously contrary to common-sense and our ordinary way of understanding sensation words[1] that leads one prominent Wittgenstein interpreter to speak of his "prejudice

---

1. C.W.K. Mundle asks rhetorically what the adjectives we normally ascribe to "pain" such as "throbbing", "stabbing", "dull", etc., could possibly describe if not the inner pain-sensation itself (*A Critique of Linguistic Philosophy, op. cit.*, p. 213).

against the inner" and his "hostility to the doctrine of privacy."[2] It is important to recognize, both here and elsewhere, that Wittgenstein is *not* suggesting, *Tractatus*-like, that the inner or private realm involves modes of experience that are too intimate or personal to be properly expressed through public language. The message he wants to convey is clear and simple: Forget about the private object so that you can direct all your attention to publicly observable things and events.

Wittgenstein, however, is not satisfied with merely denying the possibility of a public language referring to private objects; he wants also to deny that there can be even a private language whose terms refer to private objects. A truly private language, in the sense of a language which can only be understood by its user because the terms in the language not only refer to private sensations, but lack all external, publicly observable criteria for their proper use, cannot exist according to Wittgenstein. He presents his argument against the possibility of such a language in a much discussed account of a would-be diarist who tries to devise a language for recording his own inner sensations:

> Let us imagine the following case. I want to keep a diary about the recurrence of a certain sensation. To this end I associate it with the sign "S" and write this sign in a calendar for every day on which I have the sensation.—I will remark first of all that a definition of the sign cannot be formulated.—But still I can give myself a kind of ostensive definition.—How? Can I point to the sensation? Not in the ordinary sense. But I speak, or write the sign down, and at the same time I concentrate my attention on the sensation—and so, as it were, point to it inwardly.—But what is this ceremony for? for that is all it seems to be! A definition surely serves to establish the meaning of a sign.—Well, that is done precisely by the concentrating of my attention; for in this way I impress on myself the connexion between the sign and the sensation.—But "I impress it on myself" can only mean: this process brings it about that I remember the connexion *right* in the future. But in the present case I have no criterion of correctness. One would like to say: whatever is going to seem right to me is right. And that only means that here we can't talk about 'right'.
>
> (PI 258)

At the heart of Wittgenstein's argument here is the untrustworthiness of memory as a criterion for the correct use of a sensation

2. Peter Strawson, *Mind*, vol. 63, 1954, pp. 90, 91, 98.

word. If a person—a Robinson Crusoe, let us say, (to use Professor Ayer's example)[3] who has grown up alone on a desert island—tries to devise a language for his own inner sensations, he will fail at the task, according to Wittgenstein, because a true language must have regularity of reference, and in the case of an inner sensation language, there is no way of knowing that the sensation I have now is the same sensation as one I remember having previously. My memory might be deceiving me and I would have no way of knowing this. A "subjective justification" for Wittgenstein is no justification, because "justification consists in appealing to something independent" (PI 265)—by which he means something that is publicly observable. "Always get rid of the idea of the private object," says Wittgenstein, "in this way: assume that it constantly changes, but that you do not notice the change because your memory constantly deceives you" (PI II, p. 207).

The counter-common-sensical radicalism—as well as dubiousness—of Wittgenstein's view here is important to grasp. Most people find little reason to doubt the memory of private sensations in the same manner as Wittgenstein. True, no one denies that memory can err, but regarding private sensations experienced very intensely (migraine headache or excruciating sciatic nerve pains, for instance), especially when they occur at frequent intervals, few have reason to doubt the capacity of memory to recollect such sensations accurately and to group them together under a single term. And if this can take place using terms (sensation words) drawn from a public language, there would seem to be little reason why it couldn't take place using new, invented terms constitutive of a private language. As Professor Ayer says about his Robinson Crusoe: "If we allow that our Robinson Crusoe could invent words to describe the flora and fauna of his island, why not allow that he could also invent words to describe his sensations? . . . So long as Crusoe remains alone on his island, so long, that is, as he communicates only with himself, the principle distinction which he is likely to draw between 'external' objects and his 'inner' experiences is that his [inner] experiences are transient in a way that external objects are not."[4] But Wittgenstein wants so much to eliminate the private object and the activity of mind reflecting upon itself that he subjects memory and memory-contents to a degree of doubt that most people would find inordinate. He even doubts at one place memory's capacity to recollect its own thoughts.

3. "Can There Be a Private Language", in *The Concept of a Person, and Other Essays* (The Macmillan Press LTD, London, 1963), p. 44.

4. *Ibid.*, pp. 45-6.

"Let us assume," he says, "there was a man who always guessed right what I was saying to myself in my thoughts. (It does not matter how he manages it): But what is the criterion for his guessing *right*? Well, I am a truthful person and I confess that he has guessed right. But might I not be mistaken, can my memory not deceive me? And might it not always do so when— without lying—I express what I have thought within myself?" (PI II, p. 222).

Wittgenstein's attack on memory, however, is quite selective, for he shows little inclination to subject memory to doubt when its object is an object of the external world. In a later work on certainty, for instance, he suggests that "the proposition that I have been living in this room for weeks past, that my memory does not deceive me in this," is "certain beyond all reasonable doubt."[5] "Must I not begin to trust somewhere?", he asks in a rhetorical vein elsewhere in the same work in a reference to human judgment.[6] Indeed, although Wittgenstein doesn't seem to realize it, if memory were completely ruled out of court as a reliable guide to truth, not only would all statements about the no longer existing past be invalid (statements, let us say, about one's childhood concerning which no evidence or records exist), but linguistic activity itself of whatever kind, whether public or private, would be impossible. Language, according to Wittgenstein, involves following the customary rules of usage, but how, one might ask, could a person know that an utterance he was about to make was in conformity with customary usage except through reliance on memory?[7] Even if one had prior recourse to the external check of, say, a dictionary to determine what was the customary usage of a term, *after* one had done the checking, memory alone would be one's guide. There always must be some interval—and hence, some functioning of memory—between the external check on the usage of a term and the actual use of the term "in the stream of life". Moreover, how, except through memory, would one know that a dictionary is to be used to determine proper usage? In short, if the content of one's memory is to be systematically doubted or eliminated from consideration, not only language, but intelligent activity of any kind would be impossible.

Wittgenstein, in fact, only challenges memory as part of his war against the inner, private object. It is memory-beliefs about sensa-

5. *On Certainty*, edited by G.E.M. Anscombe and G.H. von Wright, translated by Denis Paul and G.E.M. Anscombe (Harper and Row, Publishers, N.Y., 1972) par. 416. Wittgenstein has used the English "certain beyond all reasonable doubt" in the original.

6. *Ibid.*, par. 150.

7. Mundle makes a similar point, *op. cit.*, p. 223.

tions and other mental phenomena, but not about publicly observable phenomena, which are the subject of his doubts. We might compare him in this respect to Descartes. Descartes systematically doubts the outer and the public in order to arrive at what for him is the more solid foundation of the inner and the private. Wittgenstein, on the other hand, systematically doubts the inner and the private in order to arrive at what he holds to be the more solid foundation of the outer and the public. The great difference between Wittgenstein and Descartes, however, is that Descartes systematically doubts the reality of the external world, only to return to it, having found the grounding he was looking for in the reality of thinking mind (inner reality) and the reality of God. Both realities, inner and outer, remain untouched. In the case of Wittgenstein, however, the result of his systematic doubt is to cut man off from his existential grounding in the inner, in order to re-establish that grounding on the basis of the outer dynamics of social interaction and public language games.

In all of this, Wittgenstein has tried to create a philosophy of language where the possibility of estrangement from society cannot emerge. The only reality that is to count as such in his later thought is public reality—we are to direct our attention away from our private feelings and mental states, and busy ourselves with participating in the collective linguistic behavior of the group. Private feelings and mental states are to be banished from our field of apperception by being denied linguistic expression. One doesn't talk about them even to oneself.

Work Therapy vs Language Therapy

The function of Wittgenstein's ordinary language therapy as a psychic stabilizing force can perhaps be better appreciated when it is compared to what might be called the work therapy that proved so crucial to Wittgenstein personally at various times in his life. To love and to work (*lieben und arbeiten*) Freud and his followers tell us, are the activities most crucial to a fulfilling, mentally healthy life, and for the truth contained in at least the latter part of this formula, one need look no farther than the cumulative social and psychological damage produced by periods of prolonged unemployment (i.e., increased divorce, depression, alcohol and drug addiction, etc.).

But in periods of threatening psychic chaos—periods when one's mind, so to speak, is on the brink—work and other forms of active interaction with the world can prove not so much a means to long-range fulfillment as a stop-gap method of "holding on", of "keeping one's head above water", to use one of Wittgenstein's metaphors. On a number of occasions in his life a solid work routine was to be a life-raft for Wittgenstein, spelling the difference between a stabilizing equilibrium and a threatening disintegration. One of these occasions, which has already been alluded to previously, occurred in the summer of 1920, when he first took on work as a gardener's assistant at a Roman Catholic monastery. The year and a half before this Wittgenstein had experienced Austria's defeat in the war and the collapse of the Hapsburg Empire; he had learned of the death in the war of his dearest friend David Pinsent, as well as the suicide of his brother Kurt; and he had not only received Russell's Introduction to the *Tractatus*, indicating Russell's total misunderstanding of its message, but experienced the rejection of his book by no less than three German publishers. As can be gathered from his letters to Engelmann during this period, Wittgenstein was in an almost continuous state of mental torment and depression, several times contemplating ending his agony through suicide. In July of 1920, less than two months after receiving word of the rejection of his manuscript by the publisher Reklam, he wrote a letter to Engelmann explaining why he would not be able to come to Engelmann's home at Olmuetz as he had originally planned. Wittgenstein had at this time been attending the Teachers' Training College in Vienna to prepare for his new vocation as a rural school teacher, but at the time he wrote the letter to Engelmann his summer vacation had already begun:

> I have broken my word. I shall not come your way, at least for the time being. . . . For in my present dubious state of mind even talking to you—much as I enjoy it—would be no more than a pastime. I was longing for some kind of regularized work (*regelmaessig Arbeit*), which, of all the things I can do in my present condition, is the most nearly bearable, if I am not mistaken. It seems I have found such a job: I have been taken on as an assistant gardener at the Klosterneuburg Monastery for the duration of my holiday. (How life is going to treat me there, we shall see).[1]

1. Engelmann, *op. cit.*, p. 37.

In early August, 1920, having begun his gardening chores, Wittgenstein wrote a letter to Russell briefly describing his work and how beneficial it was to him. He also indicated the lingering sadness Pinsent's death still had for him.

> At the moment I'm spending my holidays as a gardner's assistant in the nurseries of the monastery of Klosterneuburg near Vienna. I have to work solidly the whole day through, and that is good. . . . Every day I think of Pinsent. He took half my life away with him. The devil will take the other half.[2]

Late in August, just before completion of his work at the monastery, Wittgenstein again wrote to Engelmann explaining just how important the gardening work had been for him:

> My stay at Klosterneuburg is coming to an end; in three days I shall go back to Vienna and wait for a job. I am sure the gardening work was the most sensible thing I could have done in my holidays. In the evening when the work is done, I am tired, and then I do not feel unhappy. I have rather grim forebodings, though, about my future life. For unless all the devils in hell pull the other way, my life is bound to become very sad if not impossible.[3]

One can imagine from what is said in these letters just how important regularized work was for Wittgenstein at this time. By keeping mind and body occupied on a simple external task, the gardening work not only had its rewards in the restful physical tiredness at the end of the day, but of critical significance, it kept the mind from dwelling within itself at a time when its inner torments and suicidal urges were threatening to get out of hand. Within the context of Wittgenstein's near-chaotic state of mind then, the gardening work must be seen as a stabilizing therapeutic.

The function of regularized work as a stabilizing, chaos-avoiding therapeutic is explicitly stated by Wittgenstein in another letter to Engelmann written shortly after the commencement of his first teaching activities. Like his work at the monastery, his initial teaching work in the Austrian countryside was apparently to set his mind at ease. "At last," he wrote to Engelmann in October of 1920, "I have become a primary-school teacher, and am working in a beau-

---

2. *Letters to Russell, Keynes and Moore, op. cit.*, p. 91.
3. Engelmann, *op. cit.*, p. 37.

tiful and tiny place called Trattenbach." "I am happy in my work at school, and I do need it badly, or else all the devils in Hell break loose inside me."[4]

This early enthusiasm for his work as a school teacher, however, was soon to subside, though he did manage to stick to his various assignments for a number of years. In early 1926 though, serious conflict with the local townspeople of Otterthal led Wittgenstein to resign his teaching post and never again seek employment in elementary school teaching.[5] In the summer of that year, Wittgenstein was again to take up work as a gardener's assistant at a monastery (this time the monastery at Hutteldorf, near Vienna) and soon thereafter, together with his friend Engelmann, he was commissioned by his sister Margarethe to build a mansion for her in Vienna. Although no letters from this period are extant, it takes little imagination to see in his resumption of work as a gardener's assistant, and his subsequent acceptance of the task set before him by his sister, a desire for the same kind of work therapy that had previously proved so beneficial in the summer of 1920. His family had been concerned about his mental condition for some time, and it seems that it was at least partly for reasons of his psychic stability that his sister decided to ask him to take up work on the mansion. In his book on *The Architecture of Ludwig Wittgenstein*, Bernhard Leitner remarks: "The decision of Margarethe-Stonborough-Wittgenstein to transfer the building task to her brother, was specifically intended as therapy for the tormented state in which he had been since World War I."[6] As Leitner says, Wittgenstein had little experience as a builder or architect,[7] and his sister's decision to engage his services begins to make much more sense when it is seen within the context of her concern about his mental stability.

Thus, his activities as both a gardener and a construction engineer, as well as his early teaching chores, must be seen as a kind of work therapeutic which quite literally served as a means of keeping Wittgenstein sane. And here one can see the great similarity to his later form of linguistic therapy. By keeping the mind occupied on the external, practical affairs of life, the mind is effectively prevented from slipping into its own inner, private world, and the madness that threatens to engulf it there. The external and the practical

4. *Ibid.*, p. 38.

5. Wittgenstein's life as a rural school teacher and his conflict with the villagers of Otterthal is recounted in "Not Made to Measure", Chapter 3 of William Bartley III's *Wittgenstein, op. cit.*

6. *Op. Cit.*, p. 11.

7. *Ibid.*

must be made to dominate the mind's field of awareness so as to prevent it from dwelling upon itself in a potentially destructive manner.

The Attack on the Notion of Universal Essences

Besides its quasi-behaviorist philosophy of mind and the emphasis on seeing linguistic utterances within the context of public language games (forms of life), one of the most important features of Wittgenstein's later philosophy is its attack on the notion of there being universal essences of terms by virtue of which all the things designated by a certain term are properly so designated. The most widely quoted passage in this regard is Wittgenstein's remarks in the *Philosophical Investigations* on games:

> Consider for example the proceedings that we call "games". I mean board-games, card-games, ball-games, Olympic games, and so on. What is common to them all?—Don't say: "There *must* be something common, or they would not be called "games"—but *look and see* whether there is anything common to all.—For if you look at them you will not see something that is common to *all*, but similarities, relationships, and a whole series of them at that. To repeat: don't think, but look!
>
> (PI 66)

Look! says Wittgenstein, look at all the different types of things there are that are called games—all the board-games, card-games, ball-games. In some, he says, there are winners and losers, but not in all. A child, for instance, bouncing his ball up against a wall and catching it again, might be thought of as playing a game though he has no competitors and no one wins or loses (PI 66). In some cases, says Wittgenstein, skill plays a great deal in the outcome of the game, though in others the outcome is largely a matter of luck (PI 66). If we look for one characteristic common to all the things that are called games, we are not likely to find it, for the simple reason that no such common feature exists. There is not one characteristic common to all the things that are called games that constitute an essence of games. Games rather, like most other groups of things designated by general terms, are bound together by "family resemblances" rather than a single essence common to all.

> And the result of this examination is: we see a complicated network of similarities overlapping and criss-crossing: sometimes overall similarities, sometimes similarities of detail.
>
> I can think of no better expression to characterize these similarities than "family resemblances", for the various resemblances between members of a family: build, features, color of eyes, gait, temperament, etc. etc. overlap and criss-cross in the same way.—And I shall say: 'games' form a family.
>
> (PI 66, 67)

The "family resemblances" of which Wittgenstein speaks might be pictured as a cluster of traits, some, but not all of which are possessed by each member of the family. Thus, family member p might possess characteristics ABCD, q might have BCDE, r ABDE, s ACDE, and t ABCE, such that each family member has four of the five traits A,B,C,D,E, though no single one of the five traits is possessed by all the members of the family. In another (and somewhat different) metaphor, Wittgenstein refers to a thread formed by overlapping fibers, where none of the fibers runs through the length of the thread (PI 67). The things designated by a general term are seen by this metaphor to form a series with gradual transitions between the elements of the series. The elements next to one another always resemble each other very closely, though at opposite ends of the series the elements do not necessarily have anything in common. Element p, for instance, might possess characteristics ABCD, q BCDE, r CDEF, s DEFG, and t EFGH. Each element is closely related to the elements surrounding it, but p and t at the ends of the series have virtually nothing in common.

Wittgenstein's attack on the notion of there being universal essences of terms is closely tied to his rejection of the constructional systems of positivist logicians, at least insofar as such systems are taken to be a model or ideal to which actual language is expected to conform. Logicians like Frege, Russell, and himself in his earlier period, Wittgenstein says, had erroneously assumed that there was an "essence" of language and that this essence consisted of the discursive proposition whose purpose was to describe states of affairs. This, says Wittgenstein, was an *a priori* requirement rather than the result of an investigation of actual language. "The more narrowly we examine actual language," says Wittgenstein, "the sharper becomes the conflict between it and our requirement. (For the crystaline purity of logic was, of course, not a *result of investigation*: it was a requirement)" (PI 107). When we investigate actual linguistic usage, according to Wittgenstein, "We see that what we call 'sentence' and 'language' has not the formal unity that I imagined, but is the family of structures more or less related to one another" (PI 108). Thus, in reality many types of linguistic usages are seen to exist, and these are united by family resemblances rather than the possession of a single essence.

Using his new notion of the meaning of a term as the variety of ways in which it can be used in ordinary language (and in the case of object-designating terms, the variety of objects to which the term can refer) Wittgenstein can quite easily dispense with the *a priori* constructions of logical positivists. But he is also concerned in his new notion of meaning to dispense with the other great enemy of his later thought, namely, transcendental metaphysics and mysticism. This latter function of his theory of meaning, however, only becomes clear when it is viewed within the context of certain peculiarities of the history of Western philosophy, and more specifically, of the Platonic tradition in Western philosophy. For besides the Procrustean *a priorism* of the logical positivists, Wittgenstein's attack on the notion of universal essences is targeted directly at the Platonic doctrine of Ideas and all related forms of "realism".[1] Platonic philosophy is specifically taken to task by Wittgenstein for assuming that there is a pure, abstract entity such as knowledge, beauty, or the good, which the specific things we categorize under such terms somehow embody. Thus he writes,

> The idea that in order to get clear about the meaning of a general term one had to find the common element in all its applications has shackled philosophical investigations; for it had not only led to no result, but also made the philosopher dismiss as irrelevant the concrete cases, which alone could have helped him to understand the usage of the general term. When Socrates asks the question, 'what is knowledge?', he does not even regard it as a *preliminary* answer to enumerate cases of knowledge (*Thaetetus* 146D-147C). (BB pp. 20-21)
>
> One of the ways of looking at questions in ethics about *good* is to think that all things said to be good have something in common, just as there is a tendency to think that all things we call games have something in common. Plato's talk of looking for the essence of things was very like talk of looking for the *ingredients* in a mixture, as though qualities were ingredients of things.[2]
>
> . . . In view of the way we have learned the word "good" it would be astonishing if it had a general meaning covering all of

1. "Realism" as opposed to nominalism.
2. *Wittgenstein's Lectures, Cambridge*, 1932-1935, *op. cit.*, p. 34.

> its applications. . . . It is used in different contexts because there is a transition between similar things called "good", a transition which continues, it may be, to things which bear no similarity to earlier members of the series. We *cannot* say "If we want to find out the meaning of 'good' let's find what all cases of good have in common". They may not have anything in common.[3]
>
> The idea of a general concept being a common property of its particular instances connects up with other primitive, too simple, ideas of the structure of language. It is comparable to the idea that *properties* are *ingredients* of things which have the properties; e.g. that beauty is an ingredient of all beautiful things as alcohol is of beer and wine, and that we therefore could have pure beauty, unadulterated by anything that is beautiful. (BB p. 17)
>
> Consider how we learn such words [as "beautiful" and "ugly"]. We do not as children discover the quality of beauty or ugliness in a *face* and find that these are qualities a *tree* has in common with it. The words "beautiful" and "ugly" are bound up with the words they modify, and when applied to a face are not the same as when applied to flowers and trees.[4]
>
> The word "beauty" is used for a thousand different things. Beauty of face is different from that of flowers and animals. That one is playing utterly different games is evident from the difference that emerges in the discussion of each. We can only ascertain the meaning of the word "beauty" by seeing how we use it.[5]
>
> I cannot characterize my standpoint better than by saying that it is opposed to that which Socrates represents in the Platonic dialogues.[6]

Reading these remarks, one might naturally acquire a certain sympathy for Wittgenstein's point of view, for there is obviously something of the ridiculous in Plato's notion of ideal forms somehow embodied in the objects of the sensory world, as Plato himself may have been coming to recognize in the *Parmenides*. Under this aspect, the Wittgensteinian doctrine of polymorphism certainly has a common-sense appeal. But there is much more here than meets the eye. What is not seen is the fact that the Platonic doctrine of Ideas, as well as all similar doctrines since Plato's time (e.g. Christian and

---

3. *Ibid.*, p. 33.
4. *Ibid.*, p. 35.
5. *Ibid.*, pp. 35-36.
6. Quoted from an unpublished manuscript in Garth Hallett's *A Companion to Wittgenstein's "Philosophical Investigations"* (Cornell University Press, Ithaca, 1977), p. 771.

neo-Platonic exemplarism, medieval realism, Schelling's idealism) was not intended to serve merely as a logic of things of the sense-perceivable world, but was conceived as a speculative metaphysical device designed to relate the sense-perceivable world to a divine-transcendent Beyond.[7] And so when the Platonic Socrates says in the *Phaedo* that it only confuses him when he hears "that what makes a thing beautiful is its lovely color, or the shape, or anything else of that sort" (100 C), and when he declares that it is only through the presence of Beauty in itself (*auto kalon*) that beautiful things are made beautiful (100 D), it must be understood that he is not aiming at an immanental logic of the sense-perceivable world, but wants to direct the reader's attention away from the multiplicitous world of sense-perception and the cognitive modes appropriate to it. This process of attention re-direction, then, reaches its magnificent culmination in Diotima's speech in *Symposium*:

> Starting from individual beauties, the quest for the universal beauty must find [the lover] ever mounting the heavenly ladder, stepping from rung to rung—that is, from one to two, and from two to *every* lovely body, from bodily beauty to the beauty of institutions, from institutions to learning, and from learning in general to the special lore that pertains to nothing but the beautiful itself—until at last it comes to know what beauty is. And if, my dear Socrates, Diotima went on, man's life is even worth the living, it is when he has attained this vision of the very soul of beauty. And once you have seen it, you will never be seduced again by the charm of gold, of dress, of comely boys, or lads just ripening to manhood; you will care nothing for the beauties that used to take your breath away . . . But if it were given to man to gaze on beauty's very self—unsullied, unalloyed, and freed from the mortal taint that haunts the frailer loveliness of flesh and blood—if, I say, it were given to man to see the heavenly beauty face to face, would you call *his*, she asked me, an unenviable life, whose eyes had been opened to the vision, and who had gazed upon it in true contemplation until it had become his own forever?
>
> (211 C-E; Michael Joyce translation)

A similar *via negativa* pattern is, of course, to be found in Book VII of the *Republic*, in the ascent to the Idea of the Good. Wittgenstein, it might be contended, was merely attacking the immanental

7. I follow here the interpretation of Plato offered by Eric Voegelin in his *Plato and Aristotle* (Louisiana State University Press, Baton Rouge, 1957). In the present context, see especially pp. 274-279.

logic of Platonic essentialism, and wasn't thinking of the essentialist doctrine in terms of a transcendental metaphysics which attempts to relate the contents of an altered state of consciousness to that of more normal consciousness. After all, it might be argued, critics from Aristotle to medieval and modern nominalists have seen fit to criticize the logic of Plato's view of the Ideas without being concerned with—or even aware of—the larger transcendental issue involved. This, however, would not seem to be the case with Wittgenstein. While such an interpretation cannot be ruled out, since Wittgenstein does not link the idealist-essentialist doctrine which he attacks to mysticism or theological terminology, the following considerations would seem to argue against it. First of all, Wittgenstein, in contrast to many other critics of Plato, had a first-hand, empathetic understanding for the kinds of radically altered states of consciousness that give rise to such images and symbols as are to be found in the Cave Allegory and Diotima's speech. Secondly, Wittgenstein, who, as Georg von Wright says, was most attracted to thinkers "in the borderland between philosophy, religion, and poetry,"[8] seems to have been very attracted to Plato,[9] despite what he says in his writings against him. And finally, it must be kept in mind that Wittgenstein had himself employed a Platonic-like formulation of the problem of the ethical good ("absolute good," "absolute value") in his "Lecture on Ethics", and like Plato, saw ethics and aesthetics in the *Tractatus* as belonging to one and the same transcendental realm, which was identified with a mystical "outside-of" (*ausserhalb*) the world of space and time (6.41-6.421).

In his attack on the notion of universal essences, Wittgenstein it would seem, is consciously trying to dispense with the two great enemies of his post-*Tractatus* period—i.e., destructivistic positivism, on the one hand; mysticism, metaphysics, and the potential torments of the inner life, on the other. By constantly drawing attention to the multiplicitous-differentiated aspects of the physical world—i.e., the *variety* of games, beautiful things, etc.—the mind would be effectively prevented from any kind of unitive-abstractive activity. It would not only be prevented from forming a model or ideal of language such as that sought after by positivist logicians, but of equal importance, it would be effectively prevented from pushing its unitive-abstractive activity beyond the world of sense-perception to the realm of mind itself, and beyond this, to that transcendental horizon of consciousness where the finite, particular mind

8. Malcolm, *Memoir, op. cit.*, pp. 20-21.
9. *Ibid.*, p. 21.

begins to be drawn up into, and to become one with, the great mystery of infinite, Universal Mind.

A Comparison with Augustine

Both the *Philosophical Investigations* and the *Brown Book* begin with a criticism of St. Augustine's view of language learning as set forth in his *Confessions*. In both cases, Wittgenstein faults Augustine for using thing-words (e.g., "table", "chair", "bread") as a model for language in general. Such a picture of language, says Wittgenstein, is a description of only one narrowly circumscribed part of language, but not the whole of it (PI 3). It describes one strain within a complicated mosaic, and while valid for certain words and their uses, obviously does not do justice to others (e.g., "not", "but", "perhaps"). Norman Malcolm, in relating Wittgenstein's near reverence for Augustine, says that Wittgenstein began the *Philosophical Investigations* with a quotation from the *Confessions* because he believed that the Augustinian view of language and language learning, however mistaken, would have to be considered an important one if so great a mind as Augustine's held it.[1] While what Malcolm says here must be accepted as true—he having heard it from Wittgenstein himself—and while Wittgenstein's deep affection for Augustine is certainly not to be disputed, the fact still remains that one could hardly find a work more out of tune with the whole manner and tenor of truth seeking to be found in Augustine's *Confessions* than Wittgenstein's *Philosophical Investigations*. The latter in fact, might be aptly subtitled *Contra Augustinum*.

For Augustine, as for all those who have been deeply influenced by the Platonic and neo-Platonic tradition in philosophy, the perception of objects and events in the external world constitutes the very lowest level of human knowledge. By contrast, the highest level, which is represented by contemplation, involves for him a process in which mind alone, freed from the public world of the sense-perceivable, directly apprehends spiritual truths and its own relationship to a space-time transcending order. From start to finish the *Confessions* is an account not of outward, publicly observable things—though these, of course, come into play—but of Augustine's inward

1. *Memoir, op. cit.*, p. 71.

journeys and soul searchings. As Augustine himself explains in the work, he wrote the *Confessions* for those who "wish to hear me confess what I am within myself, where they can extend neither their eye, nor ear, nor mind."[2] "Why do I tell these things?", Augustine asks. "It is," he says, "that I myself and whoever else reads them may realize from what great depths we must cry unto [God]."[3] It is, in other words, from the introspective viewpoint that Augustine writes, and it is about personal introspective material which his friends and those who have urged him to write are most interested in hearing.

Augustine's account of his inner travail, of his great battle against his divided self and the many temptations of the world, has become, of course, one of the classics of Western spiritual and psychological literature. When one compares it to the quasi-behaviorist view of mental activities and mental terms to be found in the *Philosophical Investigations* the incompatibility of the world-views sketched in the two works becomes readily apparent. Little if any of the more important topics Augustine talks about in the *Confessions*, for instance, lends itself to being described in behavioral or dispositional terms. Augustine, one might say, assumes as a matter of course, that all readers have a beetle in their box which is more or less the same as his own. There is no attempt to prove this; it is just something which is not seriously doubted. Moreover, memory, which is accorded such a dubious status in the *Philosophical Investigations*, becomes the object in the *Confessions* of almost unbounded enthusiasm and praise:

> Great is the power of memory! An awesome thing, my God, deep and boundless and manifold in being! And this thing is the mind, and this I am myself . . . Behold! in the fields and caves and caverns of my memory, innumerable and innumerably filled with all varieties of innumerable things . . . through all these I run, I fly here and there, and I penetrate into them as far as I can, and there is no end to them. So great is the power of memory! So great is the power of life, even in man's mortal life![4]

There is no desire on Augustine's part to "get rid of the inner object", nor is there any concern that the inherently private lacks public criteria for its occurrence.

---

2. *Confessions*, Book 10, Chapter 3, John K. Ryan translation (Image Books, Garden City, N.Y., 1960).
3. *Ibid.*, Book 2, Chapter 3.
4. *Ibid.*, Book 10, Chapter 17.

The radical divergence between Augustine and Wittgenstein is also to be seen in the manner in which the ego or self-enclosure is transcended. In Augustine—and *mutatis mutandis*, in the Wittgenstein of the *Tractatus* and the "Lecture on Ethics"—man's enclosure within himself is overcome as the ego is delivered over, in loving self-surrender, to the mystical transcending power of the divine initiative. In Wittgenstein's later philosophy, while man is expected to surrender himself, the manner of man's self-surrender has radically changed. His enclosure within himself is to be overcome by surrendering, not to God and the cathartic power of *das Mystische*, but to the public language and the customs and traditions embodied in the public life-form. The *amor Dei*, one might say, has come to be replaced by the *amor populi* and the *amor traditionis.*

There is, however, one close parallel between Wittgenstein's later thought and the thought of Augustine that should not be overlooked. While the mystical and introspectivist elements are certainly strong in the *Confessions*, they are far from the only path which Augustine believes leads to truth in moral and spiritual matters. Soul-searching, examining one's conscience, the meditative exploration of the depths of the psyche—these, while important for Augustine, are overshadowed in much of his writings by his uncritical acceptance of the Bible as "scripture" and the teachings of the Roman Catholic Church as unerring authority. Just as Wittgenstein accepts without question the various forms of life involved in the language games of human cultures, so Augustine accepts without criticism both the Bible and Roman Catholic orthodoxy. These latter, one might say, constitute for Augustine the form of life that simply *must* be accepted.

Linguistic Tribalism and the Ultimate Failure of Ordinary Language Philosophy: An Evaluation

The ordinary language philosophy put forth by Wittgenstein in his later works might be described as a kind of linguistic tribalism, though a tribalism of a particularly modern sort. As we know from historical and anthropological studies, one of the chief characteristics of many pre-modern peoples is a sense of identity with the social group so overpowering, that personal consciousness—i.e., the awareness of an individual identity distinct from the group—is only present in a rudimentary form. A sense of oneness and solidarity with the collective dominates the manner in which people experience themselves. In modern times, the pervading sense of estrangement which people often feel in the more advanced industrialized societies has led to a yearning to recapture this lost sense of oneness and solidarity which once characterized man's situation. But modern man, in contrast to his pre-modern predecessors, finds it almost impossible to lose his sense of individuality in the group without at least a partial awareness of the fact that there is some aspect of his being which simply cannot be contained within the public order that is called society. There is, one might say, a certain irreducibly private aspect to human nature which resists amalgamation into any public collective. Pre-modern man, not fully conscious of this private aspect, can be fully amalgamated into society with little if any residual sense of incongruity or loss. For modern man, however, this simply is not possible. However hard modern man may try to lose his sense of individuality in the group—and in the form of the various nationalisms and class solidarity movements of the 20th century, he has certainly tried very hard—his sense of uniqueness always tends to reassert itself, even if only in the form of fleeting moments in which the tribal manner of existence temporarily begins to lose its sense of naturalness and authenticity. When modern man tries to re-establish a psychic unity on the pattern of a pre-modern tribe, the unity he achieves inevitably takes on something of the character of an artificial conformism.

One need not go along with all the obscurantist elements in Heidegger's thought to see in his analysis of *das Man* ("the they") a very perceptive critique of the tribal and conformist elements to be found in modern society. As this tribal/conformist pattern is to be found in Wittgenstein's later philosophy, it is well worth quoting a few brief passages from what Heidegger has to say on the matter in *Sein und Zeit*:

> This Being-with-one-another (*Miteinandersein*) dissolves one's own Dasein [i.e. one's own personal being] into the kind of being of "the Others", in such a way, indeed, that the Others, as distinguishable and explicit [i.e. as individual], vanish more and more. In this inconspicuousness and unascertainability, the real dictatorship of the "they" (*das Man*) is unfolded. We take pleasure and enjoy ourselves as *they* take pleasure; we read, see, and judge about literature and art as *they* see and judge; likewise we shrink back from the "great mass" as *they* shrink back, we find "shocking" what *they* find shocking. The "they", which is noth-

> ing definite, and which all are, though not as the sum, prescribes the kind of Being of everydayness (*Alltaeglichkeit*). . . .
>
> Publicness (*die Oeffentlichkeit*) proximally controls every way in which the world and Dasein get interpreted and it is always right. . . .
>
> Everyone is the other, and no one is himself. The "*they*", which supplies the answer to the question of the "who" of everyday Dasein, is the "*nobody*" to whom every Dasein has already surrendered itself in Being-among-the-other (*Untereinandersein*).[1]

"Everyone is the other, and no one is himself"—one could hardly find a more succinct characterization of Wittgenstein's later philosophy. Man's private, inner self is accorded little if any regard (indeed *Wittgenstein and Privacy, Wittgenstein and the Inner Self,* might be titles to add to the many candidates for "thinnest book in the world"); for it is only within the linguistic tribe that Wittgensteinian man lives and breathes and has his being. What counts for Wittgenstein is that a person conforms to the rules and traditions of the public language game. At every turn in the analysis an effort is made to reduce, in quasi-behaviorist fashion, private to public, mental to sense–perceivable (particularly the visually sense-perceivable), the "I" or self to the "I-as-others-see-me". Being seen and heard by others takes precedence over anything that might occur in a private sphere beyond the pale of the public. Publicness, one might say in Wittgenstein's later philosophy, proximally controls every way in which the world and one's own being get interpreted, and it is always right.

Both the *Tractatus* and the later philosophy, one might say, display an inability to maintain a proper balance between self and society. In the *Tractatus*, a radical split occurs between the philosopher and society, the Truth of the philosopher's experience being relegated to a society-transcending silence as interpersonal discourse is confined to the realm of the natural sciences. In Wittgenstein's later philosophy, the self, weary of its estrangement from society, throws itself headlong into the linguistic stream of social life, losing in the process, the inner dignity of its private sphere. In neither case do self and society, private and public, establish a proper tensional relationship. And the same pattern of radical swings is to be seen in Wittgenstein's treatment of existing language forms. In the *Tractatus*, all existing language forms, at least insofar as they try to

1. *Being and Time*, translated by John Macquarrie and Edward Robinson, (Harper and Row, Publishers, N.Y. 1962), pp. 164-166.

express "higher things" (*Hoeheres*), are rejected as unseemly corruptions. In the later philosophy though, fearing the greater corruption represented by Carnap, Neurath, and Co., Wittgenstein comes to accept existing cultural language forms without further question. From the most radical critic of social custom Wittgenstein becomes its staunchest defender.[2]

It would be a mistake, however, to see a tribalistic (or populist) frame of mind exclusively in Wittgenstein's later period. While the spirit of Wittgenstein's *Tractatus* was certainly the farthest thing from that of his later writings, a latent tribal or *voelkische* impulse is clearly to be discerned in the early Wittgenstein, and can be seen, for instance, in the manner in which he, like so many millions of his contemporaries, was drawn up into the nationalistic euphoria of the First World War—a war whose absurdity and murderous insanity non-tribalists such as Karl Kraus and Bertrand Russell had no trouble at all perceiving from the very beginning. Only in Wittgenstein's later writings, however, do these tribal or *voelkische* impulses begin to influence his thinking.

In evaluating ordinary language philosophy, while some good must certainly be said about it when seen from the perspective of its logical-positivist predecessor, from the standpoint of its own goal of saving society, it must be viewed ultimately as a great failure. This study has endeavored to show that the major concern of Wittgenstein throughout both his early and later phases—a concern which is not to be readily gathered at first glance from either of the two works for which he was to become famous—was with the moral and spiritual health of Western society. In the *Tractatus*, moral and spiritual regeneration was to take place through a reverential silence and the meditative ascent of the soul (Wittgenstein's eye point) to the height of mystical ecstasy and the vision of the world *sub specie aeternitatis*. In the later work, regeneration was to be achieved by embracing the overall world-view of the common man against the corrupting inroads of a positivist-oriented intelligentsia. With the exception of Paul Engelmann, however, the *Tractatus* and its purpose was understood by virtually no one, and so its therapeutic effect on Western society, despite the enormous influence the misunderstanding of its doctrines was to have on the members of the Vienna Circle, was virtually nil. The ordinary language philosophy worked out in Wittgenstein's later writings, on the other hand, was

2. This neat formulation would have to be qualified somewhat, in that the cultural forms he had in mind in the earlier, critical phase of his thought, were primarily those of the intellectual elite (philosophers and others), while those in his later, conservative phase, were the life-forms of the populous.

not generally misunderstood, at least not to the same extent as the *Tractatus*, and its impact on philosophy students in Britain and America was certainly considerable. Yet contrary to what Wittgenstein believed, following as he did in the paths of Tolstoy and Dostoyevsky, the peasants and the common people were not able to save Europe. It was, in fact, the common people and certainly not the intelligentsia who formed the backbone of the Fascist and National Socialist movements in Central Europe, while in Russia it was in part, at least, owing to the lethargy, confusion, and moral indecisiveness of the peasant classes that Stalin was able to consolidate his tyranny.

When the major events of European history following the First World War are taken into account, one of the great flaws in Wittgenstein's later philosophy becomes readily apparent; namely, its lack of any critical perspective. Take, for instance, the situation which emerged from the great social, political, and ideological revolution that engulfed Germany in the 1930s. Are Jews, for instance, "parasites" or "poisoned humanity" as the Nazis contended? All, it would seem, that a Wittgensteinian could say in reply to such a question once Hitler had come to power was that there was indeed a National Socialist form of life, which in Germany had become the dominant one, and that within the context of one of the language games comprising this form of life, it was certainly correct to speak of Jews as "parasites" and "poisoned humanity". In a similar manner, if one was to ask whether the kulak farmers in Russia in the 1930s were in truth "enemies of the people", a Wittgensteinian presumably, would be forced to reply that the dominant form of life in Russia at this time was Bolshevism-Stalinism, and that according to one of the language games comprising this form of life, the kulaks were clearly the "enemies of the people". Or to move the analysis over to America, if someone in the American South wanted to know whether the anti-lynching agitation and the demand for equality of treatment on the part of Southern Negroes was a question of "niggers" and "nigger-lovers" getting "uppity", the Wittgensteinian, true to his principle of keeping his linguistics "purely descriptive" and accepting all existing forms of life as given, would have to reply that there was indeed a strong anti-Negro *Lebensform* alive in America, which at various times and places, such as the Deep South in the 1920s, was clearly the dominant one, and that according to the rules of usage of one of the more popular language games comprising this *Lebensform*, it was quite correct to characterize the black protest movement in terms of "niggers" and "nigger-lovers" getting "uppity".

To state the problem simply, ordinary language philosophy offers no way out of situations in which common-sense and common decency have ceased to be common, and where this state of affairs has become sufficiently ingrained to stamp the ordinary language of the ordinary man. Wittgenstein apparently assumed in his later writings something which the events of the post-World War I world showed clearly either not to exist at all, or to exist only very precariously; namely, a general consensus among "ordinary people" (non-intellectuals) on the most fundamental moral and pragmatic issues of the day. The Wittgensteinian mode of analysis, consequently, can't begin to address itself to the very real problem of choosing between competing and mutually exclusive value-systems. As Ernest Gellner writes, the problem of the validity of social norms "simply cannot be solved by invoking the norms built into our ordinary speech or our conceptual custom, for the simple reason that our custom is but one of many, and has in any case undergone rapid change and will continue to do so."[3] In the absence of a widely shared consensus on the more important normative issues of the day, the Wittgensteinian is left with no basis for evaluating human action.

Wittgenstein, it must be said in his defense, was certainly aware that language changes. The multiplicity of the kinds of sentences, he says in the *Philosophical Investigations*, "is not something fixed, given once for all; but new types of language, new language-games, as we may say, come into existence, and others become obsolete and get forgotten" (PI 23). Elsewhere in the *Investigations* he compares language to a city that has developed over time—"a maze of little streets and squares, of old and new houses, and of houses with additions from various periods; and this surrounded by a multitude of new boroughs with straight regular streets and uniform houses" (PI 18). But while Wittgenstein acknowledges that changes in language do, in fact, occur, his later philosophy offers no means for evaluating such changes, nor any suggestion that such changes are in need of evaluation. Like the subjects in Hobbes's political philosophy, Wittgensteinian man is always obliged to submit to whatever linguistic sovereign happens to be in power.

And when this uncritical, purely descriptive mode of analysis is applied to cultures of the distant past, the result becomes almost ludicrous. What, for instance, is one to make of the practices of sortilege, astrology, and witchcraft as these have existed—and still do exist—in certain primitive cultures? A Wittgensteinian, it would seem, would have to acknowledge that practices such as these have

3. *Words and Things, op. cit.*, p. 24.

formed integral parts of the *Lebensformen* of certain societies, and insofar as these practices are thought of as language-games, they must be accepted as an aspect of the given. To be sure, not all primitive practices and beliefs are to be judged in a negative manner, as Wittgenstein rightly stresses in his "Remarks on Frazer". But the Wittgensteinian mode of analysis offers no way of distinguishing what may be of value in primitive societies from what is patently absurd. Maurice Cornforth, a Marxist critic of linguistic philosophy, presents the problem quite accurately when he writes:

> When . . . Wittgenstein set up the actual use of language as a standard, that was equivalent to accepting a certain set-up of culture and belief as a standard. And so, when he said that philosophy "may not interfere", that came to saying that it may not interfere with currently accepted culture and belief. It is lucky no such philosophy was thought of until recently, or we should still be under the sway of witch doctors, and the decorous feasts of Oxford University would be transformed into ritual sacrifices.[4]

It has often been remarked that the view of language offered by Wittgenstein in his later philosophy has been greatly influenced by his experiences in Austria teaching language to rural school children. And this, one might say, is precisely what is wrong with it: in essence, it presents a view of language fit for a child, rather than for a critically thinking, morally and intellectually mature adult. "One thing we always do when discussing a word," says Wittgenstein, "is to ask how we were taught it."[5] And in the *Philosophical Investigations* he says that when looking for the definition of a concept in such areas as ethics and aesthetics, "always ask yourself: How did we *learn* the meaning of this word ('good' for instance)? From what sort of examples? in what language-games" (PI 77). "Am I doing child psychology?", Wittgenstein asks in *Zettel*; to which he replies: "I am making a connection between the concept of teaching and the concept of meaning" (par. 412). Wittgenstein, in other words, directs all important questions in regard to language back to the uncritical and unproblematic years of childhood in which language was first learned, and there is no advancement beyond this stage.

In addition to its lack of a critical perspective, the Wittgenstein-

---

4. *Marxism and Linguistic Philosophy* (International Publishers, N.Y., 1971), p. 163.

5. *Lectures and Conversations on Aesthetics, Psychology and Religious Belief, op. cit.*, par. 5.

ian brand of ordinary language philosophy must be criticized for still another fundamental weakness, namely, its tendency to stifle all intellectual creativity and innovation. Like all ideological conservatisms, it puts its stamp of approval on all existing aspects of a given culture, while effectively destroying the creative urge to develop anything new. The role of the philosopher in this process is radically transformed from that of leader and innovator of intellectual change to that of an obsequeous follower of custom. The freedom and creativity of the philosophical spirit is replaced by an arid attachment to the linguistic *nomos*. But, as Friedrich Waismann once remarked in a late article, "a philosopher, instead of preaching the righteousness of ordinary speech, should learn to be on his guard against the pitfalls ever present in its forms."[6] "A philosophy," he says, "is an attempt to unfreeze habits of thinking, to replace them by less stiff and restricting ones."[7] In the *Republic* (562 E), Socrates accounts it as one of the symptoms of a decaying society when parents begin to imitate the ways of their children. One can hardly imagine what he would have thought of a situation in which the philosophers turn to the customs and conventions of the ordinary man for their guidance and orientation in life.

Bertrand Russell has certainly been one of the most outspoken critics of ordinary language philosophy, and in particular, of its tendency towards the intellectually sterile. "I have not found in Wittgenstein's *Philosophical Investigations*," he once declared in an autobiographical work, "anything that seemed to me interesting and I do not understand why a whole school finds important wisdom in its pages . . . The earlier Wittgenstein, whom I knew intimately, was a man addicted to passionately intense thinking . . . and possessed (or at least so I thought) of true philosophical genius. The later Wittgenstein, on the contrary, seems to have grown tired of serious thinking and to have invented a doctrine which would make such an activity unnecessary."[8] Russell goes on to say that he doesn't for one moment believe that a doctrine with such lazy consequences is true—but then he admits to an overpoweringly strong bias against it, for if it is true, he writes, "philosophy is at best, a slight help to lexicographers, and at worst, an idle tea-table amusement."[9] Russell, it would seem here, has squarely hit the mark, though one may wish to challenge the grounds for his positive eval-

6. *Contemporary British Philosophy*, Third Series, H.D. Lewis, editor (George Allen and Unwin Ltd., 1956), p. 468.

7. *Ibid.*, p. 485.

8. *My Philosophical Development, op. cit.*, pp. 216-217.

9. *Ibid.*, p. 217.

uation of Wittgenstein's early work. In any event, despite the absurdity of some of its central ideas, the *Tractatus* must be seen as above all a work of art. It had genuine musical cadence to it, and displayed all the monomaniacal passion and conviction of a man possessed—of someone *seized* by the truth, who, at all costs, sought to convey what he knew to others. The *Philosophical Investigations*, by contrast, is a tedious and boring work. It is a collection of often not-well-integrated paragraphs ("an album"), in which the author himself seems to have lost interest, as one can readily detect from the Preface. A prophet, one might say, who becomes a rabbi, is untrue to his calling, as is a philosopher who becomes an apologist for the *plethos*. While one may disagree with Russell's reasoning, his remark quoted in the previous section, suggesting that Wittgenstein abandoned his true genius in his later writings, must be taken as substantially correct.

Once again, as in Section II of this study, a major intellectual handicap under which Wittgenstein was laboring must be stressed. Contrary to the widely held view of Wittgenstein as something of a Renaissance man,[10] the fact of the matter is that Wittgenstein was not at all learned or broadly educated, and thus, was forced to conduct his battle against the *Zeitgeist* with a severely limited arsenal. His training was essentially that of an engineer, with a very limited background in the *Geistes-* and *Kulturwissenschaften*. While it is true that he did some reading in psychology (Freud, Gestalt) and modern history, in contrast to other Continental thinkers, he seems to have had little if any background in ancient and medieval history, in classical studies (Greco-Roman), in anthropology, sociology, political science, comparative religion, comparative philosophy, or even in many of the classic works of Western philosophy. He was one of the few thinkers of note from the European Continent not to have the benefit of a Gymnasium liberal arts education. (The sharp contrast between Wittgenstein and other Continental thinkers in this regard, is readily seen, for instance, if one compares a work such as Cassier's *The Philosophy of Symbolic Forms*, with its enormous erudition and its elaborately developed philosophy of lan-

---

10. This view is part of an extensive Wittgenstein hagiography which grew up in Britain and America after his death. A similar remark can be made about the view of Wittgenstein (see, for instance, Wolfgang Stegmueller, *op. cit.*, p. 424, and Georg von Wright in Malcolm, *Memoir, op. cit.*, p. 21) as a great German prose stylist. While Wittgenstein certainly wrote, as Erich Heller once phrased it, with "disciplined clarity", (no mean feat, perhaps, for a German thinker), a master prose stylist he certainly was not. One can hardly imagine future students of the German language reading Wittgenstein as they might, for instance, read Schopenhauer or Nietzsche.

guage and human communication forms, with the content and manner of presentation of any of Wittgenstein's writings). Denied the benefit of a broader historical and cross cultural perspective, Wittgenstein's battle against Western decadence and deculturation was severely handicapped from the start, and in the end could only prove feeble and indecisive.

An Exoteric Philosophy: Wittgenstein's Relationship to His Later Thought

One usually does not need to comment on a philosopher's relationship to his writings, since it is generally assumed that a philosopher writes what he does because he believes it to be true, and desires to communicate this truth to others. And Wittgenstein's philosophy, it might seem, whether in its early or later phase, offers no exception to this general rule. There are, however, certain known facts about the later period of Wittgenstein's life and work that would tend to call this simple view into question. Specifically, there is the fact that Wittgenstein never ceased to read, and apparently to draw the profoundest inspiration from, such introspectivist writers as Kierkegaard, Augustine, Tolstoy, Dostoyevsky, and George Fox. And this was the case at the very same time that Wittgenstein was formulating a quasi-behaviorist, anti-personalistic philosophy of mind which would seem to exclude, or at least to divert attention away from, the self-examination and inner meditative activities that played so prominent a role in the lives and writings of each of these men.

And here, in searching for an explanation of this apparent contradiction, everything that was said in this section about "saving oneself", the "fear of the psyche and its depth", "coming in out of the storm", etc., would have to be qualified by the knowledge that Wittgenstein, while he certainly derived his later philosophy from his own personal psychic situation, was primarily addressing himself to others. Whatever the attraction a behavioristically colored ordinary language philosophy may have held for Wittgenstein personally—and it was certainly considerable—it was not a philosophy which Wittgenstein himself could, in his profounder moments, fully accept. It is in this regard that one is justified in speaking of Wittgenstein's later work as a kind of exoteric philosophy.

Just as a man who has grown up amidst poverty and deprivation wishes an easier life for his son, so Wittgenstein wished for others a life free from the isolation and inner turmoil which he himself had to bear. His celebration of ordinary language and the common man in this regard, is like the parent telling his overly introverted child: "Go out. Live. Talk to people. Be normal." The path which he outlined, however, was not one which he himself ultimately chose to take. Not only did he live much of his life alone and apart from the mainstream, rarely participating in the public language games, but he never abandoned the introspective dimension of his own existence or his great respect for those who have tried to structure their lives according to the promptings of the soul's inner depth. For some men—and Kierkegaard is a prime example—the meaning of human existence only becomes clear at the price of intense personal suffering and loneliness. Wittgenstein was certainly one of these men who could not abandon his isolation without rejecting his insight. He could not be one with ordinary people and remain true to his higher understanding.

V

Concluding Remarks on the Nature of Language as *Spiel*

To be sure, man's life is a business which does not deserve to be taken too seriously; yet we cannot help being in earnest with it, and there's the pity. Still, as we are here in this world, no doubt, for us the becoming thing is to show this earnestness in a suitable way. . . . Why, I mean we should keep our seriousness for serious endeavor, man, as we said before, has been constructed as a [plaything] for God, and this is, in fact, the finest thing about him. All of us, then, men and women alike, must fall in with our role and spend life making our play as perfect as possible.

(Plato, *Laws*, 803 b-c,
A. E. Taylor translation)

. . . der Mensch spielt nur, wo er in voller Bedeutung des Wortes Mensch ist, und er ist nur da ganz Mensch, wo er spielt.
(. . . man plays only when he is man in the full meaning of the term, and he is wholly man only when he plays)

Friedrich Schiller, *Ueber die aesthetische Erziehung des Menschen*, 15. Brief.

Concluding Remarks

Few ideas are more important to Wittgenstein's later philosophy than the notion of language as a game or play (*Spiel*), though the significance of this comparison is not always sufficiently understood. As we have seen previously, Wittgenstein himself in the *Philosophical Investigations* (par. 66) uses the term "game" to demonstrate the lack of any unifying essence to the various referents of polymorphic terms, and the reader, seeing this, might naturally jump to the conclusion that Wittgenstein had only the vaguest notions in mind in his reference to language as a *Spiel*. This conclusion, however, would be false, for Wittgenstein has chosen the term *Spiel* rather than some other polymorphic term to be the central metaphor of his work,[1] and it is clear from what he says throughout his later writings that he has some very definite notions of language in mind when he characterizes it as a *Spiel*.

The first of these notions is the idea (1) that language is *rule-governed*. Just as, when playing a game, one doesn't make up the rules as one goes along, so with language one follows the pre-existing rules of custom and usage as these have evolved over time. Language, Wittgenstein wants to stress, is not an anarchic affair which proceeds according to the whim or dictate of the language-user, but a highly structured activity that must conform to established norms. Wittgenstein is particularly concerned here with discrediting the *a priori* approach to language of positivist logicians, at least in so far as they seek to replace ordinary language with their own constructional systems.

Another notion which Wittgenstein wants to bring out by the *Spiel*-metaphor is (2) the idea that the meaning of a linguistic utterance is intimately tied to the *situation* or *context* in which the utterance is made, the situation or context comprising both linguistic and non-linguistic elements. Just as the movement of chess pieces on a board, or of playing cards on a table, must be interpreted in terms of

1. Wittgenstein does, of course, sometimes compare language to other polymorphic terms—"tool", for instance—but none have the centrality of importance of the term *Spiel*.

the larger game-matrix of which they are a part, so linguistic utterances, according to Wittgenstein, must be seen in terms of both the linguistic context (e.g., single words must often be interpreted as part of a sentence; a sentence must often be seen in the context of the sentences which precede and the sentences which follow it), as well as the concrete life-situation in which the utterance occurs. Against the view of language which he took in the *Tractatus*, Wittgenstein now stresses that words do not exist in a vacuum, that they have no meaning *an sich*, but are only to be grasped in the actual situations of life.

A third notion which Wittgenstein has in mind by the *Spiel*-metaphor is the idea (3) that language is a *social* rather than a private activity. As rules of custom and usage, linguistic rules presuppose an existing society, and participation in linguistic activity must be understood as essentially social in character.[2] (It might be recalled in this context all of what Wittgenstein has to say about the impossibility of a private language). Just as games generally involve social interaction and social activity, so language is seen as essentially social in nature.

A fourth notion which Wittgenstein wants to bring out through the *Spiel*-metaphor is closely related to the preceding two, namely, (4) the idea that language must be grasped from an *active-participatory* perspective rather than a passive-observational one. The meaning of language, he seeks to emphasize, cannot be properly grasped from the outside, but only from the perspective of the language-user, just as a game is only to be properly grasped from the perspective of the players. Language is not to be understood from the sidelines, but only from active participation "in the stream of life."

The preceding similarities between language and *Spiel* are to be found either explicitly stated or directly implied in Wittgenstein's later writings. Much commentary has been written about them, and in general one might say, they belong to the less controvertial side of Wittgenstein's later thought. It would seem, however, that there is another similarity between language and games which Wittgenstein wants to bring out which is subtler, though at the same time more pervasive than the others, and which has not been the focus of study by commentators. This might be described as (5) the idea of language and human culture (*Lebensform*) as *play* or *make-believe*.

2. Wittgenstein does, it is true, acknowledge solitaire and other single-person activities as games, though when he thinks of language as a game he is clearly thinking of games such as chess or football, in which two or more people play.

The elements of play and make-believe are central to the conduct of most games, and are easily exemplified by the games of chess and football—the two games which seem to have had the most influence on Wittgenstein's formation of the language-game concept. In chess we move pieces about which represent medieval figures in the conduct of war-like exercises. We play alternately at being kings and queens, bishops and knights, castles and foot-soldiers, each with a freedom of movement appropriate to its rank and class. The element of make-believe is always present. In football—whether soccer, rugby, or American football—the make-believe quality manifests itself in a somewhat different manner, namely, in the seeming seriousness with which the participants throw themselves into what, from a rational or utilitarian standpoint, is a thoroughly senseless task.[3] Grown men kicking or passing a ball around a huge field, trying to keep it away from other grown men—it's a totally ludicrous activity, from whence springs its play-quality. According to a story recounted by Malcolm, it was upon seeing a football game actually being played that the idea of language as constituting a game first struck Wittgenstein:

> . . . Wittgenstein then did talk to Dyson [Freeman Dyson, an undergraduate who lived in a room adjacent to Wittgenstein's] about the nature of philosophy and his own part in it. Dyson recalled one anecdote of Wittgenstein's which is of considerable interest: One day when Wittgenstein was passing a field where a football game was in progress the thought first struck him that in language we play *games* with *words*. A central idea of his philosophy, the notion of a "language-game", apparently had its genesis in this incident.[4]

The first four similarities mentioned between language and games are all exemplified in the game of football, and Wittgenstein no doubt had some or all of these in mind when the language-game concept first occurred to him. Like other games, however, football is *played*, and the make-believe nature of games which gives rise to this play-mode must surely have struck Wittgenstein as forcefully as any of the other features of games. This play or make-believe aspect of games was then seen as a way of exemplifying human language and human culture. It was, it would seem, one of the ways Wittgenstein was to bring back to his picture of the world something of the enchantment that was missing from the *Weltanschauung* of

3. This could be said of chess too.
4. Malcolm, *Memoir, op. cit.*, p. 65.

the *Tractatus*. The *Tractatus*, as we have seen, had stripped the world of the divine in order to exalt God in his transcendence. Reverence for the Sacred manifested itself in the form of a disenchantment and de-sacralization of the physio-temporal plane of existence. In his later philosophy, however, Wittgenstein came to realize that the world cannot do without the gods, and thus a manner was sought to bring a sense of enchantment back into the world. This, it would seem, Wittgenstein hoped to achieve not only through a return to the living discourse of the common people, but, in addition, through participation in this discourse in the mode of play. A new *Lebenswelt* was to emerge which would possess all the enchanted magic of a game.

Wittgenstein was not alone among European thinkers to seek a way out of the malaise of modern times through an understanding of human culture as *Spiel*. By far the best known of these thinkers was the Dutch cultural historian Johan Huizinga, who first became interested in the relationship between culture and *Spiel* through his study of medieval society, with its ever-present tournaments, codes of honor, chivalric orders, courtly demeanor, and the like.[5] It was this element of play, Huizinga came to realize, so prominent in ages past, that had increasingly seeped out of the modern world from the 18th century onward. "More and more the sad conclusion forces itself upon us," he was to say, "that the play-element in culture has been on the wane ever since the 18th century, when it was in full flower. Civilization today is no longer played . . ."[6] In contrast to modern civilization, which Huizinga saw in a state of decline, earlier cultures, he explained, were permeated throughout by the spirit of play. "The view we take in the following pages," he wrote in his classic *Homo Ludens*, "is that culture arises in the form of play (*Spiel*), that it is played from the very beginning."[7] "By this we do not mean that play turns into culture, rather that in its earliest phases culture has the play-character, that it proceeds in the shape and the mood of play."[8] "It does not come *from* play like a babe detaching itself from the womb: it arises *in* and *as* play, and never leaves it."[9] "It is through this playing that society expresses its interpretation of life and the world."[10]

5. *Homo Ludens: A Study of the Play-Element in Culture* (Beacon Press, Boston, 1956), p. 104.
6. *Ibid.*, p. 206.
7. *Ibid.*, p. 46.
8. *Ibid.*
9. *Ibid.*, p. 173.
10. *Ibid.*, p. 46.

And so it is with Wittgenstein. Human culture, human "forms-of-life", arise *in* and *as* language-games (*Sprachspiele*), and never leave them. The play or game aspect of language—the enchanted make-believe—must never be abandoned, for it constitutes the very life of man in society. The language-game is the magic circle outside of which only meaninglessness and estrangement can exist.

With this *Spiel*-aspect of human language in mind, the otherwise compulsive element in Wittgenstein's attachment to ordinary language begins to take on an entirely different cast. For if one views language in terms of a game to be played, then the rules of the language (rules of usage, grammar, etc.), no matter how strict, will no longer possess the oppressive, spirit-destroying character they otherwise would have if taken with full seriousness. The rules are the rules of a game (*Spiel*), and are to be followed in a manner appropriate to a game—i.e., in the manner of play. There is, however, a problem here. If linguistic activity is to be conducted in the manner of play—and no doubt one of the reasons Wittgenstein defines language-games in terms of the way a child is taught language[11] is to stress this very play-element—and if linguistic activity and human culture are not to be taken with complete seriousness, the human situation, it would seem, stands in danger of being trivialized. This, however, is not what Wittgenstein intends to do. He does, it is true, wish to reduce in stature the importance of human affairs, but only in so far as the tendency exists to accord to them an ultimacy of meaning. Here, it would seem, the *Spiel*-metaphor serves to reintroduce the great theological theme of the *Tractatus* concerning the transcendence of the divine and the relative insignificance of man's achievements, while at the same time overcoming the *Tractatus* tendency to separate the realms of human and divine too rigidly. In seeing human culture in terms of *Spiel*, Wittgenstein, one might say, declares war on all misplaced seriousness. Only God, Wittgenstein might say along with Plato, is worthy of being taken with full seriousness, for human affairs partake of a lesser level of importance and reality. But once this is realized, once human existence is reoriented in such a manner that the accent of reality falls on a divine Beyond of language and culture, language and culture can be viewed in their proper role as play. Just as a theater-play takes on its character as play by virtue of the background provided by the world of "real life" beyond the theater, so human existence in society and culture takes on the character of play once it is sensed that the ultimately real and ultimately important reaches beyond the

11. BB p. 17; BrB p. 81; PI 7.

temporal world into another dimension.[12] In the symbol of play, one might say, Wittgenstein has found the proper mean between the extremes of according to the temporal world a false ultimacy of meaning, and denying it meaning altogether as an absurdity or a bad dream.

Wittgenstein himself, with his great depression and reclusiveness, found it very difficult to experience the world in terms of play. A story related by Malcolm, however, shows that Wittgenstein definitely had a sense for what he was talking about. As Malcolm describes:

> Sometimes he came to my house in Searle Street for supper. Once after supper, Wittgenstein, my wife and I went for a walk on Midsummer Common. We talked about the movements of the bodies of the solar system. It occurred to Wittgenstein that the three of us should represent the movements of the sun, earth, and moon, relative to one another. My wife was the sun and maintained a steady pace across the meadow; I was the earth and circled her at a trot. Wittgenstein took the most strenuous part of all, the moon, and ran around me while I circled my wife. Wittgenstein entered into this game with great enthusiasm and seriousness, shouting instructions at us as he ran. He became quite breathless and dizzy with exhaustion.[13]

In this delightful anecdote the element of playful make-believe is manifest. One plays at being the sun, the earth, and the moon, and in so doing, begins to enter a frame of mind from which all human endeavor can be seen in its proper perspective. Play in this sense becomes the great nemesis of all soap opera and all melodrama, of all pedantry and of misplaced seriousness of whatever description. As such, it stands functionally quite close to humor. Wittgenstein once told Malcolm that a serious philosophical work might consist entirely of jokes,[14] and while he doesn't seem to have elaborated on this cryptic remark, it is perhaps not too wild of a

---

12. *Cf.* Hugo Rahner:

> But the man who is at the exact midpoint between heaven and earth, the Christian, the true gnostic, can conceive of his life and of all the happenings in the world as something best described by the apt metaphor of Plotinus: a single great theatrical performance, for he knows something of the secrets of what is behind the stage.
>
> *Man at Play* (Herder and Herder, N.Y., 1967), p. 39.

13. Malcolm, *Memoir, op. cit.*, pp. 51-2.
14. *Memoir, op. cit.*, p. 29.

speculation to see here a similar understanding on Wittgenstein's part of humor as of *Spiel*—both serve to carry the mind to a plane of existence where normal everyday realities cease to be seen as ultimate. In a late work Wittgenstein says that "humour is not a mood but a way of looking at the world." And he then goes on to declare: "So if it is correct to say that humour was stamped out in Nazi Germany, that does not mean that people were not in good spirits, or anything of that sort, but something much deeper and more important."[15] Indeed, the Nazi was not capable of humor, for National Socialist philosophy had raised the socio-political and historical realms of existence to the level of an absolute (an eschaton or millennium in theological jargon). Wittgenstein seems to have recognized this, though he doesn't elaborate the point. From the Nazi perspective, it would seem, humor, like play, could only be viewed as boorish levity, when not a *lèse majesté*.

It can only be regretted that Wittgenstein hasn't left us with a book of jokes. For ironically, the effect of his late philosophy was to inspire a plethora of scholastic exercises thoroughly lacking for the most part in a sense of either humor or play. It was remarked in Section II that the *Tractatus* was characterized by a spirit of playfulness, which tended to balance the seriousness of its message. When this playfulness, however, was absorbed into Wittgenstein's thought in the manner of a formal doctrine (the doctrine of human life-forms as *Spiel*), the result was an actual decline in sensitivity for the play-aspect of human existence. Both Wittgenstein's own later work, and those of his followers clearly reveals this decline. Once again, however, it can be said that the situation was much worse on the side of the logical positivists. In the Carnapian attempt to restrict all language to the descriptive-observational mode used by physicists and chemists, the *Spiel* aspect of human existence was totally shut out.[16]

---

15. *Culture and Value* (translated by Peter Winch, The University of Chicago Press, 1981), p. 78e.

16. Despite a certain penchant for sarcastic or sardonic wit, rigorous positivists —like Marxists and National Socialists—are not renown for their capacity for either humor or play. Carnap's humorlessness seems to have struck even A.J. Ayer (see the latter's remarks in his autobiography, *Part of My Life: The Memoirs of a Philosopher*, Harcourt Brace Jovanovich, N.Y., 1977, p. 157).

Index

Abbott and Costello, 54-57
Absolute safety experience, 91-96
Anscombe, G.E.M., 110, 111, 111*n*
Apatheia, 102-107
Aristotle, 209
Augustine, Saint, xiii, 73-74, 82, 84, 147, 152*n*, 159, 235-237
Ayer, A.J., xi, 3, 3*n*, 38-39, 68, 68*n*, 192, 192*n*, 223

Barclay, Robert, 85-86
Barrett, William, xv*n*, 216
Bartley, William, 163*n*-164*n*
Beetle-in-the-box allegory, 221-222
Behaviorism, quasi-behaviorism, 211-225
Bergson, Henri, 62-63
Black, Max, 98, 110, 110*n*, 136, 150
Boisen, Anton, 50*n*, 208*n*
Buber, Martin, 131, 132, 132*n*

Carnap, Rudolf, 3, 4*n*, 5-18, 54-57, 61-69, 98, 129, 135, 170-171
Catherine of Siena, 73
Conservatism (of ordinary language philosophy), 182-187
Cornforth, Maurice, 243

Derealization-depersonalization, 15-29
Diary argument, 222-225
Dostoyevsky, Fyodor, xiii, 188-189, 189*n*
Drury, Maurice, 207, 208*n*
Dyson, Freeman, 253

Eckhart, Meister, 72*n*, 116, 122*n*, 154, 154*n*
Edwards, James, xv, xv*n*
Ekstasis (see "mystic-flight experience")
Engelmann, Paul, xii-xiii, 111*n*, 112*n*, 129, 129*n*, 133, 168-169, 188, 199-200
Erickson, Erik, 51*n*
Erkenntnis, 5, 131
Eternal Present, eternal Now, 153-154
Exoteric philosophy, 246-247

Fallenness, 146-148
Family resemblances, 230
Feigl, Herbert, 3, 3*n*, 4*n*, 66, 216
Fox, George, xiii, 90, 131
Frazer, Sir James, 174-175
Freud, Sigmund, 67, 68*n*

Games, 229
Gellner, Ernest, xvi, 197*n*-198*n*
Gigon, Olof, 78*n*, 79, 79*n*
Gnosticism, 142-143, 143*n*, 145, 146*n*

Habakkuk, 90
Hahn, Hans, 3, 4*n*
Hampshire, Stuart, 217-218
Harrison, Jane, 132*n*
Heidegger, Martin, 10-13, 15-29, 39-42, 52-53, 209
Hierarchical ontology, 156-158
History, 152-155
Hooker, Richard, 87*n*
Hudson, W. Donald, xv*n*, 116*n*-117*n*
Huizinga, Johan, 254
Hume, David, 83, 120, 120*n*
Humor, 256-257

Inwardness, 211-220
Isaiah (Second-Isaiah), 81-82

Jaeger, Werner, 80
James, William, xiii, 17*n*, 20, 77*n*
Jamnia, 184
Janik, Allan, ix, xi, 155*n*
Jaspers, Karl, 50*n*
John of the Cross, 43-52, 118*n*
Jonas, Hans, 143*n*

Kant, Immanuel, 99, 100, 104, 107, 124
Kaufmann, Walter, xvi
Keightley, Alan, xv*n*
Kelsen, Hans, 130-131
Keynes, John Maynard, 187-188
Kierkegaard, Soren, xiii, 24-26, 24*n*-26*n*, 247

Kimura, Bin, 17*n*, 46*n*
Koestler, Arthur, 92-93, 125, 125*n*, 133
Kolakowski, Leszek, 131*n*
Kraft, Victor, 3
Kraus, Karl, xi, 240

Ladder metaphor, 117-118, 118*n*
Laing, R.D., 50*n*-51*n*, 71, 121*n*, 208*n*
Langer, Susanne, 151*n*
Legislative linguistics, 148-152
Leibnitz, Gottfried, 209
Leitner, Bernhard, 228
Loewith, Karl, 41, 41*n*
Logical form, 115-116
Logical positivism, 3-57, 61-69, 170-173

McGuinness, Brian F., xi, 69*n*-70*n*
Madness, 204-211, 219-220, 226-229
Maisky, Ivan, 187
Malcolm, Norman, 95-96, 163*n*, 235, 253, 256
Maslow, Abraham, 70, 126
Maxwell, Grover, 216
Maya, 100, 104, 106
Memory, 222-225, 236
Menger, Karl, 3
Mental activities, mental terms, 212-220
Mental health metaphors, 205-211
Metaphysics, 3-53, 61-69, 82-88, 127-139, 159, 209-211
Moore, G.E., 185-186, 209
Mundle, C.W.K., xvi, 197*n*, 217, 221*n*
Mystic-flight experience (*ekstasis*), 69-158

Neurath, Otto, 3, 4, 4*n*, 5, 6, 68, 109, 171-172, 172*n*
Nietzsche, Friedrich, 15, 17*n*
Nirvana, 72*n*, 107
Nothing, experience of, 10-53

Obscurantism, 127-128
Ordinary language philosophy, 176-182, 190-193, 237-246
Otto, Rudolf, 71*n*-72*n*, 81, 108*n*

Pascal, Blaise, 87, 181
Pears, David, 178*n*
Picture theory of language, 114-116
Pitcher, George, 110-110*n*
Plato, 106, 137, 184-185, 231-235
Play (see *Spiel*)
Plotinus, 121, 146*n*-147*n*
Plutarch, 89*n*
Popper, Karl, 5-6, 136, 136*n*, 150*n*
Porphyry, 89*n*
Privacy, private language, 220-225
Profanation, 128-139
Pseudo-Dionysius (Dionysius the Aereopagite), 74-75, 84-85, 89, 109
Puritans, 82

Russell, Bertrand, xvi, 69, 113, 115, 119, 156, 165-166, 180-181, 180*n*-181*n*, 189, 192, 240, 244-245
Russia, 187-190
Ryle, Gilbert, ix, 211

Sartre, Jean-Paul, 29-39
Say/show-itself distinction, 108-118
Schlick, Moritz, 3, 3*n*, 65, 66*n*, 129, 131
Schopenhauer, Arthur, 98-107, 128
Shamanism, 94, 94*n*-95*n*
Silence, and religious experience, 88-91
Smith, John, 86-87
Solipsism, 118-123
Spiel (game or play), 251-257
Stace, Walter, 72*n*, 122*n*
Stalin, Joseph, 4, 189
Stenius, Erick, 107
Strawson, Peter, 210*n*-211*n*, 221-222
Suso, Henry, 72

Tagore, Rabindranath, 66, 106
Tauler, John, 48*n*
Teresa of Avila, Saint, 45
Theologia Germanica, 49*n*
Tillich, Paul, 127*n*
Tolstoy, Leo, xiii, 108*n*, 133-134, 133*n*, 154*n*-155*n*, 164, 166-167
Toulmin, Stephen, ix, xi, 155*n*
Tribalism, 237-240

Underhill, Evelyn, xiii
Universal essences, 229-235
Urge to the mystical, 124-127

Verification principle, 8
via negativa, xii, 73-75, 135, 153*n*, 210
Vienna Circle, 1-57
Voelker, Walter, 75*n*
Voegelin, Eric, ix-x

Waismann, Friedrich, 3, 64, 173, 244
Watts, Alan, xiii
Whitman, Walt, 122-123
Will, and ethics, 140-142
Wittgenstein, Hermine, 96*n*
Work therapy, 225-229
World, meaning in *Tractatus*, 97-99, 107-108
Wright, George von, 69*n*, 205

Xenophanes, 78-81

Made in the USA
Middletown, DE
02 October 2018